PARALLEL
LIVES

Drawings by David Schorr

VINTAGE BOOKS
A DIVISION OF RANDOM HOUSE
NEW YORK

PARALLEL

LIVES

Five Victorian Marriages

PHYLLIS

ROSE

First Vintage Books Edition, November 1984

Copyright © 1983 by Phyllis Rose
Illustrations copyright © 1983 by David Schorr

Library of Congress Cataloging in Publication Data

Rose, Phyllis, 1942–
Parallel lives.

Bibliography: p.
Includes index.
1. Marriage–Great Britain–History–19th century–
Case studies.
2. Married People–Great Britain–Biography.
3. Authors, English–19th century–Biography–Marriage.
I. Title
[HQ613. R67 1984]   306.8'1'0941   84-40026

ISBN 978-0-394-725580-2

Cover painting of Carlyle's house in London by Robert Tait.
Courtesy of a private collection, London.

Manufactured in the United States of America

33

To
D. S.

"Marriage affords great collective excitations: if we managed to suppress the Oedipus complex and marriage, what would be left for us to *tell*?"

—ROLAND BARTHES, *Roland Barthes*

Contents

Contents

Acknowledgments

My biggest debt is to the scholars, living and dead, who have made the private writings of the great Victorians available to us. I could not have considered doing a book such as this one if the biographical materials on which I base my own writing had still to be sought, found, deciphered, catalogued, indexed, footnoted, and printed, or if fine biographies of the people I write about did not already exist. The publication of correspondences and collected papers and the writing of authoritative biographies depend upon the labors of so many people that I will merely touch the tip of Leviathan in naming a dozen names, but in doing so I will at least signify my gratitude to the whole enterprise of biographical scholarship. For the Carlyles: Carlyle himself; J. A. Froude; and the editors of the ongoing Duke-Edinburgh Edition of *The Collected Letters of Thomas and Jane Welsh Carlyle*, including Charles Richard Sanders, Kenneth J. Fielding, Ian Campbell, John Clubbe, and Aileen Christianson. For the Ruskins: supremely, Mary Lutyens. For Dickens: John Forster; Ada Nisbet; Walter Dexter; and the editors of the Pilgrim Edition of Dickens's letters, in progress, Madeline House, Graham Storey, Kathleen Tillotson, and (again) K. J. Fielding. For Mill: Michael St. John Packe; F. A. Hayek; and the editors of Mill's collected letters, Francis E. Minetka and Dwight N. Lindley. For George Eliot: Gordon Haight, with particular warmth. In a more general way, I owe thanks to Diane Johnson for the inspiration provided by her biography of Mary Ellen Peacock, the first Mrs. Meredith.

Friends who have helped me by reading and commenting on various parts of the manuscript include Paul Alpers, Svetlana Alpers, Georges Borchardt, Catherine Gallagher, Leslie Garis, William I. Miller, Richard Ohmann, Iris Slotkin, and Alex Zwerdling. Bryan Fuermann helped me with research, and Henry Abelove has left genial tracks of his learning throughout the book. Joseph W. Reed has read my manuscripts for longer and at earlier stages than anyone else, and for that alone he deserves special thanks. Moreover, his encouragement of this project was crucial. I also want especially to thank Annie Dillard for precious gifts of time, friendship, intelligence, and candor. Another friend, Nancy Nicholas, is also my editor—as excellent a friend as an editor and dazzlingly graceful at juggling the two roles.

For many kinds of support, I am grateful to the faculty, staff, students, and administration of Wesleyan University.

I wish I wrote books faster so I could more often have the pleasure of recording in print my gratitude to Teddy Rose. This time I want to thank him particularly for teaching me—with the help of his Atari—how to overcome obstacles either by speeding up to go round them or by blasting them out of the way. Thanks, too, to Danny Dries and to David Schorr for the happiness of the past ten years.

PARALLEL
LIVES

Prologue

When Leslie Stephen, the Victorian man of letters, read Froude's biography of Carlyle in the early 1880s, he was shocked—as were many people—by its portrait of the Carlyles' marriage. He asked himself if he had treated *his* wife as badly as it seemed to him that Thomas Carlyle had treated Jane. With the Carlyles in his mind, Stephen, after his wife's death, enshrined his self-exoneration in a lugubrious record of his domestic life which posterity has dubbed *The Mausoleum Book*, and I, reading it, conceived the idea for this book.[1] Froude's life of Carlyle is a masterpiece, but much biography shares its power to inspire comparison. Have I lived that way? Do I want to live that way? Could I make myself live that way if I wanted to? Nineteenth-century Englishmen read Plutarch's *Parallel Lives of the Greeks and Romans* to learn about the perils and pitfalls of public life, but it occurred to me that there was no equivalent or even vaguely similar series of domestic portraits.

So this book began with a desire to tell the stories of some marriages as unsentimentally as possible, with attention to the shifting tides of power between a man and a woman joined, presumably, for life. My purposes were partly feminist (since marriage is so often the context within which a woman works out her destiny, it has always been an object of feminist scrutiny) and partly, in ways I shall explain, literary.

I believe, first of all, that living is an act of creativity and that, at certain moments of our lives, our creative imaginations are more conspicuously demanded than at others. At certain moments, the need to decide upon the story of our own lives becomes particularly pressing—when we choose a mate, for example, or embark upon a career. Decisions like that make sense, retroactively, of the past and project a meaning onto the future, knit past and future together, and create, suspended between the two, the present. Questions we have all asked of ourselves such as Why am I doing this? or the even more basic What am I doing? suggest the way in which living forces us to look for and forces us to find a design within the primal stew of data which is our daily experience. There is a kind of arranging and telling and choosing of detail—of narration, in short—which we must do so that one day will prepare for the next day, one week prepare for the next week. In some way we all decide when we have grown up and what event will symbolize for us that state of maturity —leaving home, getting married, becoming a parent, losing our parents, making a million, writing a book. To the extent that we impose some narrative form onto our lives, each of us in the ordinary process of living is a fitful novelist, and the biographer is a literary critic.

Marriages, or parallel lives as I have chosen to call them, hold a particular fascination for the biographer-critic because they set two imaginations to work constructing narratives about experience presumed to be the same for both. In using the word *parallel*, however, I hope to call attention to the gap between the narrative lines as well as to their similarity.

An older school of literary biography was concerned to show how "life" had influenced an author's work. My own assumption is that certain imaginative patterns—call them mythologies or ideologies— determine the shape of a writer's life as well as his or her work. I therefore look for connections between the two without assuming that reality is the template for fiction—assuming, if anything, the reverse. In first approaching this material, I looked for evidence that what people read helped form their views of their own experience. Some emerged. Jane Welsh, for example, being courted by Thomas Carlyle, derived her view of their relationship from reading *La Nouvelle Héloïse*. Dickens's management of his separation from his wife seemed influenced by the melodramas in which he was fond of acting. But what came to interest me more was the way in which every marriage was a narrative construct—or two narrative constructs. In unhappy marriages, for example, I see two versions of reality rather than two people in conflict. I see a struggle for imaginative dominance going on. Happy marriages seem to me those in which the two partners agree on the scenario they are enacting, even if, as was the case with Mr. and Mrs. Mill, their own idea of their relationship is totally at variance with the facts. I speak with great trepidation about "facts" in such matters, but, speaking loosely, the facts in the Mills' case—that a woman of strong and uncomplicated will dominated a guilt-ridden man—were less important than their shared imaginative view of the facts, that their marriage fitted their shared ideal of a marriage of equals. I assume, then, as little objective truth as possible about these parallel lives, for every marriage seems to me a subjectivist fiction with two points of view often deeply in conflict, sometimes fortuitously congruent.

That, sketchily, is the ground of my literary interest in parallel lives, but there is a political dimension as well. On the basis of family life, we form our expectations about power and powerlessness, about authority and obedience in other spheres, and in that sense the family is, as has so often been insisted, the building block of society. The idea of the family as a school for civic life goes back to the ancient Romans, and feminist criticism of the family as such a school—the charge that it is a school for despots and slaves—goes back at least to John Stuart Mill.[2] I cite this tradition to locate, in part, my own position: like Mill, I believe marriage to be the primary political experience in which most of us engage as adults, and so I am interested in the management of power between men and women in that microcosmic relationship. Whatever the balance, every marriage is based upon some understanding, articulated or not, about the relative importance, the priority of desires, between its two partners. Marriages go bad not when love fades—love can modulate into affection without driving two people apart—but when this understanding about the balance of power breaks down, when the weaker member feels exploited or the stronger feels unrewarded for his or her strength.

People who find this a chilling way to talk about one of our most treasured human bonds will object that "power struggle" is a flawed circumstance into which relationships fall when love fails. (For some people it is impossible to discuss power without adding the word *struggle*.) I would counter by pointing out the human tendency to invoke love at moments when we want to disguise transactions involving power. Like the aged Lear handing over his kingdom to his daughters, when we resign power, or assume new power, we insist it is not happening and demand to be talked to about love. Perhaps that is what love is—the momentary or prolonged refusal to think of another person in terms of power. Like an enzyme which blocks momentarily a normal biological process, what we call love may inhibit the process of power negotiation—from which inhibition comes the illusion of equality so characteristic of lovers. If the impulse to abjure measurement and negotiation comes from within, unbidden, it is one of life's graces and blessings. But if it is culturally induced, and more particularly desired of one segment of humanity than another, then we may perhaps find it repugnant and call it a mask for exploitation. Surely, in regard to marriage, love has received its fair share of attention, power less than its share.[3] For every social scientist discussing the family as a psychopolitical structure,[4] for every John Stuart Mill talking about "subjection" in marriage, how many pieties are daily uttered about love? Who can resist the thought that love is the ideological bone thrown to women to distract their attention from the powerlessness of their lives? Only millions of romantics can resist it—and other millions who might see it as the bone thrown to men to distract them from the bondage of *their* lives.

In unconscious states, as we know from Freud, the mind is astonishingly fertile and inventive in its fiction-making, but in conscious states this is not so. The plots we choose to impose on our own lives are limited and limiting. And in no area are they so banal and sterile as in this of love and marriage. Nothing else being available to our imaginations, we will filter our experience through the romantic clichés with which popular culture bombards us. And because the callowness and conventionality of the plots we impose on ourselves are a betrayal of our inner richness and complexity, we feel anxious and unhappy. We may turn to therapy for help, but the plots *it* evokes, if done less than expertly, are also fairly limiting.

Easy stories drive out hard ones. Simple paradigms prevail over complicated ones. If, within marriage, power is the ability to impose one's imaginative vision and make it prevail, then power is more easily obtained if one has a simple and widely accepted paradigm at hand. The patriarchal paradigm has long enforced men's power within marriage: a man works hard to make himself worthy of a woman; they marry; he heads the family; she serves him, working to please him and care for him, getting protection in return. This plot regularly generates its opposite, the plot of female power through weakness: the woman, somehow wounded by family life, needs to be cared for and requires an offering of guilt. Mrs. Rochester, the madwoman in the attic in *Jane Eyre*, is a fairly spectacular example.[5] The suffering female demanding care has often proved stronger than the conquering male deserving care—a dialectic of imaginative visions of which the Carlyles provide a good example—but neither side of the patriarchal paradigm seems to bring out the best in humanity. In regard to marriage, we need more and more complex plots. I reveal my literary bias in saying I believe we need literature, which, by allowing us to experience more fully, to imagine more fully, enables us to live more freely. In a pragmatic way, we can profit from an immersion in the nineteenth-century novel which took the various stages of marriage as its central subject.

We tend to talk informally about other people's marriages and to disparage our own talk as gossip. But gossip may be the beginning of moral inquiry, the low end of the platonic ladder which leads to self-understanding. We are desperate for information about how other people live because we want to know how to live ourselves, yet we are taught to see this desire as an illegitimate form of prying. If marriage is, as Mill suggested, a political experience, then discussion of it ought to be taken as seriously as talk about national elections. Cultural pressure to avoid such talk as "gossip" ought to be resisted, in a spirit of good citizenship. In that spirit, then, I offer some private lives for examination and discussion. I will try to tell these stories in such a way as to raise questions about the role of power and the nature of equality within marriage, for I assume a connection between politics and sex. In the interests of objectivity, I offer the joint lives of some Victorian men and women for whom the rules of the game were perhaps clearer than they are for us.

To many people the word *Victorian* means prudish, repressive, asexual, and little more. This popular understanding has been wholly unaffected by over two decades of scholarship which have tried to destroy the notion of a monolithic Victorian culture in Britain, pointing out, to begin with, that a span of over sixty years (Victoria ruled from 1837 to 1901) is highly resistant to responsible generalization. It has also been unaffected by a surge of memoirs, biographies, and scholarly studies, led off by Steven Marcus's *The Other Victorians*, whose goal as a group has been, speaking crudely, to show the kinky side of Victorian life. (More accurately, I'd describe Marcus's study of pornography and sexuality as aiming to suggest the tremendous amount of sexual energy which the Victorians were sublimating in the interests of civilization.) Strange and marvelous stories have come to light, a remarkable number having to do with double or hidden lives. Arthur Munby (*Munby: Man of Two Worlds*), a respectable barrister, was obsessed with working-class women, collected their life stories and photographs, and was secretly married to his household servant for many years. J. R. Ackerley (*My Father and Myself*) discovered that his father, another person of seemingly irreproachable respectability, had maintained a separate household, with second wife and children, a few blocks from the family home. But even more important to Ackerley, a homosexual, was the discovery that his father, like many other Guardsmen, had been enthusiastically homosexual in his youth.

Such books (I have mentioned a couple I found particularly absorbing) get talked about now in the amused or astonished tones children use for discussing evidence of their parents' sexuality. The comparison is appropriate, since the Victorians—or more precisely our imagined condensation of Victorian culture—still constitute our parental generation in the largest sense and we rebel against a partly real, partly invented nineteenth-century sexual code. But we are the flip side of the same pancake. If Marcus began the process of re-sexualizing the Victorians by suggesting the power of what they repressed, Foucault has more recently and from a more radical perspective attacked the whole notion of Victorian prudery.[6] Whether one talks about sex encouragingly (as we do) or discouragingly (as the Victorians did) is of no significance to Foucault; the Victorians, like every generation since the eighteenth century, participated in the transformation of sex into "discourse."

When I said that the rules of the game were somewhat clearer for the Victorians than for us, I had in mind primarily the difficulty of divorce. Before the Matrimonial Causes Act of 1857, divorce was possible in England only by Act of Parliament, a process so expensive and unusual as to place it virtually out of reach of the middle class, although, in special cases such as non-consummation, annulments were possible through the ecclesiastical courts. Even after 1857, when secular courts were established to grant divorces, relatively few people could bring themselves to submit to the scandalous procedure: adultery had invariably to be one of the grounds. So these unions, however haphazardly undertaken, were intended to last for life. Comparatively, our easy recourse to divorce seems—to adopt Robert Frost's image—like playing tennis without the net. John Stuart Mill, who advocated divorce, nevertheless believed that re-marriage was an inefficient remedy for certain kinds of marital distress, those caused by the human tendency to grow unhappy in the course of years and to blame this unhappiness on one's spouse. The sufferer, after the initial elation brought by change, would reach the same point eventually with a second mate, said Mill, and at what a cost of disrupted life! It has become a story familiar enough today. But the Victorians, with no easy escape from difficult domestic situations, were forced to be more inventive.

Few were more inventive than Mill's eventual wife, Harriet Taylor, who, for twenty years, arranged to live in a virtual *ménage à trois* with her husband and Mill, a companion to both, lover to neither. Her inventiveness depended on a de-emphasis of sexual fulfillment which it requires effort to perceive as useful rather than merely pinched. But I think the effort must be made. Of the five marriages I discuss, at least two of them, and possibly a third, were sexless, and it will not do just to say "How bizarre."

In fact, scholars in our own post-liberated age who interest themselves in innovative living arrangements are beginning to discover
that people a hundred years ago may have had *more* flexibility than
we do now. Lillian Faderman, for example, has described with great
sympathy the nineteenth-century American practice of the "Boston
marriage," a long-term monogamous relationship between two women
who are otherwise unmarried.[7] The emotional and even financial
advantages of such a relationship are immediately evident, whether
or not—and this is something we shall never know—sex was involved.
The important point is that such relationships were seen as healthy
and useful. Henry James, for one, was delighted that his sister Alice
had some joy in her life, in the form of her Boston marriage to
Katherine Loring. But what seemed healthy and useful to the nineteenth century suddenly became "abnormal" after the impact, in the
early twentieth century, of popular Freudianism. With all experience
sexualized, living arrangements such as those Boston marriages could
not be so easily entered upon or easily discussed; they became outlaw,
suppressed, matters to hide. By the mid-1920s, it was no longer possible
to mention a Boston marriage without embarrassment. By sexualizing
experience, popular Freudianism had the moralistic result of limiting
possibilities.

I prefer to see the sexless marriages I discuss as examples of
flexibility rather than of abnormality. Some people might say they
are not really marriages because they are sexless; it's a point I'd
want to argue. There must be other models of marriage—of long-
term association between two people—than the very narrow one we
are all familiar with, beginning with a white wedding gown, leading
to children, and ending in death, or, these days increasingly often, in
divorce.

Many cultural circumstances worked against the likelihood of sexual satisfaction within Victorian marriages. The inflexible taboo on
pre-marital sex for middle-class women meant, among other things,
that it was impossible to determine sexual compatibility before marriage. The law then made the wife absolute property of her husband
and sexual performance one of her duties. Imagine a young woman
married to a man she finds physically repulsive. She is in the position
of being raped nightly—and with the law's consent. The legendary

Victorian advice about sex, "Lie back and think of England," may be seen as not entirely comical if we realize that in many cases a distaste for sex developed from a distaste for the first sexual partner and from sexual performance which was essentially forced. In addition, the absence of birth control made it impossible to separate sex from its reproductive function, so that to be sexually active meant also the discomforts of pregnancy, the pain of childbirth, and the burden of children. For men, the middle-class taboo on pre-marital sex meant sexual experience could be obtained only with prostitutes or working-class women, an early conditioning which Freud said breeds dangers in the erotic life, by encouraging a split between objects of desire and objects of respect.[8]

We would seem to have a greater chance of happiness now. Theoretically, men and women can get to know each other in casual, relaxed circumstances before marrying. More young people feel free to sleep together, to live together before marriage. They do not have to wait until they are irrevocably joined to discover they are incompatible. Nor are they so irrevocably joined. If we discover, as we seem to, early and late, that despite all our opportunity to test compatibility, we have married someone with whom we are not compatible, we can disconnect ourselves and try again. Perhaps most important, women can hold jobs, earn a living, own property, thereby gaining a chance for some status in the family. Birth control is reliable and available, so women needn't be, quite so much as formerly, the slaves of children. Nor need men be so oppressed by the obligation of supporting large and expensive families. We can separate sex from reproduction; it can be purely a source of pleasure. If all this does not ensure that, cumulatively, we are happier in our domesticity than the Victorians, then perhaps we expect even more of our marriages than the Victorians did—perhaps we place too much of a burden on our personal relationships, as Christopher Lasch, among others, has suggested.[9] Or perhaps the deep tendency of human nature to unhappiness is even harder to reach by legislation and technology than one might have thought.

Neither in novels nor in biographical material can I find much evidence that people of the last century placed less emphasis on their personal relationships than we do. Romantic expectations seem to

know no season, except the season of life. Dickens and Carlyle offer
examples of one connubial dream: that an idealized woman will
reward the young man for his professional labors. Of the five Victorian couples I have written about, the Mills and the Leweses, for
various reasons, expected less out of marriage and found greater
satisfaction in it than the others. Temperament and ideological bent
seem more important in determining happiness than whether one
lived in the nineteenth or the twentieth century.

We should remind ourselves, I think, of the romantic bias in
Anglo-American attitudes towards marriage, whether of the nineteenth or the twentieth century. Effie Ruskin, travelling in Italy,
discovered how much more comfortable Continental ways of being
married were than English. For the English assumed you loved your
husband and were loved by him and wanted to be with him as much
as possible, whereas the Europeans made no such extraordinary
assumption. They knew they were making the best of a difficult
situation often arranged by people other than the participants and
for reasons quite apart from love, and so they gave each other
considerable latitude. One hardly knows whether the Victorians suffered more from their lack of easy recourse to divorce or from the
disappearance of the brisk assumptions of arranged marriages. At
least when marriages were frankly arrangements of property, no
one expected them to float on an unceasing love-tide, whereas we
and the Victorians have been in the same boat on that romantic
flood.

In general, the similarities between marriages then and now seem
to me greater than the differences. Then as now certain problems of
adjustment, focussing usually on sex or relatives, seem typical of
early stages of marriage, and others, for example absence of excitement, seem typical of later stages. In good marriages then as now
shared experience forms a bond increasingly important with time,
making discontents seem minor. And then as now, love also tends to
walk out the door when poverty flies in the window. Conditions I
would have thought unreproducible today—Ruskin's total innocence
of the female nude and consequent shock when confronted by one—
turn out to have been reproduced in the lives of people I know. I
have been reminded continually in these Victorian marriages of mar-

riages of friends: strong women still adopt a protective coloring of weakness as George Eliot did; earnest men with strongly egalitarian politics are still subject to domination by shrews, as John Mill was; men like Dickens still divorce in middle age the wives they have used up and outdistanced; clever women like Jane Carlyle still solace themselves for their powerlessness by mocking their husbands. Moreover, attitudes towards marriage which I would have thought outdated prove not to be. Apparently it is still possible to assume that the man is without question the more important partner in a marriage. That is, the patriarchal paradigm still prevails. Indeed, as fundamentalist religion and morality revive in contemporary America's ethical vacuum, we are likely to find ourselves fighting the nineteenth-century wars of personal morality all over again. Since we have not come so far as some of us fear and some of us hope we have, people who want to legislate morality back to an imagined ideal should, at the least, learn some humility in the face of the conservatism of human nature.

The following chapters on the marriages of Jane and Thomas Carlyle, of Effie Gray and John Ruskin, of George Eliot and George Henry Lewes, of Harriet and John Stuart Mill, and of Catherine and Charles Dickens are selective. That is, I do not attempt to cover the chronology of any marriage. If every marriage is, as Jessie Bernard puts it, two marriages—the man's and the woman's—a satisfactory treatment would require two books, one from his point of view and one from hers, or at least one novel with a high degree of complexity. So I have focussed on one period or problem per chapter, providing for the most part two chapters on each couple. These chapters are consecutive except for the ones on the Carlyles, which frame the others—the first on their courtship and Thomas's ascendance, the second on the later stages and Jane's. When read in sequence, the chapters offer a somewhat chronological spectrum of marriage. That it is a perverse spectrum I hardly need underline. Not all courtships are quite so epistolary as the Carlyles', nor conclude with quite so dramatic a reversal of all the conventions of the preceding months. Not all wedding nights are so traumatic as the Ruskins', and not all newlyweds have quite so much trouble adjusting to each other's families. The Ruskins allow me to write about the triangle, that recurrent feature of marriage, although many triangles prove to be more stable arrangements than that of the Ruskins and John Everett Millais. In the chapters on Harriet Taylor and John Stuart Mill, I deal with the lassitude that develops after some years of marriage and one scenario for coping with it. Departing from chronology, I also deal with the issue of equality in marriage, which was important to the Mills and must be to anyone who thinks critically about marriage. Dickens comes next, as an example of what we would now call "mid-life crisis" and one way of dealing with it—taking out his dissatisfactions entirely on his wife and ending his marriage. George Eliot and George Henry Lewes follow, providing an example of a couple who stayed together happily until death parted them. I admit this is my favorite couple, and I do not find it accidental to their happiness (or to my pleasure) that their marriage wasn't a legal one. The book concludes with an exploration of the Carlyles' marriage at a late stage, when tensions and jealousy had entered it, and an exploration of how, after Jane's death, she avenged herself, through her diary, for all the wounds her husband gave her when she was alive.

I set out to choose my subjects on the grounds of variety and intrinsic narrative interest. My two goals were not entirely compatible, and narrative interest won out. Still, two of my subjects (Dickens and George Eliot) are novelists and three, in different ways, are social critics (Carlyle, Ruskin, Mill). Two are liberal (George Eliot and Mill) and three are what I would call romantic authoritarians (Dickens, Ruskin, Carlyle). I wanted happy and wretched couples, stable and unstable couples, couples with children and couples without. I wanted examples of various configurations of power—dominant men, dominant women, and, if it existed, equality. But my couples are more unhappy than happy, more unstable than stable, more childless than parental, more sexless than sexually fulfilled. Perhaps my own mythology appears in my choices, but I feel, too, that I discovered for myself the specific truth of Tolstoy's generalization: "happy families are all alike"—in offering the world less interesting stories than the unhappy families. This rule of narrative is a shame, leading to the proliferation of images of misery and a paucity of models of happiness. For my part, to counteract it, I have included Mr. and Mrs. Darwin (about whom I had originally intended to write a long chapter) in the concluding chronology, Mrs. Darwin regularly giving birth to another child with Mr. Darwin, dear, loving, unable to witness her pain without pain to himself, hovering over her, anxious and concerned.

Finally, I have chosen to write about writers not because they live more intelligently—or less so—than other people, nor in the belief that they are representative. I expect, quite the contrary, that writers, like other people who must push their psychic development to extremes, are less able than most people to live comfortably within the constraints of the customary. But, however they live, writers tend to report on it more amply than most people—in their letters and journals, and, to some extent, in their imaginative work. I wanted to work with couples about whom a lot was known so that I could direct my efforts, biographically, to the shaping of narratives rather than archival research. To Victorianists, no new facts will be revealed, yet I hope the work as a whole will suggest new truths, especially the extent to which all living is a creative act of greater or lesser authenticity, hindered or helped by the fictions to which we submit ourselves.

Although I began the book with no thesis to prove, merely with a feminist skepticism about marriage, a taste for the higher gossip, a distaste for the rhetoric of romantic love, and a desire to look at marriages as imaginative projections and arrangements of power, I ended with a bewildered respect for the durability of the pair, in all its variations. Perhaps predictably, I became more convinced than ever about the sterility, for men as well as women, of the patriarchal ideal of marriage and more skeptical about the chances of any particular marriage to escape its influence.

Psychologically, the purpose of marriage is not obscure. It provides limits within which one defines oneself, against which one can usefully rebel. It enforces depth. One's relationship to a person known over years is unlikely to be "happier" than one's relationship with a stranger (hence the perpetual appeal of strangers), but it is qualitatively richer, deeper. As in the relationship between parents and children, meaning develops simply because of time and intimacy. The social purpose of marriage, however, has gotten increasingly murky since the mid-nineteenth century. (By the end of the century, George Bernard Shaw could get a laugh, in *Misalliance*, from the refreshingly simple idea that couples should marry for money. Shaw had no truck with the sentimental burden which the institution of marriage has been made to bear.) Divorce, far from clarifying things, makes marriage even more problematic. What does the promise of a permanent commitment mean when everyone knows it's provisional?

I am tempted to say that divorce makes marriage meaningless—which doesn't mean I would wish there to be less divorce, just less marriage. When divorce is possible, people no longer need to conform themselves to the discipline of the marital relationship. Instead the law is presssured to authorize more personalized and meaningful forms of relationship. This is the wrong way round. People should be able to hide within the thickets of the law, in Thomas More's phrase. The attempt to make laws supple enough to accommodate the wrinkles of their personalities and desires may be quixotic. Since it was in the nineteenth century that the attempt was first made to humanize the marriage laws, it was in the nineteenth century that marriage as an institution began to lose meaning. Bad enough to choose once in a lifetime whom to live with; to go on choosing, to reaffirm one's choice day after day, as one must when it is culturally possible to divorce, is really asking a lot of people. Perhaps better the old way, indissoluble unions with a great deal of civilized behavior—in other words, secrecy, even lying—for the sake of harmony.[10] Or the way of the future, frankly personal unions entered into personally, with carefully articulated and individualized pledges of fidelity, if any.

Late-nineteenth-century feminists urged the public to accept the idea that all women were not made for marriage, that other ways of living should be encouraged. This was the point of George Gissing's novel *The Odd Women*; the oddness of the protagonists consists in their not wanting to marry. But despite Gissing and feminist interest, remote and more recent, in unmarried lives, the pressure to marry has not much abated. Since the 1890s society has seen to it that it is easier and easier to get out of marriage, but it has made it only a little easier to avoid getting into it in the first place. My own feeling is that marriage still displaces too many other possibilities in our culture, at least in part because of its narrative appeal, the clear-cut beginnings and endings it offers, the richly complicated middle. As Barthes says, if we managed to suppress marriage, what would we have left to tell? Perhaps someday this will change, and our descendants, looking back at us from a marriage-less, anarchic, free-form or post-modern future, will find our attempts to live parallel lives deliciously quaint.

I hope this book will have a mirroring effect similar to the effect that Froude's biography of Carlyle had on Leslie Stephen, but not exactly. For I do not want to move readers either to self-blame or the blame of others. I *would* like them to be prompted by these stories to question how the presumption of marriage, the fiction of marriage, has affected the shape of their lives, for I believe that marriage, whether we see it as a psychological relationship or a political one, has determined the story of all our lives more than we have generally acknowledged. The extent to which these particular marriages serve as parallels to lives closer to their own in time and place readers must of course decide for themselves.

JANE

WELSH

and

THOMAS

CARLYLE

1821–1866

The Carlyles' Courtship

Take the case of an heiress, handsome, clever, and rich, with a comfortable home and a happy disposition, who has lived some twenty years in the world with very little to distress or vex her. I borrow Jane Austen's description of her most willful heroine, Emma Woodhouse, in order to present another heiress, Jane Baillie Welsh, roughly her contemporary, living in the Scottish town of Haddington, and, like Emma, a young woman with rather too much the habit of having her own way.

Jane Welsh at eighteen seemed a fortunate being. She was the only child of prosperous parents who adored her. They were kindly people, between whom there was no discord, who lived comfortably but not ostentatiously, who were well respected in Haddington, a thriving county seat, some sixteen miles from Edinburgh. The Welshes indulged Jane, but she knew how far her power went with them. Unquestioning and absolute obedience to her parents, she said in later years, was the foundation of everything valuable in her character.

Jane particularly loved her father, a physician, and wanted to please him. Since what seemed to please him most were precocious displays of wit, that was what Jane labored to produce. At the age of thirteen she wrote a novel. At fourteen she wrote a five-act tragedy which Dr. Welsh admired so much that he sent it on to a friend. Words, clever words, written and spoken, were Jane's way of winning her father's approval, an approval she came to depend on. In 1819, when Jane was eighteen, Dr. Welsh died suddenly. He contracted typhoid fever from a patient and was dead within four days. It was a devastating blow to Jane, who was left with no one to work for, no one to improve herself for. "I had no counselor that could direct me," she wrote, "no friend that understood me—the pole-star of my life was lost, and the world looked a dreary blank."[1]

Her misery was profound, her consolations superficial; but there were consolations. Jane was attractive, with perky good looks and a liveliness of spirit which made her dark eyes sparkle and caused her to look even prettier than she was. Her light body, her small face with its pointed uptilting chin, her mocking eyes—everything about her suggested sprightliness and a buoyant confidence in her social worth. Her best friend in later life, Geraldine Jewsbury, was to say that Jane enjoyed flirtation. Thomas Carlyle vehemently denied it. No, Jane was simply a charming woman who liked to charm young men. She was witty, playful, irresistible. She was also moderately rich, for her father had passed most of his property on to her. No wonder so many men were attracted to her, and Jane enjoyed the attention, however much she liked to present herself as a Penelope, bothered by pesky suitors, kept by them from her serious business, the making of her web. For her, the life of the mind would always exist in tension with, resisting as it were, her social existence.

Like many other women raised in the Anglo-Saxon tradition until very recently, Jane assumed that the life of the mind was basically a male preserve. In her childhood, she wanted to study Latin, as boys did. Her parents would not allow it. Furtively, Jane consulted a local scholar and managed to teach herself the declension of a Latin noun, choosing—with unerring emphasis—the word *penna*. One night, when she was presumed to have gone to bed, she hid herself under a table in the drawing room and surprised her parents by reciting the purloined declension. "*Penna*, the pen; *pennae*, of the pen." In conclusion, she said, "I want to learn Latin; please let me be a boy."[2] Jane got her wish, at least to the extent that she was allowed to study Latin, but her pen envy did not diminish with the years. Until she decided to marry a writer, she wanted to be a writer herself, and from time to time it occurred to her that her courage and daring, her lively intelligence and ambition were wasted on a girl. She was fond of quoting an old woman of Haddington who said, after watching her skip along the mill-dam, that in Jane nature had "stickit a fine callant," that is, thwarted a fine boy. A feminist consciousness flickers in Jane's letters. But flickers merely. She saw the way that women were encouraged to waste themselves in social trivia, and she envied the cultural advantages of men, but she never realized that the barriers to achievement for women were internal as well as external. She would come to blame a lack of talent for her failure to achieve her goals, whereas the problem may have been a lack of confidence in her talent. Ignoring the difference between provincial Scotland and cosmopolitan France, between the middle class and the aristocracy, she took as her heroine and inspiration Madame de Staël.

If Jane was to turn herself into Madame de Staël, education was necessary—not such an education as a boy would get, but better than that given to most girls. The man whom Dr. Welsh engaged to teach Latin to the ten-year-old Jane was Edward Irving, then nineteen and master at the Haddington school. He was fair-skinned, dark-haired, and, except for a squint, very handsome, a man of some charisma. He spent two years in Haddington before moving in 1812 to another school in Kirkcaldy, where his appointment proved to be controversial. Some of the parents of his pupils disliked his methods. They broke away and hired a rival schoolmaster, recommended by the same professors in Edinburgh who had recommended Irving. This man was Thomas Carlyle, three years Irving's junior, and, like him, an Annandale lad. He had followed Irving's educational path and arrived at the same place.

Irving chose to treat Carlyle not as a competitor but as a friend, a fellow countryman happily met in a town far from home. They discussed books; they went on walking trips together. It was from Irving, who was probably in love with her at the time, that Carlyle first heard of Jane Welsh and her father. Irving spoke of Dr. Welsh as "one of the wisest, truest and most dignified of men," and Jane as "a paragon of gifted young girls." To Carlyle they became "objects of distant reverence and unattainable longing."[3] The seeds, it seems, had been planted before he ever met Jane, and it is not surprising that he fell in love with her immediately.

By May of 1821, Dr. Welsh was dead, Irving was preaching in

Glasgow, and Carlyle, who was to say that it was better to perish than to continue schoolmastering, had abandoned the school at Kirkcaldy for a wretched but independent life in Edinburgh. He was studying law halfheartedly and writing reviews to make money. His only pleasure was reading Goethe. He was lonely. He couldn't sleep. His health was poor. When Edward Irving came by on a visit and proposed a brief jaunt to Haddington, he agreed with pleasure. They walked out on a sunny afternoon and paid a call on Mrs. Welsh and Jane. The ladies seemed sad, still conscious of their loss. Carlyle found Mrs. Welsh beautiful but "not of an intellectual or specially distinguished physiognomy." The drawing room, however, seemed to him the finest apartment he had ever been in, bearing the stamp of the late owner's solid temper. "Clean, all of it, as spring water; solid and correct," although there was perhaps on the tables of the drawing room "a superfluity of elegant whim-whams." He felt "as one walking transiently in upper spheres," where he had "little right even to make transit."[4]

That night, back in the room they had taken at the George Inn, Carlyle and Irving discussed young ladies, beginning with Augusta Sibbald, a tall and shapely person, but giggly and foolish.

"What would you take to marry Miss Augusta now?" Irving asked.

"Not for an entire and perfect chrysolite the size of this terraqueous globe."

"And what would you take to marry Miss Jeannie?"

"Hah, I should not be so hard to deal with there I should imagine."

They stayed for three days, with daily visits to the Welshes. The two ladies were "very humane" and listened benevolently while the young men talked, Jane managing to convey even while silent, as intelligent people can, a lively understanding of all shades of meaning. Upon returning to Edinburgh, Carlyle wrote to his brother, "I came back so full of joy, that I have done nothing since but dream of it."[5]

He sent Jane a parcel of books and included a letter, a mixture of pedagogy, sentimentality, and absurdity in the form of a reading list, some flattering comparisons of Jane to Madame de Staël, and some references to the "Elysian hours" they had spent together in Haddington. In returning the books a few weeks later, Jane cut off his attempt to establish a romantic correspondence with the curtest of notes: "with Miss Welsh's compliments and very best thanks."[6] She misspelled his name. If it was not apparent to him that he was ineligible, it was clear enough to her. He was the son of a stonemason in the meager town of Ecclefechan. She was the daughter of the leading man of Haddington. The superfluity of elegant whimwhams in the drawing room ought to have suggested to Carlyle, if nothing else did, that more was respected in the Welsh household than intelligence, and Jane was enough her conventional mother's daughter to find unthinkable marriage with a man who had no station, no money, no prospects of improving his worldly position—nor even much ambition to do so.

But if Jane did not want Thomas as a suitor, she wanted him very much as an intellectual companion. Her aspirations for literary achievement were serious, and there was no one in Haddington with whom to share them. It was pleasant, of course, to have young men admiring one's person and wanting to marry one, but it was tedious, too. None of them cared about serious books or ideas. None of them valued her, as she wanted to be valued, for her judgment. Even Edward Irving thought that she was a little too snobbish, tended to cut herself off too much from the people around her, and he feared that more learning would only aggravate the problem.

So I suspect there was something of a struggle between Jane and Mrs. Welsh on the subject of the brilliant young man who knew so much about German literature. Jane would claim that she did not think of him in the light of a suitor, but Mrs. Welsh knew better, foresaw danger, and made Jane promise to correspond with him as little as possible, without absolutely cutting off the welcome flow of books from Edinburgh. So the curt note was succeeded, in response to the next parcel, by a note only slightly less curt, and when Carlyle asked if he might visit, Jane sent a polite refusal on her mother's behalf. But she herself agreed to see him when she was in Edinburgh, in July of 1821 and again in November, and she had only to be in his presence to become his pupil. His idealism and largeness of mind overwhelmed her. With her eager, responsive intelligence, she adopted his way of seeing things, changed her vocabulary, forgot to be concerned with "prudence" and "the reasonable," and agreed to a "Romantic Friendship." No sooner did she get back to Haddington and her mother's influence than the forces of prudence and the reasonable reasserted themselves, and she begged Carlyle not to make her honor the promise he had extracted to write to him, a promise involving "disobedience and deceit" to her mother.[7] And yet, so great was her interest in Carlyle's work, so great her need for him to be interested in hers, that she could not prevent herself from leaving a loophole: when he finished his essay on *Faust*, he might send it to her along with a letter.

Carlyle, lonely, poor, hopeless, liked the idea of working, in a sense, to win Jane. She was the grail, the object of his quest. If he were successful, if he made himself a name, perhaps he could gain her love. The very idea was enough to make him more buoyant than he had been in a long time. When he finished *Faust*, fulfilling the conditions for writing, he recklessly hinted at his secret hopes to Jane. "When I compare the aspect of the world to me now with what it was twelve months ago, I am far from desponding or complaining. I seem to have a motive and a rallying-word in the fight of life: . . . *Alles für Ruhm und Ihr!*"[8]

Jane replied with all the force of her wit.

"Alles für Ruhm und Ihr"!!—On my word, most gay and gallantly said—One would almost believe the man fancies I have fallen in love with him, and entertain the splendid project of rewarding his literary labours with myself. Really Sir I do not design for you a recompense so worthless. If you render yourself an honoured member of society . . . I will be to you a true, a constant, a devoted *friend*—but not a Mistress—a Sister—but not a Wife—*Falling in love* and marrying like other Misses is quite out of the question.[9]

Already a formidable prose stylist at the age of twenty-one, Jane deploys her mockery like a knife, slashing through Carlyle's solemn Teutonic motto, cutting its idealism to ribbons. Like most of Jane's letters, this one displays its cleverness self-consciously, and its primary message is "Admire me." Carlyle saw this clearly enough and acknowledged it to be "very spirited and very satirical and altogether very clever."[10] His letter is sad, earnest. He doesn't understand why their friendship can't proceed directly. He sees her as lonely, knows he is lonely. Why can't they solace one another? He does not understand that he is a danger. He does not feel dangerous at all. Nor will he immediately allow himself to be contained by the role Jane and her mother are creating for him, the emasculated tutor of German.

Jane was not being coy. Her interest in Carlyle was not romantic. Letters to her cousin Eliza Stodart show that the romantic drama she imagined herself enacting involved George Rennie, a year younger than Jane, who was later to achieve some distinction as a sculptor, a member of Parliament, and governor of the Falkland Islands. He had made some sort of declaration to Jane, exchanged letters with her, but now was leaving her to travel abroad. Jane wrote for her cousin a description of their leave-taking which features strong feeling at war with correct behavior—the kind of scene Jane Austen so loved to depict.

> He took leave of my Mother then looked at me as if uncertain what to do—I held out my hand he took it and said *"Good bye"!* I answered him *"Farewell"* He left the house!—such was the concluding scene of our *Romance!*—Great God He left the house —the *very room* where—no matter—as if he had never been in it in his life before—unfeeling wretch!—It was a dreadful trial to me to be obliged to save appearances even for some minutes *after* he was gone but I went through it bravely![11]

She returned his letters, scorning to keep them "like a sword over his head." One doubts the weight of the sword, the depth of the romance, but not Jane's delight in portraying herself the stoic, dignified, and tragically disappointed heroine of this domestic drama.

At about the same time, a much more powerful and unconventional paradigm of romance began to inform the way she imagined her own experience. She was reading Rousseau's *La Nouvelle Héloïse* and was immensely moved by Julie's passionate love for her tutor, Saint-Preux, whom she cannot marry because of his social inferiority, and by her resolution to marry the man of her father's choice, M. de Wolmar. Julie's passion is so strong that she cannot keep herself from yielding to Saint-Preux, but the instinct of duty is stronger yet, and she nobly compels herself to live the rest of her life as a virtuous wife and mother.

The first impact of this reading on Jane was to strengthen her resolve never to marry.

> No lover will Jane Welsh ever find like St Preux—no Husband like Wolmar ... and to no man will she give her heart and pretty hand who bears to these no resemblance—George Rennie! James Aitken! Robert MacTurk! James Baird!!! Robby Angus!—O Lord O Lord! where is the St Preux? Where is the Wolmar?[12]

A little further thought, however, suggested that Scottish reality might after all have something to measure up to the fictional world of Rousseau. Craig Buchanan was too lame, too bald, too given to puns and flattery to pass for Wolmar, but Thomas Carlyle was not a bad Saint-Preux. "He has *his* talents—*his* vast and cultivated mind —*his* vivid imagination—*his* independence of soul and *his* high souled principles of honour—But then Ah these *buts!* St Preux never kicked the fire irons—nor made puddings in his teacup."[13] "Want of elegance," which Rousseau said was a defect no woman could overlook, was decidedly an obstacle in raising Carlyle to the level of a *beau idéal*. Imagination? Yes, he had that. Genius, brilliance, passion of a sort. But elegance? By no stretch of the imagination. The roughness, the cragginess of his physical appearance, so attractive to contemporary eyes, was not attractive to Jane. He was awkward, his manners uncouth. His physical presence—particularly his tendency to flail about with his arms and legs—made Jane so uncomfortable that she wished she could tie up all his "members," leaving at liberty only his tongue.[14]

Against Jane's wishes, Carlyle went to Haddington for a visit in early February of 1822. She had not wanted him to come because of the gossip it would provoke: people would think she was receiving him as a suitor. Since he insisted on coming, Jane made sure he would not mistake the nature of his reception. She was cold and formal. This visit, along with a few more letters of elegant mockery and a two-month silence, finally made Carlyle understand that if his friendship with Jane were to continue, he must accept the purely tutorial role she offered. And so, by a year after their first meeting, they had settled into a comfortable relationship based on the exchange of books and responses to books, a relationship which satisfied Jane entirely. By a judicious wielding of anger, mockery, and coolness, she had won the initial struggle for power between them, and it was a long time before the stronger power of his imagination could impose itself on hers.

The letters which Jane and Thomas wrote between 1821 when they met and 1826 when they were married are called by their first editor "love letters," but that is misleading. Jane ruled out love or even passionate friendship as a subject for much of the correspondence, and if the letters form an epistolary novel, the genre they belong to is not romance but *Bildungsroman,* the novel of education. Carlyle had thought that if he worked hard to improve himself he might win Jane. That was not to be. His task instead was to educate Jane so that finally she would appreciate him. Without consciously setting out to do so, he trained his pupil so well, so transformed her values, that she was able to perceive him finally as the only fit object for her love.

And what an education he gave her! He corrected her translations of German, he set subjects on which they were both to write poems, he sent her books, he suggested others, they exchanged comments on their reading, he encouraged, criticized, cajoled. She must force herself to read more history, for which she had little inclination. Four hours of study every morning, held to regularly, would double her mental capacity within months. But Jane, who preferred the heroic cavalry charge to successful trench warfare, replied that four hours were not enough. She would do eight. Well, six, if she must, he countered, but no more than six. Regular application was the chief thing. Repeatedly, insistently, he urged her to set herself a large task of composition. Too much reading, too much research, too much intaking with no creative reconstruction was, he told her wisely, not a good thing. Write a play, write an essay on Madame de Staël, do a translation of *Don Carlos.* The subjects he chose were cannily suited to appeal to Jane and to make use of her talents, of which he gave her a shrewd assessment. He saw that she was a keen observer of human foibles and concluded that her talent was essentially dramatic. Why not, then, write a tragedy on the subject of Queen Boadicea? He outlined the structure, spelled out the conflicts implicit in the action, gave her what film people call a complete "treatment" of the material, and you understand his hope that in this strong and high-spirited heroine of the British past his high-spirited friend would see a kindred soul.

But Jane's talent—which he rightly saw was dramatic, wrongly hoped would be tragic—was already expressing itself in the only form it would ever take and in a form which suited it perfectly—her letters. For Jane was not disposed to write a tragedy on Queen Boadicea. She did not seem disposed to write a tragedy at all. And much as she adored Madame de Staël, she did not think she could write an essay on her. In fact she doubted she could write anything, and it is on this subject—the obstacles to her writing—that Jane produces her best and most characteristic prose.

I have neither genius taste nor commonsense—I have no courage no industry no perseverance—and how in the name of wonder can I write a tragedy—I am not at all the sort of person you and I took me for—I begin to think that I was actually meant by nature to be a fine Lady—My friends that is my acquaintances have told me this all along but I would not believe them—For the last month however I have shown lamentable symptoms of a tendency that way—I have spent all my time in riding on horseback, dressing three times a day, singing Italian airs, and playing at shuttlecock! Dear Sir what will cure me? I have just enough of reason left to perceive I am in a bad way—if another such month passes over me—I am a lost woman—even my ambition is expiring very fast. I am as proud of striking the shuttlecock two hundred times as if I had written two hundred admirable verses — . . . Oh dear me! I shall never hold a respectable place among literary ladies—but I know I can be a first rate fine Lady whenever I please—the temptation is strong; furnish me with an antidote if you can.[15]

The writing is fast-paced, lively, riotously specific. Her equation of the two hundred strokes at shuttlecock with two hundred lines of poetry reduces both accomplishments to equal absurdity. With Jane, aspiration is a subject for comedy, not tragedy, and the comedy is dazzling. Spirit tries to soar and is plucked back to earth by dresses that must be changed, shuttlecocks that must be batted, tunes that must be sung. Another day: "I opened 'Mary Stewart' after breakfast but Dr. Fiffe interrupted me, and teazed me to play at shuttlecock till I consented—When we had finished: I observed the Piano open and Lord Byron's 'fare thee well' (my favorite song) staring me in the face: I sat down and played and sung badly till dinner time. The evening I spent as I spend too many, at an odious tea party. . . . Since my return I have read Atala, *twelve lines* of Mary Stewart; written two pages of *two Novels*, and four lines of an ode to Whilhelmina and moreover I have darned two rents in my gown behold the fruit of my resolution—the sum total of my labours."[16] Her comedy works by juxtaposing intellectual concerns and domestic demands. Exasperation is her constant mode.

Although his sense of humor could not be called playful, the author of *Sartor Resartus* was to prove no mean comic writer himself, and he fully appreciated the art of Jane Welsh's letters. But however much he treasured them, he never considered her letters enough of a goal for her talents. He was a demanding teacher. She must not waste herself in trifles. She must write something serious and sustained. Carlyle bestowed upon her, in letter after letter, some of the best advice about starting to write that an aspiring writer has ever received. "You really magnify the matter too much: never think of the press or public when you are writing: . . . If you cannot think of any proper theme, cannot get in motion for whatever cause; then let the business rest for a week; cease to vex yourself about it, in time materials will come unsought."[17] But at last it occurred to him to wonder why Jane was having so much trouble getting down to business. Where was the difficulty? As he saw it, she had not only talent but a comfortable home and total freedom from the "heartbreaking isolation" and the "thousand vulgar cares" which oppress so many writers—that is to say, himself. He imagined her surrounded by friends and relations who loved her and gave her the emotional support he missed. In this, however, he was wrong. People sought her company, but none was a companion of the soul; no one—except him—urged her to achievement. She had gardened her mind for her father's sake, but her father had died. "I am *alone*, and no one loves me better for my industry." Without constant reassurance, she succumbed to despair about her own talent. "I do fear I am fit for nothing—I wish I could refrain from teazing you with this incessant subject." And again, "I can feel but I cannot write; the more I try it the more I am convinced that nature has raised some insurmountable obstacle to my desires—it is very hard! for I am sure I have known more ignorant and more senseless people than myself that scribble away delightfully."[18] There was something dependent —something that had been made dependent—in Jane's creativity. Letter writing was a congenial form for her, because in correspondence feedback comes quickly and the impulse to write for immediate response is wholly legitimate. Her need to be validated intellectually explains, too, why Carlyle was becoming more and more important to her, despite her infatuations and flirtations—none of which she concealed from him—with more eligible men.

Increasingly, the correspondence with Carlyle was the only thing of intellectual substance in her life. Often at the end of the week, she wrote her cousin, her spirits and industry would start to flag, but then one of Mr. Carlyle's brilliant letters would arrive to inspire her with new resolution, to brighten all her prospects and hopes with "the golden hue of his own imagination." To Carlyle himself, her expressions of affection and appreciation grew ever warmer. "I owe you so much! feelings and sentiments that ennoble my character, that give dignity interest and enjoyment to my life—in return, I can only love you, and *that* I do, from the bottom of my heart." Understandably, Thomas interpreted this as the declaration of love he so long had hoped for, and he responded with exuberance, symphonic delight, dark notes about the peril they faced, and a rich resolution: "If your happiness be shipwrecked by my means, then woe, woe is to me without end! But it will not: no, you will yet be blessed yourself in making me more blessed than man has right to look for being upon Earth."[19]

Jane panicked. She had been misunderstood. The love she bore him was a sisterly love, deep, delightful, but not impassioned enough to reconcile her to the existence of a married woman, the cares and occupations of which were her disgust. Was it possible that he, too, thought her an ordinary female, incapable of feeling strong affection for a man her own age without having as its object their union for life? She would be his truest friend while she breathed the breath of life, but she would never marry him. "Never, never! Not though you were as rich as Croesus, as honoured and renowned as you yet shall be."[20] Carlyle replied with patient compliance. He was content to continue their friendship just as it had been. So long as she had charity to listen, he would pour out his affections and his plans. If she married, he would cease writing to her, but not loving her. And so the flurry of anxiety on her part, of hope on his, subsided. But I think this "misunderstanding" was a turning point in their relationship, for the words *love* and *marriage* had been spoken between them. She might reject the idea of marrying him, but she had conceived it, and it seems that no matter how impossible a thing appears, if it can be imagined, it can be enacted.

We should remember at this point the extent to which the Carlyles' courtship was conducted by correspondence. They were rarely in each other's physical presence. After the disastrous visit of February 1822, a full year went by before Jane and Thomas saw each other again, a year in which Jane waited for the capricious Mrs. Welsh, who had taken an immense dislike to Carlyle, to veer around with another wind and wonder why Thomas Carlyle never came out to visit any more. Even after they were engaged, an entire year passed in which they did not see each other once. Clearly, this was no union of sensualists, but of people who create with words their own experience. Indeed, one fascination of this epistolary courtship is that, with such a mass of material, with so many bulletins on the state of the soul, it is possible to see how change occurs, how language is eventually found to describe what has been felt, how with the finding of the language the feelings begin to change again.

For a year and a half (April 1823 to January 1825) the correspondence continues at the same pitch of heightened platonism. Love on both sides is fervently expressed but is understood not to be the sort of love that leads to marriage. Thomas imagines their idyl will end when Jane agrees to marry someone else. He has said that their correspondence must cease upon her marriage. Jane cannot imagine herself giving up their correspondence, which has become her chief pleasure, but she also cannot imagine marrying Carlyle. Nothing seems likely to change. And then something changes. Because of a joke.

Thomas had long cherished the idea of abandoning the haunts of men and establishing for himself a kind of hermitage in a wild and desolate part of the country. In his heart of hearts, he hoped that Jane would accompany him, making the hermitage more like the Garden of Eden. By the end of 1824, his fantasy had crystallized into a semi-rational plan to support himself by farming, so that, in country quiet, he could write his books and improve his health. When he mentioned his plan to Jane, she offhandedly—jestingly, as it turned out—suggested that he farm her estate of Craigenputtock, which was just then in need of a tenant. To Thomas, this was no joke but a hint that Jane might be persuaded to involve herself in his fantasy. He wrote back immediately, in a letter too rife with purpose to waste time on sentiment, proposing that they marry and live at Craigenputtock together.

Now Jane's father had gone to considerable trouble to escape from the southern Scottish moorlands. Farming had been his family heritage; he left it and turned himself into a physician and a town man. Jane was, like him, sociable and urban in her tastes, and Craigenputtock, an hour by horse from the nearest town, set among treeless hills, a house completely isolated in a countryside which seems fitter for cows and sheep than for people, was truly one of the most desolate spots in the British Isles. Jane insisted that she had been joking and begged Thomas to think of a plan more promising than farming the most barren spot in Dumfriesshire. "What a thing that would be to be sure! you and I keeping house at Craigenputtock! . . . I would not spend a month on it with an Angel."[21] They were to spend six years there.

But for now Jane gave various reasons—some good, some silly— for refusing to marry him. She denied aspiring to marry a rich man, but she would not marry someone who would force her to live more meanly than she was accustomed to; the sacrifice would make her resent him. Besides, Providence had assigned her to a certain station, and she could not abandon it without the approval of her "judgment." Beneath these prudential considerations, one senses that Jane is unsure of her feelings. Carlyle still does not quite measure up to Saint-Preux. And then too, though Julie gave herself sexually to Saint-Preux (a matter that seems by no means at issue between Jane and Thomas), she never would consent to marry him. So let Thomas apply himself to improving his circumstances, let him use his talents to make up for the inequality in their births, and then they would talk of marrying. "If all this were realized I *think* I should have good sense enough to abate something of my romantic ideal, and to content myself with stopping short on this side idolatry."[22]

She tried to highlight the inadequacies of his circumstances out of tact, to avoid mentioning his inadequacies of person, but Carlyle, by accusing her of following the vulgar counsels of prudence, forced her to speak even more frankly about her reservations of feeling.

> I am *prudent*, I fear, only because I am not strongly tempted to be otherwise—My heart is capable (I feel it is) of a love to which *no* deprivation would be a sacrifice—a love which . . . would bear down all the restraints which *duty* and *expediency* might throw in the way, . . . But the all-perfect Mortal, who could inspire me with a love so extravagant, is nowhere to be found—exists nowhere but in the Romance of my own imagination! . . . In the mean time, I should be very mad, were I to act as if from the influence of such a passion, while my affections are in a state of perfect tranquillity.[23]

Jane was trying wholeheartedly to understand herself, but language was failing her: she loved Carlyle, but she was not in love with him; her sentiments were such as one would feel for a brother but not for a husband. She could not imagine marrying anyone else, she could not imagine life without him, but was this strong attachment to him "passion"? There are certain experiences to which language gives names—"being in love" is perhaps the most interesting—which are never precisely described. Worldly wisdom says you will know when it happens, but worldly wisdom is often wrong. Jane, sensibly if dangerously, made behavior a test of experience. Passionate love was the kind of love that would move her to ignore the demands of duty and expediency. Her formulation is sensible, because it is easier to describe and consequently to understand behavior than it is to describe experience, easier to say what you did for a man than what you felt for him. Her formulation is dangerous, because, if a person can bring herself to behave in the way defined, then she can *deduce* the feeling that inspired it—that is, if Jane could make herself agree to marry Thomas, then she must, according to her emotional syllogism, be in love with him. Perhaps more "being in love" is of this kind—deduced—than we might care to admit. The calm, delightful affection one has enjoyed without being made untranquil, suddenly seems deeper, more turbulent, after certain words are uttered. Commitment grows when you begin to use the language of commitment.

A further stumbling block was the institution of marriage itself. To Jane it had always presented itself as a pitiful waste of her talents, a squandering of genius on the ordinary. In this she had been encouraged by Thomas, who imagined her—until very late—marrying someone else. In the common world, he told her, the great object of a woman's existence was to "get a rich husband, and a fine house, and give dinners, just as it is the great object of ravens to find carrion." To him it appeared "more enviable to be a sister of Madame de Staël's for half a year, than 'to suckle fools and chronicle small beer' for half a century."[24] But vulgar marriage with a common rich man was one thing, marriage with Carlyle, a heroic spiritual undertaking, quite another. Jane's imagination finally rose to the challenge, although it was perhaps the hardest part of her education, as it is for many ambitious young women, to acknowledge that the traditional institution of marriage could apply to her, too; that even capacious spirits could submit to that ancient containment. But this common, vulgar custom, so shockingly interruptive of her plans, was her only way out of an intolerable situation —perpetual childhood, perpetual life with her mother, perpetual inability to pursue her own plans—even if it led to another equally draining. In late January of 1825 she wrote to Thomas, "Not many months ago, I would have said it was impossible that I should ever be your wife; at present I consider this the most *probable de*stiny for me; and in a year or so, perhaps, I shall consider it the only one."[25]

She over-estimated the time. The big step, as I have said, is between not conceiving something at all and conceiving it to be impossible. Once you have conceived it as impossible, it is but a short step to finding it possible—probable—certain. And so, without being wholly in control of the process at the last, Jane found herself after this flurry of letters, somewhat to her own surprise, "*half en-gaged*." "*I* who have such a natural horror at engagements! it gives me asthma every time I think of it."[26] She did not know, she said, how his spirit had gained such a mastery over hers, in spite of her pride and stubbornness, but so it was. Looking backward, we can say that the stronger, more resolute imagination was bound to prevail, but it is also true that social reality left her few alternatives. How long could she go on playing shuttlecocks and being unable to read when there were visitors in the house? And how could she live, except as the technical dependent of her mother or of some man?

Carlyle received the good news in London, where he had been for many months overseeing the publication of his life of Schiller and beginning to establish himself in the literary world. He wrote that he would return to Scotland directly. That was January. It was April before they had their reunion. Between that encounter and the next, a visit Jane paid to the Carlyle family in Dumfriesshire, four months went by. Their eighteen-month engagement was every bit as epistolary as their prior acquaintanceship had been. The incidents of drama, too, were transacted by mail. Carlyle, for example, had scruples to deal with. He did not want it thought that he was marrying Jane for her money. He urged her to make over to her mother her inheritance, largely the property at Haddington and the farm of Craigenputtock, with its yearly rent of some £200. This, accordingly, Jane did in July 1825, leaving herself as penniless as her future husband.

Mrs. Welsh acted the good parent. By objecting to the marriage, she drove her daughter into the arms of her fiancé and solidified the young people's commitment to each other. So long as Mrs. Welsh had been the feeble, incompetent widow, Jane had been her protector. So long as she refrained from comment, Jane supplied her place and urged caution on her lover. But when Mrs. Welsh objected to the marriage on the grounds of Thomas's bad temper, Jane replied that she preferred to suffer from temper of her own choosing than from temper—like her mother's—thrust upon her.

> No! my own Darling! we shall not be parted on this account. Your irritability is the very natural consequence of continual suffering; when you are well, and happy . . . you will be the best humoured man alive. And tho' you should never be good-humoured, what then? Do we not love each other? And what is love if it cannot make all rough places smooth![27]

From which will be seen the extent to which Jane has lost her detachment, her irony, and much of her instinct for self-preservation in the process of scrambling from the maternal nest.

Carlyle was more and more disposed to assert himself. This was evident during the next crisis, deciding where Mrs. Welsh was to live after the wedding. Jane, concerned about her mother's loneliness, no doubt feeling guilt about leaving her, suggested that she live with them. But Thomas objected strenuously. Mrs. Welsh, as the older party, might think the household was hers to rule, whereas in fact, man was born to command and woman to obey. He could consent to live with Mrs. Welsh only on condition that she thoroughly accept this.

His metamorphosis from humble suitor to arrogant cock of the walk is distressing. His encouragement of Jane's ambition ceases. No more talk of Madame de Staël. He assumes with cool majesty that taking care of him is a full-time affair. He imagines the duties of their household rigorously divided:

> Do you not think, that when you on one side of our household shall have faithfully gone thro your housewife duties, and I on the other shall have written my allotted pages, we shall meet

over our frugal meal with far happier and prouder hearts than thousands that are not blessed with any duties, and whose agony is the bitterest of all, "the agony of a too easy bed?" . . . I predict that we shall be the finest little pair imaginable! A true-hearted dainty lady-wife; a sick and sulky, but diligent, and not false-hearted or fundamentally unkind goodman: and these two fronting the hardships of life in faithful and eternal union.[28]

If Jane was not to know the agony of a too easy bed, there is no saying that she was not warned. When his right to be sick and sulky but not *fundamentally* unkind is built into their understanding of the marriage, whereas she is only given leave to be true-hearted and dainty, how could her lot be too easy? Yet, so complete has Jane's education been in the five years since her meeting with Carlyle, that she accepts this picture without a single wisecrack or splinter of elegant mockery. In fact Jane considered this the best-natured letter she had received from Thomas in some time.

She was indeed his pupil, and the subject on which, above all, he had instructed her most eloquently—giving her a credo she proved ready to receive—was the superiority of intellectual power to any other kind of power and the superiority of glory achieved by writing to any other kind of glory. Years before, he had written her:

Kings & Potentates are a gaudy folk that flaunt about with plumes & ribbons to decorate them, and catch the coarse admiration of the many-headed monster, for a brief season—then sink into forgetfulness . . . but the Miltons, the de Staëls—these *are* the very salt of the Earth; they derive their "patents of Nobility direct from Almighty God," and live in the bosoms of all true men to all ages.[29]

So, when she finally brought herself around to the resolution of marrying Carlyle, she knew well enough how to defend her choice. She knew that people would think the match unequal, with all the advantages on her side. She knew they would say that he was poor and not well born and not even good-looking, tending towards the rough. "But a hundred chances to one, they would not tell you he is

among the cleverest men of his day; and not the cleverest only but
the most enlightened! that he possesses all the qualities I deem essential in *my* husband—a warm true heart to love me, a towering
intellect to command me, and a spirit of fire to be the guiding star-
light of my life. . . . Such then is this future husband of mine; not a
great man according to the most common sense of the word, but
truly great in its natural, proper sense—a scholar, a poet, a philosopher, a wise and noble man, one who holds his patent of nobility
from Almighty God, and whose high stature of manhood is not to be
measured by the inch-rule of Lilliputs!—Will you like him? no matter whether you do or not—since *I* like him in the deepest part of my
soul."[30]

This letter, sent to her uncle's wife in 1826, at the time of their
wedding, made its way after Jane's death forty years later to Carlyle,
who used it, along with the rest of their correspondence, as fodder
for his monumental remorse.

EFFIE

GRAY

and

JOHN

RUSKIN

1848–1854

Prelude:
Carlyle and the Gentleman
from Paisley

The day was, for different reasons, a significant one—as famous in English history as July 4 is to Americans—for April 10 in that revolutionary year of 1848, when monarchies disappeared all over Europe, was the day of the Chartist demonstration, the day that revolution did not take place in England. Two hundred thousand people were to march through the streets of London for a rally at Kennington Common, then back to the House of Commons to present *en masse* a petition for various democratic reforms endorsed with five million signatures. The streets of London were deserted in anticipation of violence; the government had called upon the old duke of Wellington to arrange the guarding of the Custom House, the Bank, the Exchange, the Post Office, and all other important public buildings. Downing Street was barricaded and the gates of the Admiralty closed. Soldiers and mounted Guardsmen were posted at Kennington Common and in strategic places throughout the city. But no force was needed to keep the demonstrators in order. On April 10, 1848, it rained.[1]

Thomas Carlyle, who walked out to see the revolution, hoping to describe it for his wife, in the country for her health, saw very little before the rain and fiercely cold wind forced him to take shelter in the Burlington Arcade. He struck up a conversation with a gentleman from Paisley who was able to inform him that the Chartist leaders had asked the crowd to disperse and return home peacefully, without marching to the Houses of Parliament. And so, cold and disappointed, the author of *Chartism*, the prophet of destruction to

sham forms of government, took the omnibus back to his house in
Chelsea and wrote a letter to his wife about the day's events. Later he
would learn that the crowd on Kennington Common had been closer
to twenty thousand than the two hundred thousand predicted and
that the famous petition bore closer to two than five million signatures, many of them—such as the signatures of the queen and the
prince consort—obviously fake.

Newlyweds

The Chartist demonstration prevented John James Ruskin, prosperous importer of sherry, and his wife, Margaret, from travelling to Scotland for the wedding of their son, already famous as the author of the first two volumes of *Modern Painters*. At any rate, the shutdown of London and the fear of violence provided an acceptable excuse for Mr. and Mrs. Ruskin's absence. In fact, they had never planned to attend their son's wedding in Perth. Scottish by birth and upbringing, both Mr. and Mrs. Ruskin hated Scotland and she, in particular, dreaded going there. In earlier days, when she was just a poor relation in the Ruskin household, her future husband's father had killed himself by cutting his throat and it was Margaret who discovered him and held the throat together with her hands while screaming for help. In later years, the closer she got to the site of Mr. Ruskin's suicide, the greater was her dread, the greater her reluctance to proceed. She crossed the Scottish border unwillingly, entered the city of Perth even more so, and drew the line absolutely at the threshold of Bowerswell, even after it was sold to their distant relations, the Grays, even after the old house was torn down and another with the same name erected on the same land. As for Mr. Ruskin, who travelled widely throughout England on business and the continent for pleasure, he claimed to be unable to sleep anywhere but under his own roof. In other words, the Ruskins had many and excellent reasons for avoiding the wedding of their only child, none of which had anything to do with disappointment that John had not married more spectacularly—had not secured, for example, Charlotte Lockhart, Sir Walter Scott's granddaughter—and was allying himself merely with Effie Gray, of the Bowerswell Grays, whose father was a lawyer and whose grandfather, though a decent man, was not Sir Walter Scott.

So, without the immediate blessing of the senior Ruskins, who were not only their twenty-nine-year-old son's sole source of financial support but also his most intimate friends, John Ruskin was married to nineteen-year-old Euphemia Gray, in the drawing room of the bride's parents' home at four in the afternoon of April 10, 1848. The Reverend Mr. John Edward Touch, minister of Kinnoull, presided. The bride's cousin, Eliza Jameson, and two little sisters, Sophie and Alice Gray, served as bridesmaids. The bride and groom "bore up with the greatest firmness throughout the trying ceremony,"[2] as the bride's mother reported to the absent mother of the groom, and immediately departed for their honeymoon while the rest of the wedding party sat down to dinner, in the course of which many toasts were offered and compliments spoken in honor of the newly married pair and those most dear to them.

Night had fallen when, after a tiring journey of several hours by carriage, the new Mr. and Mrs. Ruskin reached Blair Atholl in the Scottish Highlands, their place to stop for the night before journeying to the Lake District. Both of them were far from relaxed. Like any large social ceremony, the wedding had been a strain. In the months preceding it, an even more serious cause of distress had been Effie's father's finances. Mr. Gray had lost a great deal of money in railway shares (the revolution in France having made his stock in the Boulogne railway almost worthless) and seemed on the brink of bankruptcy. He was unable to give Effie the customary dowry. Mr. Ruskin took up the slack by bestowing upon the couple the sum of £10,000, on the income of which they could live comfortably. He also promised to provide them with an additional allowance and subsidies for travel, which he saw as essential to his son's work. Money was not the problem. Mr. Ruskin could afford to be generous, and he did not mind being generous—but only to the members of his narrowly defined family group, his wife, his son, and now, grudgingly, his son's wife. But *not* her father, who had been so foolish as to speculate in railway shares. The young couple were caught in the middle, each loyal to his or her parents, and their loyalties directly in conflict. Effie, an affectionate eldest child, accustomed to helping her parents with their large family, shared their worry and longed to help them, but the only way she could do so was through the Ruskins. And John, who understood his father's feelings about self-sufficiency—understood that requests for help would only produce irritation—resented Effie's pressure to intercede on her father's behalf.

The revolution of 1848, which played so large a part in Mr. Gray's financial downfall, had provokingly upset the wedding plans in other ways. When John had proposed to Effie by letter in the fall of 1847 and been accepted, he imagined them spending their honeymoon in the Alps, which he was in the habit of visiting annually with his parents. He expected that the elder Ruskins would join them on their honeymoon. But now travel in France was impossible and he was journeying away from the mountains of his soul's home and away from his parents in the company of a woman he hardly knew to whom he was joined for life.

Ruskin had spent his lonely childhood making much out of meager materials. Allowed almost no toys, he fastened his eyes on patterns on the floor, wall, and ceiling of his room and satisfied himself with imaginative games. Allowed almost no playmates, because his status-conscious parents wanted neither to be guilty of social climbing nor to have their son play with children of families beneath them, he reacted strongly to the few who got by his parents' screen. As an adolescent, he fell passionately in love with one of the daughters of his father's partner, Pedro Domecq, and became ill with frustration at losing her. He had known Effie from the time she was a child (a fairy tale, later published as *The King of the Golden River*, was written for her when she was twelve) but did not see her often. She sometimes stayed at the Ruskins' house in Denmark Hill on her way back to Scotland from school in England, and it was on one such visit, in 1846, that John developed a fancy for her. That the fancy developed into a passion suggests the depth of his need for a companion and the activity of his imagination. It had little to do with a deepening knowledge of vivacious, sociable, practical, and worldly Effie Gray. His letters to her during their engagement, in contrast with Carlyle's to Jane, recorded fantasies:

You are like a sweet forest of pleasant glades and whispering branches—where people wander on and on in its playing shadows they know not how far—and when they come near the centre of it, it is all cold and impenetrable. . . . You are like the bright—soft—swelling—lovely fields of a high glacier covered with fresh morning snow—which is lovely to the eye—and soft and winning on the foot—but beneath, there are winding clefts and dark places in its cold—cold ice—where men fall and rise not again.[3]

From which we may conclude that he loved Effie (a point later disputed), that his love was more for mythic woman than a particular Miss Gray, and that his passion for this woman was compounded with a terror of female sexuality so transparently revealed it is almost embarrassing to mention it.

Both John and Effie Ruskin were virgins, and as they sat in their carriage on the way to Blair Atholl, glaringly alone, their greatest source of anxiety was possibly the scene of intimacy that lay before them. Of course they did not discuss the matter at this point—such discussion would have been highly indelicate—yet both expected to consummate their marriage that night. Effie, having been told almost nothing about sex by her mother, expected in this adventure to follow her husband's lead, and John, having married a beautiful woman he had wanted very much, had fought with his parents in order to marry, and had written to passionately, fully intended in the Victorian phrase to "make her his wife." But as he rode in the carriage, as they arrived at their hotel and dined and started getting ready for bed, he found himself strangely uneager. His state was nervous and anxious rather than ardent. He wished somehow he did not have to endure the scene he saw no way to avoid. And when the time came, when they were alone in their room, when they had changed into their night clothes and John had slipped Effie's dress from her shoulders, the great event did not take place. They embraced and fell asleep chastely in the same bed, as they were to do for the rest of their married life, giving no indication, even to those closest to them, that their relationship was in any way unusual.

By the time they discussed the matter, in the days that followed,

John had as many good reasons for deferring the consummation of his marriage as his parents had for not attending the ceremony. Most centered around his aversion to children and the hindrance they would be to his work. Moreover, he had married principally for companionship, and if Effie were pregnant or nursing a child she would be unable to accompany him on his travels abroad. Moreover, children would ruin her beauty. If he knew of any methods besides abstinence for limiting birth, he certainly did not let on. When Effie ventured to suggest that the production of children was the purpose of matrimony and that to abstain from having them was unnatural, perhaps sacrilegious, John cited the Church's sanction of chastity and reminded her that the holiest people in the history of Christianity had been chaste. He was eloquent in conversation, a master of argument. Effie fell into a somewhat bewildered, somewhat relieved, acquiescent silence. Tolstoy talks of the psychological law "which compels a man who commits actions under the greatest compulsion, to supply in his imagination a whole series of retrospective reflections to prove his freedom to himself." Certainly this crucial event in Ruskin's life was produced under compulsion; but so quickly and effectively did his conscious mind go to work supplying reasons why it ought to have happened that he never in later months and years seems to have doubted that *not* consummating his marriage was the rational and obvious thing to do.

In the interests of a broad and yet specific understanding of Victorian sexuality, let us return to the Ruskins' room at Blair Atholl and the moment of greatest ambiguity, that between the removal of Effie's dress and the chaste embrace. What did Ruskin feel at that moment? What was going through his mind? Incredibly, we may know this. Unprotected by post-Freudian self-consciousness, Ruskin limpidly admitted to his lawyer, years later, that when he slipped the dress from Effie's shoulders, he did not like what he saw. He had imagined women to be different from what he saw she was. He believed there was something wrong with her body: it was not as lovely as her face; it was "not formed to excite passion"; it checked passion completely. Effie's body disgusted him.[4]

No one who has thought about this surprising turn of events has seriously entertained the possibility that Effie's body was deformed or blemished in any way. Neither the doctors who examined her in her divorce suit nor her second husband seems to have found anything unusual about her body; she would become the mother of eight children. According to Mary Lutyens, who has spent years studying the Ruskins' marriage, what disgusted John about Effie's body was probably her pubic hair. She reasons that John had never seen a naked woman in his life and that even the representations of the female nude he had seen in art were either censored or highly idealized, like classical statues. He expected therefore a smooth, hairless, small-breasted body, essentially a pre-adolescent body, and the signs of sexual maturity on Effie's body (it may have been no more than her breasts—the gown may never have slipped much below her shoulders) disconcerted and dismayed him. The fact that Ruskin in later life was attracted to very young girls, falling in love at the age of forty with a ten-year-old, supports the conjecture that his image of the ideal female body was immature.[5]

This explanation of what happened on Ruskin's wedding night is almost too good to be true. It offers proof of the radical innocence of the Victorians, a state of mind so unfamiliar as to be positively quaint, a state of culture more exotic than the promiscuity of Margaret Mead's Samoans. It offers what to my mind is an even more seductive proof, that art has a more powerful hold on the imagination than experience, that we realize only what we are prepared to know. The story is so good that one resists accepting it, and Mary Lutyens herself has come to distrust it, having discovered evidence that Ruskin was not so innocent about mature female nudity as she had previously believed. In a taunting letter to his parents, he mentions having seen drawings of "naked bawds," presumably pornographic drawings, in the possession of his rakish friends Lords March and Ware when he was at Oxford. But Ruskin's purpose in flinging the "naked bawds" in his parents' faces was to rebuke them for their snobbish encouragement of his friendship with the great and titled, to suggest that aristocrats could be a corrupting influence. The drawings Lords March and Ware showed him may have been pornographic in intent without being explicit about female anatomy; the women depicted might have been shielding themselves in tantalizing ways; even *Playboy* centerfolds don't reveal everything (or didn't until recently).

In any case, the theory of body hair trauma, while probably valid to some extent, is insufficient to explain what happened on the Ruskins' wedding night. The ignorance in the case was not so clear and simple. It was ignorance mixed with self-deception, an unfamiliarity with women combined with a vivid and yet wholly unrealistic imaginative vision of what they should be—both physically and morally—added to motives and aversions so deeply buried in the subconscious that I hardly dare speculate upon them, except to say that a man who has been brought up virtually alone, who was rarely allowed playmates, whose mother followed him to Oxford, taking lodgings there for the term, and saw him every evening after dinner as well as for prayers on Sundays, a man who has had the greatest experiences of his life in the company of his parents and still lives in their house at an age close to thirty will not have an easy time in following the Biblical injunction to leave his father and mother and cleave unto his wife, an injunction no one would have bothered to write down had it been an easy thing to do in the best of circumstances.[6] Rarely has unconscious motivation beckoned so invitingly as in the case of Ruskin, who cared more about stones than people, who preferred little girls to grown women, who instructed a nation in taste and morality, who went mad and saw snakes. Ruskin's sexuality is a rich field for psychoanalytic speculation, but I for one would not venture to guess why one child, kept under close guard by overprotective and earnest parents, should grow up sexually disturbed, perhaps impotent, and another, raised similarly, should develop into healthy sexual maturity. Moreover, I am concerned more generally with Victorian sexuality and with the light poor Ruskin's fiasco sheds on it. So instead of seeking the peculiarly Ruskinian in Ruskin's wedding night, I would like to look for the typical.

With pre-marital chastity demanded absolutely of middle-class women (suggested but not required for men), the Victorian wedding night, a supercharged transition from innocence to experience, could hardly have been easy, may well have been a barbaric trial for at least one, and sometimes for both, of the newly married pair. Ignorance about sex, too often made the guarantee of innocence, increased a woman's terror; all her training in purity was suddenly countered by a demand for the performance of dark deeds about which she had no specific knowledge. Edith Jones, for one, on the verge of becoming Edith Wharton, confronted her mother and begged to be told "what marriage was really like." "I'm afraid, Mamma—I want to know what will happen to me." Mrs. Jones said that surely Edith had seen pictures and statues. Hadn't she noticed that men were different from women? According to her biographer, Edith still understood nothing, but her mother had gone the limit. "Then for heaven's sake," she said, "don't ask me any more silly questions. You can't be as stupid as you pretend."[7] Marie Stopes, the great propagandist for sex education, wrote her best-selling *Married Love* in the belief that ignorance about sex, which she perceived to be widespread (this is after World War I), was an obstacle to marital happiness. Her passion on this subject stemmed from her own early experiences. This highly educated Englishwoman, with an advanced degree from a German university, was married in 1911 to a botanist. It took six months before she realized that something was lacking in her marriage and more time and research in the British Museum before she realized what it was. Like Effie Ruskin over fifty years before her, she was found to be a virgin and granted an annulment of her marriage.

One Victorian couple confronted the problem of wedding-night trauma with amazing candor. Charles Kingsley, the clergyman-novelist, wrote to his fiancée, Frances Grenfell: "I have been thinking over your terror at seeing me undressed, and I feel that I should have the same feeling in a minor degree to you, till I had learnt to bear the blaze of your naked beauty. You do not know how often a man is struck powerless in body and mind on his wedding night."[8] The Kingsleys were perhaps unusual in their reverence for marital sex: both of them had flirted with Puseyism and been drawn to celibacy, so that the sexual side of marriage represented for both an important religious commitment.[9] Partly as religious self-mortification, partly in response to his fear that too sudden intimacy would lead to impotence, they decided to defer the consummation of their marriage. A few weeks before their wedding in 1844, the future Mrs. Kingsley sent her fiancé a scenario for their wedding night:

After dinner I shall perhaps feel worn out so I shall just lie on your bosom and say nothing but feel a great deal, and you will be very loving and call me your poor child. And then you will perhaps show me your *Life of St. Elizabeth*, your wedding gift. And then after tea we will go up to rest! We will undress and bathe and then you will come to my room, and we will kiss and love very much and read psalms aloud together, and then we will kneel down and pray in our night dresses. Oh! What solemn bliss! How hallowing! And then you will take me up in your arms, will you not? And lay me down in bed. And then you will extinguish our light and *come to me!* How I will open my arms to you and then sink into yours! And you will kiss me and clasp me and we will praise God alone in the dark night with His eye shining down upon us and His love enclosing us. After a time we shall sleep!

And yet I fear you will yearn so for *fuller* communion that you will not be so happy as me. And I too perhaps shall yearn, frightened as I am! But every yearning will remind me of our self-denial, your sorrow for sin, your strength of repentance. And I shall glory in my yearning, *please God!*[10]

The Kingsleys devoted the first four weeks of their honeymoon to becoming comfortable with each other. They studied German, they prayed, they indulged in little acts of tenderness. In the fifth week, their marriage was consummated and a child almost immediately conceived. Lady Susan Chitty, Kingsley's biographer, believes that a stranger wedding night than his was never passed, but I am struck by the good sense with which the Kingsleys orchestrated their intimacy, modifying a harsh custom with intelligence and flexibility. For the custom of isolating for an extended period of time a newly married couple and asking them to concentrate on what they had been brought up to ignore *was* a harsh one, and its harshness may explain why Queen Victoria, who had a way of invoking the good of the country to avoid what she didn't want to do, refused to spend more than three days on honeymoon. The country, she said, could not spare her any longer.

I began by describing a revolution that did not take place and will now suggest that the sexual failure of the Ruskins' marriage can be seen as another case of revolution *manqué*, in that the young Ruskins were, like every newly wed Victorian couple, in the position of having to rebel against all their previous training. Suddenly sex, after years of being proscribed, was approved, encouraged, indeed required. What resulted was sometimes impotence and frigidity, with their attendant train of misunderstandings and hurt feelings, or, less drastically, sex that was not very pleasurable. The Ruskins' plight was probably less extraordinary and eccentric than one might think at first.[11]

The writers whose domestic lives I have chosen to present are by no means a statistically meaningful sample, and I make no claims for their being representative, but it must be mentioned at this point that Thomas Carlyle, too, was probably impotent and his marriage, like Ruskin's, unconsummated. When Geraldine Jewsbury, the novelist and Jane's close friend, heard that Froude had been asked to write a biography of Carlyle, she went to him and confided that Carlyle had been "one of those persons who ought never to have married," which she intended and Froude understood to mean that Carlyle was impotent. Froude was not surprised. There had been rumors in the circle of people focussed upon the Carlyles' house in Chelsea that the marriage was not a real marriage, that it was a marriage for companionship only. Froude had even heard that Jane had thought of leaving Carlyle "and as if she had a right to leave him if she pleased." Once, Carlyle had told Froude that he had a secret which no one would ever know, and that without a knowledge of it, no true biography of him was possible. So Geraldine's revelations were not unexpected. Froude had thought that perhaps the Carlyles had agreed to do without sex, not wanting children, being so poor, but Geraldine said no. Jane had longed for children, and children were denied her. She never forgave Carlyle the injury which she believed herself to have received.[12]

You could call it a solution to the difficulties of sexual adjustment early in marriage that the Ruskins decided to have no sex at all. But "solving" in this unusual way the "problem" of sex threw all the more weight upon the other classic area of conflict between newly married people, their relations with their parents. Modern family therapy talks about a newly wed couple's need to establish clear boundaries around itself and to assert its new social identity.[18] Not surprisingly, Ruskin had as much trouble leaving his father and mother and cleaving to his wife in the social sense as he did in the sexual, and Effie, loyal daughter in a large and loving family, had ties of her own she was loath to undo. When, in 1854, John explained to his lawyer why his wife grew to dislike him with an intensity that amounted to hatred, he said the aversion had nothing to do with their "mode of living together," by which he meant the absence of sex.

It arose from the steady endeavours of my wife to withdraw me from the influence of my parents, and to get me into close alliance with her own family. She tried to get me to persuade my father to put her brother into his counting house; and was much offended at my refusal to do so; she then lost no opportunity of speaking against both my parents, and, every day, was more bitterly mortified at her failure in influencing me. On one occasion, she having been rude to my mother, I rebuked her firmly; and she never forgave either my mother or me.

I married her thinking her so young and affectionate that I might influence her as I chose, and make of her just such a wife as I wanted. It appeared that *she* married *me* thinking she could make of me just the *husband she* wanted. I was grieved and disappointed at finding I could not change her, and she was humiliated and irritated at finding she could not change me.[14]

Over what pitiful pieces of ground these unheroic matrimonial battles were fought! One might be embarrassed to write of such trivialities were it not for the example and encouragement of George Eliot, who believed it was precisely "in these acts called trivialities that the seeds of joy are forever wasted, until men and women look round with haggard faces at the devastation their own waste had made, and say, the earth bears no harvest of sweetness."[15] For example, one of the Ruskins' most violent early disagreements, the first round in Effie's protracted battle with her mother-in-law, concerned the care and treatment of a common cold.

In July of 1848, when the newlyweds were staying with his parents, John developed a cold, and Effie wrote about it to her mother.

John's cold is not away yet but it is not so bad as he had with us and I think it would go away with care if Mr. and Mrs. Ruskin would only let him alone. They are telling him twenty times a day that it is very slight and only nervous, which I think it is. At the same time they talk constantly to him about what he ought to do, and in the morning Mrs. Ruskin begins with "don't sit near these towels John they're damp" and in the forenoon "John you must not read these papers till they are dried."[16]

Effie observed that when John was with her and she refrained from inquiring about it, his health was fine, but that when his parents asked how he was, he would start to cough, giving his father the chance to say, "that cough is not going away—I wish you would take care." Effie was convinced that all the old folks' fussing about John did more harm than good and that some of their remedies were positively dangerous.

There was a certain blue pill from which Mrs. Ruskin expected great things. She told John to take one before going to bed. Effie distrusted medicines, preferring not to use them herself, and she stood up with particular vigor against the little blue pill. She said no. Mrs. Ruskin said yes. With choice so clearly before him, John, obeying his mother, took the medicine. A year later, trying to explain to his father-in-law the disintegration of his affection for his wife, he would assert that the matter of the little blue pill had been one "of very grave importance."[17] It was, he said, the first time since his marriage that his mother had tried to influence him, and Effie had reacted with "causeless petulance." He had rebuked her for it, and Effie had conceived from that moment an implacable resentment of her mother-in-law.

It was Effie's turn to be sick at Christmas of 1848, while they were staying at the elder Ruskins' house at Denmark Hill. She passed a bad two days with cough, cold, and a fever at night that left her alternately burning hot and shivering under her blankets. Again Mrs. Ruskin was challenged to exercise her medical skill, but this time her prescription was "no coddling." On January 1 the Ruskins had an important dinner party at which J. M. W. Turner was one of the guests. They particularly wanted Effie to come down to dinner. Still feeling ill, but slightly less feverish, Effie managed, when evening came, to go downstairs. But whatever effort she made to leave her room at all was not appreciated by Mr. Ruskin, who noted in his diary, "*Effie not down* till Evening."[18] Three days later, another party, and Effie, just as sick, wished to remain in her room. Mrs. Ruskin found her in tears when she ought to have been dressing for dinner and scolded her for it. Effie dressed and descended but looked so miserable that one of the guests, a doctor, thinking she was on the verge of fainting, sent her back to bed and prescribed loathsome medicines which she was too weak to refuse. Effie felt all the resentment of those who are not allowed to be miserable in peace. She felt pressured to be cheerful and to fulfill unimportant social obligations when doing so cost her great pain. She thought the Ruskins' social habits—guests for dinner every night at six and bedtime at one—not conducive to health and believed that in her own home, managing things for herself, she would get well much sooner.

Who was really sick, and who was just being indulged and thereby made worse was clearly a vexing issue. Each family thought the other had produced a spoiled child who used illness as a way of getting attention. Could it be that both were right? John, like his parents, thought Effie was carrying on—needlessly, petulantly nourishing ill humor rather than genuinely being sick. Should a request to come down to dinner with a happy face be considered a tyranny? Old Mr. Ruskin went further. He saw that at stake in his wife's desire to exercise her medical skills and Effie's resistance was the question of supremacy between the two women. He could understand Effie's resentment. He knew his wife was disposed to lecture and would sometimes address a young person "in a way that is not pleasant before others," but on the whole Mr. Ruskin thought it the young person's duty to defer to the one over sixty. That his model of deference conflicted with modes of young people's independence he fully realized. He guessed that Effie had been schooled by worldly people "to be sure to assert at once the full authority of a married person and especially against that awful personage, a Mother in Law."[19] But he, for one, considered such rebellion vulgar.

He did not mention it, but it could also have been considered ungrateful. The young Ruskins were living at 31 Park Street near Grosvenor Square, in the most fashionable part of London, in a townhouse leased for them at considerable cost by Mr. Ruskin. They had their own brougham and horses stabled around the corner. They had a full complement of servants. In short, they lived a luxurious life, entirely at the expense of Mr. Ruskin, who wanted his son to have a home and equipage suitable for entertaining people of rank, people his son was entitled by his education and accomplishments to know, such people as he himself, a mere tradesman, was not fit to mix with. John and Effie believed that neither of them needed nor even wanted such luxury and merely put up with it to please Mr. Ruskin. For John, who was naturally disposed to be close to his parents and to follow their wishes in every way, there was nothing galling about accepting money from his father. It merely increased his gratitude and affection. But Effie was caught between gratitude— she liked pretty dresses and jewelry, and her own father had barely been able to pay for her trousseau—and a less pleasant feeling which inspired her to show through her behavior that the money entailed no obligation.

After the disastrous bout of flu at Denmark Hill, Effie longed to return to her own house in Park Street, where her mother was to join her for a long visit. In Park Street, presumably, she could run her own life. But once more, Mrs. Ruskin had opinions which had to be listened to, this time on the subject of the proper place for the guest room. There were two extra sleeping rooms in the Park Street house, a guest room on the top floor with the servants, and John's dressing room, next to the bedroom he shared with Effie. Effie wanted to put her mother in John's dressing room and move his dressing area to the top floor. Mrs. Ruskin thought that the top-floor room with the servants was good enough for Mrs. Gray and resented the slight to her son. Effie equally resented the slight to her mother. Had it been a question of slicing carrots, no doubt Mrs. Ruskin would have advised the unique utility of the horizontal and Effie just as strongly urged the vertical. But while this analogy suggests the inevitability of the squabbles between Effie and Mrs. Ruskin, it does not capture the gravity with which they were conducted, as though two sovereign nations were negotiating mineral rights.

And then, Effie fled the field abruptly. She decided, perhaps out of pique at not being able to receive her mother as she chose, to return with her mother to Scotland. As soon as she left, John returned to Denmark Hill to live with his parents and soon thereafter left with them on the tour of the Alps he had hoped to make as his honeymoon, but which had been aborted by the revolution of 1848. They had been married less than a year, a time at which it may seem surprising for a young married woman to pay a three-month visit to her parents, and for a husband, without making any effort to see her, to take off with *his* parents on a six-month tour of the Continent. Even in that age of long visits and extended absences of spouses, the Ruskins' separation was considered unusual.

Effie's friends in Perth were appalled at John for abandoning his wife, while John's friends were indignant with her for abandoning him. Both sets of parents felt something was wrong but tried to act as though the situation were perfectly normal. Mr. Ruskin wrote to Mr. Gray, "I hear she may remain with you a few months—whilst my Son goes abroad—I should disapprove entirely of this, were my Son going abroad for his pleasure—but it seems as much a matter of Business as my travelling to Liverpool."[20] Perth rumor said that Effie was so unhappy in her marriage that she was arranging a trial separation, but folk wisdom and common gossip were in this case years ahead in insight about the parties concerned, who still believed themselves to be happily married. There is, I think, a kind of natural astonishment at the moments when one's personal life coincides with the great, public, recurring events of mankind, when one marries, for example, or produces a child. One is so amazed to have done it at all that one can by no means perceive it has been done badly. I suppose this to be the case with the Ruskins, for otherwise I cannot explain Effie's bewilderment at the rumors of her marital unhappiness and the extraordinary series of love letters which John now began to write. "Do you know, pet, it seems almost a dream to me that we have ever been married: I look forward to meeting you: and to your *next* bridal night: and to the time when I shall again draw your dress from your snowy shoulders: and lean my cheek upon them, as if you were still my betrothed only: and I had never held you in my arms."[21]

In this time of assessment and reappraisal, Effie had been thinking about their wedding night, too. It was a year after the event, and she could at last tell her husband—perhaps admit to herself for the first time—that it had been a "trial" for her, the experience at Blair Atholl a "cruel one." Moreover snowy shoulders and the adolescent love talk of her husband's letters were all very well, but she knew something was missing. Affectionate, sociable, daughter of fecund parents (her mother at the age of forty was pregnant with her thirteenth child when Effie got engaged), Effie had become a wife fully expecting to be a mother soon as well. To be deprived of children meant a very real loss to her, in status, and in a kind of companionship and activity which would have been all the more welcome in the face of her husband's coldness. If a more instinctual disappointment underlay the one she could articulate, we have no way of knowing it. Probably she had no way of knowing it herself. For well-brought-up women the vocabulary for discussing sexual experience was the vocabulary for discussing the production of babies. There was widespread belief that for a woman to enjoy full physical health, she had to fulfill her biological function, maternity; and Effie, perhaps for this reason, took advantage of her residence in Scotland to consult the distinguished physician James Simpson about her now chronic bad health. Simpson, who discovered the use of chloroform as an anaesthetic in childbirth, was professor of midwifery at Edinburgh. He confirmed that something was definitely wrong with Effie. She received the diagnosis with a glee that Ruskin found irritatingly misplaced, for of course he did not understand that official recognition of her illness meant to her official recognition that something was wrong with *him*. We do not know what specific cures Dr. Simpson suggested, but soon after her visit to him Effie wrote to her husband that seeing her little sister Alice made her want to have "a little Alice" of her own. She could not have been much reassured by his jocular reply that he too wanted a little Alice—or a little Effie—only wished that they weren't so small and unattractive. (Ruskin was made physically ill by his friend Acland's habit of having his baby sit with the adults at the breakfast table.) But he also told her that their next wedding night would be better than the first: neither of them would be so frightened.[22]

Something had clearly gone wrong with the marriage, and both "sides"—the elder Grays and Ruskins as well as the married pair—attempted to fix the blame. Neither set of parents knew the marriage was unconsummated, but they found plenty of other problems to discuss. From Mr. Ruskin's point of view, Effie was an undutiful wife, unsupportive of her husband's work. She had unaccountably withdrawn from them and gone to Perth, where she knew John would not follow. She seemed unsympathetic to his stay in Europe, perversely wanting him home. Didn't she realize that going home would mean giving up the "Haunts where his Genius finds food and occupation"?[23] Ordinary people might find John's business in the Alps incomprehensible, but didn't Effie realize that only by such labor could he do the work he'd been put on earth to do? Mr. Ruskin recommended (to her father) that she sacrifice all other feelings to duty and attempt to find pleasure in causing her husband no anxiety.

But Mr. Gray saw it differently. He knew that his daughter was not jealous of her husband's work. That was a false issue. There was only one problem in the young people's marriage: the elder Ruskins. If he might offer a word of advice, it was that Mr. and Mrs. Ruskin should leave John and Effie to themselves as much as possible. "Married people," he ventured to say, "are rather restive under the control and supervision of Parents tho' proceeding from the kindest and most affectionate motives."[24]

How one warms to Mr. Gray! How right he seems! While Mr. Ruskin with his notions of duty and submissiveness sounds archaic, Mr. Gray expresses the wisdom a contemporary upper-middle-class American would offer in response to the same situation. Freedom. Independence. Not for nothing did we cut the ties with the Mother Country. But Ruskin, in the opening paragraph of his autobiography, proclaims that he was, like his father before him, a Tory of the old school, of the school of Homer and Sir Walter Scott, men who believed in kings, in some people being better fit to rule than others, in such people exercising power for the good of their followers without the right to expect anything in return except deference. But deference they could expect. This political model applies to the family as well as the state, and one should see that the battle between John and Effie, between the Ruskins and the Grays, was to some extent an ideological battle, a clash of two sets of assumptions about power and authority.

A great number of domestic manuals about woman's place appeared in the 1830s and 1840s—suggesting, perhaps, that some people were beginning to forget what woman's place was. It was a commonplace of such books that a woman gained power by surrendering power, that by asking for nothing, she won immense influence over her husband. According to *Female Improvement,* for example, it was a woman's duty to "raise herself, by every means, in the esteem of her husband . . . and thus, far more than by insisting upon her way, or urging her own claims, she will secure a voice in her husband's counsels, and a place in his tenderest consideration."[25] This paternalistic paradox—surrender power that it may be gained—informs a typical critique by old Mr. Ruskin of Effie's behavior and her father's domestic politics.

> The ideas you express about married peoples Love of Independence makes me sore afraid that these very ideas, instilled into Phemy and encouraged, have been the cause of all the mischief —one thing I am sure of that had Phemy thrown herself entirely on our generosity and sought no independent authority, her Dominion over all our affections would have been greater at this day, and of all I know of my Son, her authority with him would have been great exactly in proportion as she had not sought to establish it on the exclusion of that of his parents. . . . The absence of petty jealousies which so beset young married women in their struggles for a childish authority would have certainly increased his Respect for his Wifes character.[26]

A woman's desire for independence and autonomy—like that of a colonial state—is childish, petty, petulantly rebellious.

John's political assumptions, like his dear father's, were rooted ultimately in the Biblical description of how woman was created after man, subordinate to him, intended for his pleasure and service. This natural hierarchy applied also to age, and if John's parents had interfered in his life and Effie's, it seemed to him they had every right to do so. Or did Effie think that in return for all the care and energy he had devoted to his son, Mr. Ruskin should receive in return nothing but a demand to stand aside, "that he should hint nothing—ask nothing—blame nothing—and expect nothing?"

> I should indeed dread to think that such were the deliberate principles on which my wife intended to act—or was encouraged to act by her parents—and I hope to see her outgrow with her girls frocks—that contemptible dread of interference and petulant resistance to authority which begins in pride—and is nourished in folly—and ends in pain. "Restiveness" I am accustomed to regard as unpromising character even in horses and asses—I look for meekness and gentleness in woman.[27]

It was her duty to attend to him, not his, as she seemed to expect, to attend to her. Ruskin could never see the disintegration of his marriage in any other light and consequently felt not the slightest remorse for his behavior. (Perhaps we should not expect self-awareness from a man who, in writing to his wife, compares her to a horse—to the horse's advantage.) In 1854 he sent a letter to his old friend at Oxford, Dr. Acland, which he believed to vindicate himself completely. "Most men, I suppose, find their wives a comfort, & a help. I found mine perpetually in need of comfort—& in need of help, and as far as was in my power, I gave her both. I found however that the more I gave the less I was thanked—and I would not allow the main work of my life to be interfered with. I would not spend my days in leaving cards, nor my nights in leaning against the walls of drawing rooms." All in all, he did not think many husbands could look back upon their married lives with more security of having done all they could for their wives than he.

The pathos of the Ruskins' marriage is in the absolute irreconcilability of their points of view. Effie was aware of being constantly criticized and told how to behave. Nothing she did was right: she dressed too loudly and was too social, or she was not social enough.

It was hard for her to separate in her mind her husband from his parents, but when she did, she wondered why he had married her. He did not want children, and he did not want much of her company. He was always secluded in his study, writing, or sketching or measuring some cathedral. Her presence gave him no pleasure. He avoided her, using work as an excuse. Cut off from her family, from children, from her husband, Effie found in marriage nothing but emotional starvation. But no more than any man had John Ruskin married for misery or to make his wife miserable. He looked for solace in marriage and found none. His wife seemed to be constantly accusing him of failure and was grateful for nothing he did for her. The plot from his point of view weirdly pre-figures (by some twenty years) the story of Lydgate and Rosamund Vincy in *Middlemarch*: a high-minded man, dedicated to his work, is seduced by a pretty face and appealing manners and thinks he can annex the charming creature for life without seriously altering his pattern of living. But he underestimates her will and the triviality of her goals. She needs his connections for her petty social purposes and treats the gold of his intelligence as though it were no more than common, serviceable tin. If, however, we can sympathize with Ruskin as a Lydgate married to a Rosamund Vincy, the story of their marriage from Effie's point of view is uncannily similar to that of Dorothea Brooke's marriage to Casaubon—the story of an ardent, high-spirited woman who married an emotionally and sexually defective man. The anticipations of *Middlemarch* are all the more uncanny because the novelistic vision this material seems to me to demand is that of George Eliot, whose great theme was the egotism of perception and who assumed that all action rightly portrayed was a tragic—or comic—clash of understandings.

It is George Eliot's tolerant, stereoscopic gaze, with its refusal to see in the most inviting circumstances anything so simple as a villain, that I should wish to direct upon the small series of well-intentioned divergences ending up in a giant disaster which was the Ruskins' marriage. When marriages go wrong, the people concerned may be excused if they seek a clear and simple reason for their misery, but we—observers, readers, friends—should try to achieve a more complicated view and a more embracing sympathy. We should try to. And yet, I find myself rooting for Effie. Perhaps she *was* frivolous. She never pretended to be anything more than a well-bred young lady, and such young ladies were frivolous by vocation, by education, by social definition. What would have convinced Ruskin of her seriousness? Nothing short of total devotion and submission to himself. Later, he would say she was crazy. One deplores the flinging about of such judgmental terms. Still, it must be said that if either of them was crazy, he was.

Triangle

After their eight-month separation, during which Effie stayed with her parents in Perth and John travelled with his on the Continent, the Ruskins were reunited—but only after an argument about whether John should travel to Perth to meet Effie and escort her back to London or whether instead Effie should travel alone to London in order to greet her husband upon his return from abroad. John, as it turned out, went to Perth, reluctant, resentful, convinced that his wife confused him with the pincushion she wore around her waist. Soon after their reunion, Effie suggested that the two of them live for a while in Venice. Her plan was to escape the senior Ruskins, whom she believed to be at the root of her problems with John. Since he already had *The Stones of Venice* in mind, he liked the idea of living in Venice where he could continue to gather material. So off they went, leaving vacant again for months the ill-fated house in Park Street, which was costing old Mr. Ruskin so much money.

They were happy in Venice, and although the absence of the elder Ruskins was surely an important factor in their happiness, the social climate of the Italian city figured importantly, too. John and Effie developed a way of living together which was satisfactory to both of them, but which would not have been so easily tolerated in England.

They went different ways, meeting only for meals and sleep. John examined Venice inch by inch, standing on ladders to look closely at places that had not been closely examined since they were carved; Effie walked, toured the city less strenuously than her husband, and visited friends or received visitors. In the evening, she went out alone to small soirées or receptions. Pretty, lively, and interestingly neglected, she was a great social success. Particularly during their second stay in Venice in 1851–52, she was welcomed by the highest circles of Venetian society. Her eccentric husband was free to get on with his work, and she was free to amuse herself. Within limits. Sometimes she went to the opera house, the Fenice, which was a center of social activity, but she behaved in a manner impeccably and peculiarly British: if John was not with her, she would receive no visitors in her box. Since the making of such visits was, for Venetians, the point of going to the opera, Effie's behavior was generally considered strange. But John's behavior on the few occasions he accompanied her was even stranger. One night, listening to Donizetti's music, he leaned against the railing of their box and wrote his chapter on chamfered edges.

At first it mortified Effie that her husband left her constantly alone and forced her to face the public unaccompanied, but gradually she got used to it and even found compensations. Venice had just survived the Austrian bombardment and was in Austrian hands; the city was filled with soldiers. The officers were well bred and well dressed. Effie had many interesting, exotic young men to talk to; as a married woman and a foreigner, she was in the position to have them as friends. Venice was certainly not Perth. Effie learned to cherish her un-English freedom and to appreciate, too, her husband's absence of jealousy. She and her companion, Charlotte Ker, were continually amazed at how much John would tolerate. He never got jealous when Effie talked to another man. He was a "model" husband, "so free from petty faults & narrow mindedness although peculiar in many ways."[28] All this put a new coloring on her relations with the elder Ruskins:

For all I care they may have John as much with them as they please for I could hardly see less of him than I do at present with his work, and I think it is much better, for we follow our different occupations and never interfere with one another and are always happy.[29]

When they went back to London in 1850, before returning to Venice for a longer stay, they continued their Venetian way of living. John accepted no invitations. Effie went out alone. Hostesses who sought her famous husband had to admit that he was somewhat boorish on social occasions; by entertaining Effie, one had the best of everything, his name and her charming social presence. Both Effie and her mother realized how careful, in such circumstances, she had to be about her reputation. But she *was* careful.

Along with Venetian glass and laces, Effie brought independence back with her from Italy; it adapted to London but could not have grown there in the first place. Italian manners were different from English—not looser, as Effie thought at first, just different. Arranged marriages and the code of behavior which allowed them to function were still the rule in the circles in which Effie moved in Venice. More divergence was allowed between husband and wife. In Venice she met many people who made gracious adjustments to bad situations, among them her closest friend on the second visit, the Countess Pallavicini, a young woman raised in Austria who had been married against her will to a rich and stupid Italian nobleman. Unhappy at first, she eventually found comfort in a child and in the brilliant group of people she entertained night after night at her home. In Paris John and Effie visited one of the Domecq sisters who had a separate suite of rooms from her husband and whose husband never entered her rooms except to take her out in the evening or to dine with her there. Everything seemed to be done differently on the Continent—they ordered these matters much better.[30]

That British propriety was narrower than that of the Italians was constantly being brought to Effie's notice by letters from home. One day the weather was so beautiful that she went walking in the Piazza San Marco without a bonnet. She told her mother about this in a letter which Mrs. Gray passed on to Mrs. Ruskin and Mrs. Ruskin showed to her husband who in turn wrote to his son to say that he was shocked to hear that Effie had been walking in the piazza without her bonnet. Or, again, one day, in an excess of energy and high spirits, she took a turn poling a gondola, but when report of this, offered as proof of what a good time they were having, reached England, Mr. Ruskin wrote back reprovingly to say there could be nothing beautiful about a lady poling a gondola on the Grand Canal. It was not only Mr. Ruskin who objected to Effie's behavior. Her brother George never could get used to the idea of his sister being left alone as much as she was. With a brother's suspiciousness, he became acutely apprehensive when a certain gentleman's name kept turning up in Effie's letters. Conviction grew that his perverse brother-in-law was deliberately throwing men in Effie's way in order to compromise her.

In 1850 the particular object of George Gray's concern was an Austrian officer named Paulizza, a friend of both the Ruskins but especially of Effie. Paulizza was a young man of scientific inclinations and considerable expertise, extremely gifted and intelligent. He was one of the few people in Venice (or elsewhere) whose company John Ruskin enjoyed. Indeed, as John told Effie, he respected her more, finding that so talented a man as Paulizza liked her.

The Austrian was suffering from a malady which made it difficult for him to endure light, so that he could not read, write, or draw, but lay for hours with a wet cloth on his forehead, thinking melancholy thoughts. He was very lonely and seemed to cheer up only in Effie's presence. Probably he loved her, but it is clear from the way she wrote home about him, freely and guiltlessly, even self-righteously, that it hadn't yet occurred to her she *could* love him. In February 1850 Effie offered her mother this description of her feelings about Paulizza and his about her:

He says he would like to be with us every moment in the day. He is very fond of me, and, as you say, were John unkind to me and not so perfectly amiable & good as he is, such excessive devotion might be somewhat dangerous from so handsome & gifted a man, but I am a strange person and Charlotte thinks I have a perfect heart of ice, for she sees him speaking to me until the tears come into his eyes and I looking and answering without the slightest discomposure, but I really feel none. I never could love anybody else in the world but John and the way these Italian women go on is so perfectly disgusting to me that it even removes from me any desire to coquetry which John declares I possess very highly, but he thinks it charming, so do not I. I tell him every word Paulizza says to me and tell the latter so too, so that they perfectly understand each other and after me I think that Paulizza likes John better than any one else here. However, be sorry for Paulizza if you like, but do not fear for me. I am one of the odd of the earth and have no talent whatever for intrigue as every thing with me must be open as the day.[31]

Nevertheless, Effie asked Charlotte not to write home about her friendship with Paulizza "as one does not know, amongst so many, what construction might be put upon what she says." The situation, as everyone but Effie saw, was perfect for "intrigue": the neglected wife in a foreign country, the handsome, devoted young officer, also far from home. But as far as Effie was concerned, such impropriety was only for Italians and bad novels.

When John and Effie were in London between stays in Venice, she saw a great deal of a man named Clare Ford, the son of their neighbor in Park Street. Again, brother George believed that John was purposely throwing his wife in the way of attractive men in order to tempt her to compromise herself, but Effie thought George was merely jealous. She might allow herself the pleasure of male company if she vigorously guarded her integrity. "What you say is perfectly true," she wrote in reply to one of many warnings from her mother, "and I am so peculiarly situated as a married woman that being much alone and most men thinking that I live quite alone I am more exposed to their attentions, but I assure you I never allow such people to enter the house and stop everything of the kind which might be hurtful to my reputation."[32] Her parents, however, continued to worry, particularly about frequent visits from Clare Ford, and eventually Ruskin himself had to write to his in-laws to defend his wife's behavior.

I quite agree in all you say of the necessity of great caution in a young married lady of Effie's beauty and natural liveliness, but

I am happy to be able to assure you that I have never seen the slightest want of caution on her part in the course of her various relations with young men of every character, but on the contrary, the greatest shrewdness and quickness in detecting the slightest want of proper feeling on their part followed by fearless decision in forbidding or otherwise preventing their farther intrusion upon her in cases which required such severity—so that she runs much more chance of being found fault with for prudery than coquetry.[33]

Paulizza died, and Clare Ford, with Effie's persuasion, pulled himself together, abandoned his dandyish life in London, and entered himself in the Foreign Service, where he would have a distinguished career. But there were others. And how are we to understand Ruskin's attitude towards them? It is hard to accept George Gray's accusation that Ruskin was knowingly, consciously, throwing men in his wife's way in order to compromise her. Nevertheless, his total absence of jealousy, which Effie purported to find such a relief, the very opposite of small-mindedness, must have seemed at times a wounding absence of concern. If he cared about her, would he not have been just a little disturbed about the attractive men who took up so much of her time? It would take a villain to have done what George believed Ruskin was doing, and true villainy is as rare as true genius. But, without consciously pushing Effie onto other men, John may have welcomed it when another came along to take her off his hands, to relieve any guilt he felt at leaving her alone, and to revive his flagging interest in her. For his liking for his wife increased in proportion with his admiration of *her* new admirer.

Ruskin very much admired John Everett Millais, the young painter behind whose work he had thrown his prestige as an art critic by writing a complimentary letter to the *Times* in 1851.[34] Millais, along with D. G. Rossetti and William Holman Hunt, was one of the leading members of the Pre-Raphaelite Brotherhood, a group of young artists who banded together in 1848 in opposition to the

Establishment art of their day, adopting the Ruskinian credo of truth to nature.[35]

Millais and Holman Hunt wrote to thank Ruskin for his defense of their work in the *Times*, and in return Mr. and Mrs. Ruskin paid a call on Millais at his parents' home in Gower Street, where he lived and had his studio. Millais was then twenty-two, a year younger than Effie, ten years younger than Ruskin. From early childhood he had dazzled people with his draftsmanship, and his career at the Royal Academy school was impressive; indeed he was something of a *wunderkind* in the art world. By the time he met the Ruskins, he had already painted *Lorenzo and Isabella* and the controversial *Jesus in the House of his Parents*, which emphasized Christ's earthly ties with the working class by painting him in a carpenter's shop. Before he saw them again, in 1852, he would create *Ophelia* with the tangled river-bank background painted from life in the country and the figure of a drowning Ophelia painted from Elizabeth Siddal lying in a tub of water in his studio.

Upon their return from Italy, the younger Ruskins moved into a house which Mr. Ruskin had rented for them in Herne Hill, near the house in which John had grown up and, more to the point, near the elder Ruskins' house in Denmark Hill. Not only had Mr. Ruskin picked out his son's house for him, he had ordered it furnished at exorbitant cost (£300) in taste both John and Effie found excruciating. John got into the habit of walking daily to his parents' house in Denmark Hill and working in his old study. Effie was given the Ruskin carriage one day a week to go into central London, a hefty distance away. When Millais asked her to pose for one of the figures in a painting he was working on, she must have been delighted for the chance to escape from her suburban imprisonment, all the more galling after the delights and freedom of Venice.

The painting was prophetically titled *The Order of Release*. It was a historical piece, drawing on the Jacobite rebellion for inspiration. It depicts a kilted Scots soldier whose wife (Effie) presents the order for his release to a jailer. She has a rapturous, triumphant look on her face. She carries a baby on her arm. Presumably overwhelmed with emotion, he buries his head in her shoulder. A dog leaps up to share their joy. The likeness of Effie is exact, except for a change of hair color from auburn to black, and when the painting was displayed in the Academy Exhibition in May of 1853, everyone who knew her recognized her. The painting was a great success: crowds of people always stood before it, straining to see. The critics by and large approved it, too, although one said the dog took up too much room, and another objected to Effie's face, going so far as to say that he would rather stay in prison all his life or even be hanged than to live with such a woman. But his reaction was unique. Most people seemed aware of the special intimacy that can develop between artist and model, and from this moment gossip about Effie and John Millais started. Mr. Ruskin, for one, told Effie that she was looking so beautiful at this stage of her life, he found it no wonder Millais was so interested in her. Mr. Ruskin had a devastating way of offering praise which barely concealed a critique, and Effie, on whom nothing the Ruskins did was lost, believed that Mr. Ruskin was trying to draw her attention to Millais's interest in her in order to get her "into a scrape."

Both John and Effie seemed to want to adopt Millais as a protégé. Effie had done this to good effect with Clare Ford; she had made him pull himself together and get serious about his career. Millais needed a different kind of handling. He was brilliantly talented, but somewhat nervous and fragile. Effie thought he needed a physical cure and sent him to her doctor in Edinburgh. John Ruskin decided his problem was a lack of education: Millais hadn't read enough, his training was too exclusively visual, he needed to be taught mental discipline and method. So, for health and for the training of the mind, in the spirit of Oxford reading parties, the Ruskins planned a summer vacation in the company of Millais, his brother, William, and Holman Hunt. John had finished three volumes of *The Stones of Venice* and needed a rest. On June 21, 1853, the party left London (without Hunt, as it happened) and after a short stay with Sir Walter and Lady Trevelyan in Northumberland, reached Brig O'Turk, in the Scottish Trossachs, in early July. This was no weekend jaunt. They were to be together for four months.

Early on, Millais conceived the idea of painting Ruskin in quite a novel way—outdoors, standing in front of a rushing mountain stream. Ruskin, who had written that truth to nature was the highest goal of art and who described natural beauty so superbly in *Modern Painters*, would be pictured in the kind of setting he himself loved to write about—the rock, the rushing water, the lichens, all rendered with meticulous precision, just as he would wish. In the finished portrait Ruskin looks downstream away from the viewer, smiling slightly, wholly self-possessed. When he began working on the painting and still thought Ruskin a good fellow, Millais wrote to a friend that Ruskin looked "sweet and benign standing calmly looking into the turbulent sluice beneath."[36] Perhaps it is only when one knows the story of the Ruskins' marriage that the contrast between the calmness of the figure in this painting and the turbulence of what he impassively regards seems intentional, ominous.

The painting of this portrait now became the ostensible focus of the trip. They all spent a couple of days walking about looking for the perfect place and found it, "a lovely piece of worn rock, with foaming water and weeds and moss and a noble overhanging bank of dark crag"[37] at a spot called Glenfinlas, which would provide the title for the painting. Then they had to wait for the canvas to arrive from Edinburgh. It was to be lunette-shaped, and white, in the PRB fashion. Every day it rained, the implacable rain of the Highlands. To save money, the Ruskins and John Millais moved from the inn, where they were each paying £13 per week, to the schoolmaster's house, where their quarters, though very cramped (Millais could open his bedroom door and shave without ever leaving his bed), were cheap, a pound per person per week. Millais still found Ruskin a "good fellow" but regarded him warily. He was "not of our kind, his soul is always with the clouds and out of reach of ordinary mortals—I mean that he theorises about the vastness of space and looks at every little stream with practical contempt."[38] The acquaintance of Mrs. Ruskin was a blessing. She was a delightful person, wonderfully kind. He painted her sitting by a waterfall. The canvas for Ruskin's portrait came, but it was not white enough, and Millais sent to London for another. Swimming in a rocky pool, he banged his nose against some rocks and hurt it badly. The same day, piling rocks across a stream to make a bridge (such minor engineering feats were among their favorite diversions), he hurt his left thumb so badly that the nail came off. Mrs. Ruskin succored him in his distress. The day after his accidents, she cut his hair. He began to give her drawing lessons and found her remarkably talented. Ruskin was working on the index for *The Stones of Venice*.

At last the lunette-shaped, sufficiently white canvas arrived and work began on the portrait. The Ruskins, their servant Crawley, Millais and his brother, William, all went out to the rocks of Glenfinlas. Effie read Dante aloud while John posed and Millais painted. William and Crawley fished. Millais painted very slowly, no more than a square inch a day, but what he painted was exquisite. However, the rains returned, and the painting, which had to be done *en plein air*, was perforce put aside. There was little to do but play battledore and shuttlecock inside the barn. Ruskin worked on his index. He was in a wonderful mood. He had begun to record snatches of Effie's conversation, preserving the disgusting things she said.

In that tiny cottage, the three of them lived together in disconcerting proximity. Millais could not help but see the neglect which Ruskin bestowed so lavishly upon his wife. He saw her unhappiness. Once, he suggested delicately to Ruskin that his wife ought not to be left alone so much, but Ruskin told him plainly that it was a woman's business to keep herself occupied. By the end of the summer, Millais knew, too, about the absence of a sexual tie between the Ruskins; either he deduced it from their living arrangement or was told about it by Effie. As they passed wet day after wet day in each other's company, Millais became her confidant.

In the evening, Ruskin and Millais started discussing architectural detail. Millais sketched some ornamental details for churches, and Ruskin was stunned by his talent in this field. One of Millais's designs was of a magnificent window in which three pairs of angels strain towards each other, their arched bodies framing the main sections of the window, their joined lips forming the pointed tops, their clasped hands defining other edges. All the angels have Effie's face. The erotic intensity of this drawing says more than all of Millais's letters about what was going on inside him. To Holman Hunt he complained about depression, low spirits, absence of enjoyment in everything but Mrs. Ruskin's drawing lessons. To Ruskin he explained his despair as resulting from Holman Hunt's decision to travel in the Holy Land: he would miss Hunt dreadfully. A letter arrived with the news that Deverell, a friend of his, an unsuccessful painter, was in dire straits, and the news provided Millais with an outlet and excuse for his grief. He spent a whole morning in tears. Then an evening.

That Ruskin remained unconcerned about the sexually charged situation in the little cottage is best explained by his own apparent immunity to sexual feeling. But, in addition, Millais did not seem to him a threatening presence, being on the verge of hysteria much of the time. Ruskin saw him painting until his limbs were numb and his back ached, refusing to take exercise in the usual way, but then taking off, on sudden whims, for seven-mile runs. "Sometimes he is all excitement, sometimes depressed, sick and faint as a woman, always restless and unhappy. I think I never saw such a miserable person on the whole,"[39] he wrote to his father. Ruskin perceived the despair but not the cause. It did not occur to him one could get so upset about a woman. That Hunt was behind it seemed more plausible, and Ruskin became sufficiently concerned about Millais's state to write Hunt and beg him to defer his trip to the Middle East. "I never saw so strange a person, I could not answer for his reason if you leave him."[40] Millais, alerted by Effie about this letter, quickly wrote to Hunt to say that he was naturally sad at his going away, but by no means to postpone the trip on his account.

In the third week of August, William Millais departed, his vacation over. Effie accompanied him as far as Perth in order to visit her mother, taking along the landlord's wife as chaperone, especially for the return to the Trossachs, when she would otherwise have been alone. Ruskin had suggested that instead of the landlord's wife Effie take Millais for company. Millais, astonished at the impropriety, firmly refused, and at this point, he, too, became convinced that Ruskin was trying to throw him and Effie together and to provoke her to compromise herself. After his brother's departure, Millais moved back into his rooms at the inn, despite their higher cost.

As the summer drew to its end, the painting of the portrait went on, meticulous inch by meticulous inch. The weather got worse, and Millais constructed a kind of tent to protect him from the elements—which served only to funnel the wind onto his back. He was working on the background, leaving the figure of Ruskin to be filled in later. Even Ruskin was aware that the summer had produced a change and now thought of his marriage as a mistake he had made. "When we married, I expected to change *her*—she expected to change me. Neither have succeeded and both are displeased. When I came down to Scotland with Millais, I expected to do great things for him. I saw he was uneducated, little able to follow out a train of thought—proud and impatient. I thought to make him read Euclid and bring him back a meek and methodical man. I might as well have tried to make a Highland stream read Euclid, or be methodical."[41]

The little group which had been together for so long finally disbanded in late October, the Ruskins heading for Edinburgh, where John was to deliver a series of lectures to the Philosophical Society. Millais was supposed to remain behind to finish the portrait, but he soon decided the project was hopeless and headed back to London after a brief stop in Edinburgh to see Effie. He would have given up the painting altogether, but Ruskin informed him that he would consider it an insult to his father as well as himself if Millais left it unfinished.

Millais's thoughts were on Effie and the terrible position she was in. He imagined her back in London besieged by rakes who would take advantage of Ruskin's neglect in the way he had not allowed himself to do. He imagined her succumbing at last to one of her admirers, giving Ruskin the chance he wanted to get rid of her with all the dishonor on her head. He begged her mother to make sure that one of her sisters was always with her for the sake of her reputation.

This paranoia, which Effie shared, was not entirely unjustified. Effie knew by now that Ruskin had no intention ever of consummating their marriage. When they had discussed the matter on her twenty-fifth birthday, which was in May of 1853—in other words, before the summer in the Highlands—he told her his feelings had changed since they had set this date for consummation six years before. As Effie reported it to her mother, he said it would be "*sinful* to enter into such a connexion, as if I was not very *wicked* I was at least insane and the responsibility that I might have children was too great, as I was quite unfit to bring them up."[42] They hated each other so much they could hardly talk. Ruskin offered his friend Furnival the follow-ing conversation, recorded at about this time, as evidence of Effie's depravity.

> Effie is looking abstractedly out of the window.
> John. "What are you looking at, Effie?"
> E. "Nothing."
> J. "What are you thinking of then?"
> E. "A great many things."
> J. "Tell me some of them."
> E. "I was thinking of operas—and excitement—and—(angrily) a great many things."
> J. "And what conclusions did you come to?"
> E. "None—because *you* interrupted me."[43]

This record of domestic bickering may not prove Effie's depravity, but it vividly shows what a stalemate the Ruskins had reached—from his point of view, every question kindly asked and every reply given with a snap, all day long, an unpleasantness in small things matched by obstinate opposition in large ones and combined with a vulgar ingratitude which led her to refer to him and his parents as that "batch of Ruskins"; from her point of view, constant neglect, an inhuman coldness that amounted to brutality, implacable dislike and disapproval which considered itself charitable in calling her insane, a cruel desire to break her spirit. In Edinburgh, she threatened him with the law, and he taunted her in reply—even if he did take all the blame, she would have to go home, lose her position, and "make a great piece of work" for her father.[44]

Effie, who had told her husband in Scotland that she could face with greater equanimity the prospect of going to Hell than returning to live with him in Camberwell, returned to Camberwell in the winter of 1853. In her eyes, her situation was that of the heroine of a Gothic novel, trapped in a castle where everyone is hostile to her, trying to drive her mad. Everyone wanted her to compromise herself, so she could be divorced. The elder Ruskins were determined to get rid of her in order to have John to themselves. On the afternoon of New Year's Day 1854, she and John visited his parents; the "batch of

Ruskins" planned a trip abroad in which she was not to be included. When they got home to Herne Hill, Effie told John she did not wish to begin the new year in the uncomfortable state they had been in and tried to negotiate a sort of truce. John said that his marriage to her was the greatest crime he had ever committed, because he had acted in opposition to his parents. His pity and polite behavior to her were adopted, he said, because he considered it a duty to be kind to one "so unhappily diseased."[45] He had already revealed to her the "true reason" why he had not consummated their marriage on the first night—that he found her body disgusting. He had also told her it would be sinful to have children with such a deranged, vile, and unnatural woman. Now he taunted her to renew her friendship with Millais.

At the same time, he continued to sit for Millais for the Glenfinlas portrait. "Surely such a quiet scoundrel as this man never existed," Millais wrote to Effie's mother. "He comes here sitting as blandly as ever, talking the whole time in apparently a most interested way."[46] Millais now continued to work on the painting in fear that if he stopped the Ruskins would somehow hurt Effie.

How much of this frenzied villainy was in the heads of the two lovers? It is a strange fact of the moral life that we never attribute bad motives to ourselves and yet do so most readily to everyone else we know. In the matter of the Ruskins, people would say—Queen Victoria among them—that Millais was an evil man who seduced a woman while painting her and while she was married to another man. Others would say that Effie left Ruskin when someone better came along. Others, in defense of Effie and Millais, would say that Ruskin had thrown them together in an attempt to get rid of Effie. All these things happened, and yet all the statements are in some measure untrue, because they imply a conscious intentionality that was lacking. Ruskin *did* bring his wife together with Millais, *did* encourage their intimacy, and *did* wish to be rid of her. Yet he could hardly have known when he took Effie to Gower Street to meet Millais, when he defended the Pre-Raphaelites, even when he suggested the party in the Trossachs, that Millais, that frail, under-educated child, would steal his wife away from him. Millais may have taken a liking to Effie while he was painting her and become enamored of her after spending four months with her in Scotland, but he did not press himself on her. Indeed, he consciously kept out of her way: after their meeting in Edinburgh in the fall of 1853, he did not see her again for eighteen months. And can we believe of Effie that she decided to get free of Ruskin when someone better came along? No doubt the idea of marrying Millais crossed her mind, but as reassurance, not motivation. Had she not had such a hope, her position would have been appalling—to return to her father's house with (as she saw it) the best of her youth gone, her reputation ruined, no prospects for marriage, which was the only way of supporting herself she had, not only deprived of the luxuries she had become used to, but a positive burden on her hard-pressed father. None of them, moving from day to day, taking advantage of now this, now that situation offered by life for the increase of their comfort and diminution of their misery, saw or planned the whole sequence of events upon which they were embarked. If they had acted upon consideration and not on instinct, from one moment to the next, from one small decision to the next, they could not have behaved so naturally in the melodramatic and scandalous situations they found themselves in. If Ruskin, for example, had seriously thought of foisting Effie onto Millais, he could hardly have suggested as nonchalantly as he did that Millais accompany Effie to Perth from Brig O'Turk and back again, alone.

On March 1, 1854, Effie went to her friend Lady Eastlake, whose husband, Sir Charles, was president of the Royal Academy, and disclosed her marital situation, asking what course to take and whether the law could help her. If economic considerations—her reluctance to place another financial burden on her father—played a part in keeping Effie from trying to get out of her marriage any earlier, sheer ignorance of the legal possibilities played a part, too: any kind of divorce was uncommon; of her own situation she could have been aware of no analogues, no precedents for action. But Lady Eastlake rather thought the law *could* help her and instructed Effie to bring her parents into her confidence, which she did in a letter of March 7, signed "Effie Gray." She had more faith in Lady Eastlake's practical savvy than in her parents', but for the sake of her future reputation she had to act in concert with them. Her father decided he must come to London and talk to Mr. Ruskin. Effie convinced him he had to talk to lawyers first. She also persuaded him that Mrs. Gray must come to London, too, despite the expense of another fare. While the Grays were making arrangements for Effie's return to her parents, worried always that their letters would fall into the hands of the Ruskins, war had been declared in the Crimea and John Ruskin went on sitting for his portrait by Millais.

On April 14 the Grays arrived by boat from Dundee. (Mr. Gray as a director of a shipping company could get sea passage more cheaply than railway seats.) He consulted lawyers, who reassured him that the case would not be difficult to make: an annulment was possible if the marriage had lasted three years without being consummated. Effie was examined by one of the two doctors whose evidence was necessary for the proceeding and was found to be a virgin. The doctor was "thunderstruck." A reader of Ruskin's books, he had always thought the man something of a Jesuit, but now he thought him mad.

Although Effie went into London almost every day to see her parents, Ruskin had no idea they were in town. Since he was spending all day, from breakfast to dinner, in his parents' house at Denmark Hill and returning to his own house only to sleep, it was not hard to evade his scrutiny. He and his parents were planning a tour of Switzerland in early May, and Effie was to go stay in Perth with her parents. When she sent off her luggage, he did not notice her sending more than usual. On the morning of April 25, he accompanied her and Sophie, her little sister, who had been staying with them, to King's Cross Station and put them on the train for Edinburgh, unaware that Effie was leaving for anything more than what had become, for them, a routine stay with her parents while he went abroad. He did not know that the Grays had left London by an earlier train and were waiting for Effie at Hitchin, the first stop outside of London.

At Hitchin, Sophie jumped out of the train and embraced her parents. Mrs. Gray took her place on the train to the north, and Mr. Gray, with Sophie, returned to London in order to deliver a package from Effie to the lawyers and to take advantage of the cheaper steamer fares on their own return trip the next day. At six o'clock that evening, two lawyers visited the home of the elder Ruskins and asked to see Mr. Ruskin and his son. One served John with a citation to court in Effie's of nullity, and the other handed to Mr. Ruskin (for forwarding to his wife) a packet from Effie containing her keys, her account book, her wedding ring, and a letter of explanation.

Effie's escape had been planned with a foresight and executed with a smoothness to gladden the heart of a general, but then, the enemy had been unaware of the state of war, and some people would blame the Grays for deceitfulness. The forthright thing to do, many people thought, would have been to inform Mr. Ruskin of the suit before the lawyers' appearance. But as Effie conceived the event she was like a fairy-tale princess, caught in an evil enchantment, and when dealing with witches, goblins, or evil monks, one doesn't stop to discuss things in a civilized manner. For his part, Millais rejoiced that Effie seemed likely to obtain her own "order of release," and, with perhaps dubious taste, said he trusted it would bring her as much satisfaction as the reverse situation—getting a husband *back*—does in the painting.

The day after the dramatic flight and serving of the papers, Mr. Ruskin called upon his solicitor, Mr. Rutter, and a proctor (a solicitor for the ecclesiastical courts) named Mr. Pott. Between them old Ruskin and Rutter managed the case; John did not involve himself. Since he had no wish to get Effie back, he was advised not to defend himself. Nevertheless, he felt moved to write for the proctor a statement of his side of the case, including an offer to prove his virility at the court's request. The document was never used in court and remained in the solicitor's desk for seventy years.[47] This self-defense is oddly moving, for its childish, one-eyed certainty as much as for its bewildered inability to trace the disintegration of the marriage.

Had she treated me as a kind and devoted wife would have done, I should soon have longed to possess her, body and heart. But every day that we lived together, there was less sympathy between us, and I soon began to observe characteristics which gave me so much grief and anxiety that I wrote to her father saying they could be accounted for by no other way than by supposing that there was slight nervous affection of the brain. It is of no use to trace the progress of alienation. Perhaps the principal cause of it

—next to her resolute effort to detach me from my parents—was her always thinking that I ought to attend *her*, instead of *herself* attending me.[48]

Ruskin was neither the first nor last to charge insanity in the face of unacceptable behavior, but in this case the lawyer rejected it as a possible defense for reasons which shed an interesting light on Victorian assumptions about sex: he argued that the irritation of Effie's brain might just as easily be understood as the *result* of the lack of consummation as its cause.

When the truth about the Ruskin marriage became known, the general indignation it aroused suggests that for certain segments of London society, sexlessness after marriage was every bit as shocking as sex before marriage. Ruskin was called a scoundrel, a blackguard, a wicked man, for all the world as though he had been keeping a string of mistresses or a second wife and family in Chelsea. Indeed there were some, like old Lady Charlemont, lady-in-waiting to the queen and wife of a notoriously unfaithful husband, who could scarcely comprehend the nature of this sexual offense. When Lady Eastlake called upon her to tell her the news (as Lady Eastlake did with a great many people in her selfless effort to purvey Effie's side of the story), Lady Charlemont heaped upon Ruskin "every possible and impossible wickedness of motive and aim that has characterized the *roué* part of the novels of the last half century," but not Ruskin's particular wickedness, which novels had not yet caught up with.[49]

Effie sat in Perth receiving reports of people's reactions. Millais reported, via Mrs. Gray, that George Richmond, the painter, who had always been a friend of Ruskin's, professed to be quite turned round by the news, and, after having thought of Effie as frivolous and unworthy of such a mighty man of intellect, had now begun to think better of her. Earnest, good Dr. Acland of Oxford, whose habit of allowing his baby to breakfast with them when the Ruskins came to visit had made Ruskin so ill, took a long time to make up his mind. He was sympathetic to Effie's plight and believed Ruskin guilty, but his conscience forced him to cite the fifth chapter of Matthew to the effect that there were no grounds for divorce but fornication. Thomas Carlyle, whose position in marriage was so similar to Ruskin's, gave an interesting opinion: no woman, he said, has any right to complain of any treatment whatsoever and should patiently undergo all misery inflicted upon her by her husband.

April was a good month that year for news to spread in the London art world: the Royal Academy was having the private viewing of its annual exhibition—where *everyone* who counted made an appearance—on April 28. The story wafted through the crowded rooms. Lady Eastlake talked about Effie with a blushing Millais. The irony was lost on few people that the year before they had been discussing *The Order of Release* and now were discussing the model, the artist, and the critic.

At the Water Colour Exhibition on April 29, the landscape painter David Roberts caught sight of John Ruskin himself, accompanied by his father. Roberts made his way to them through the crowd, engaged them in conversation, and did not shrink from the delicate subject. Ruskin, unwilling to admit that anything was wrong, merely said that his wife was in Scotland, but old Mr. Ruskin provided a complete account of his son's marriage: John had been trapped into marriage, being at the time attached to a French countess who had refused him, so that he was not hard to catch; they had overlooked that; they had overlooked Mr. Gray's lack of money; they had overlooked Effie's extravagance. Mr. Ruskin told Roberts more about Effie's temper and her father's railway shares and then said, "Come along, John. We shall have to *pay* for it—but never mind we have you to ourselves now."[50] Naturally the reference to the French countess made Effie smile when the story got to Perth, for she knew the lady was only plain Miss Domecq, whose fortune had procured her as husband a French baron of questionable character. Of all the gossip, Millais had this to say: "One great battle with the Russians will swamp the little talk there will be for the present."[51]

Millais had had a sitting scheduled with Ruskin for April 27, two days after Effie's escape, but Ruskin wrote to request a postponement until the following week. He cancelled that date, too, and postponed the final sittings—only his hands remained to be painted—until he returned from his trip to Europe with his parents. Millais worked with the greatest reluctance. He had more to do on the background, and, instead of returning to the memory-laden site at Glenfinlas, he wanted to find a similar waterfall in Wales and finish the background there. Ruskin would have none of that. Truth to nature was truth to nature, and you could not paint the gneiss of Scotland from different rocks in Wales. In another desperate attempt to wind up the wretched business and to avoid Ruskin, Millais suggested that he use another model for the hands. Again, Ruskin was indignant and held Millais to the strictest Pre-Raphaelite fidelity. His hands were unique, he said, and it would be absurd to stick other people's fingers onto his body, as indeed it would have been.

At moments, Millais thought about refusing to paint the hands at all—his hands would refuse to immortalize Ruskin's. He fantasized about using his hands to throttle Ruskin, not to paint him. At other times he consoled himself that no man living could do a better painting. But he would not be happy until the picture was finished. "It really is a misery to me and prevents me from thinking of other things. I almost fancy sometimes it will never be finished but will last all my life."[52] One has heard of tribes with rituals of sympathetic labor, but surely this is an unusual case of sympathetic separation: Millais had to effect his own divorce from Ruskin.

Effie's divorce was expedited quickly. Accompanied by her father, she returned secretly to London to make her deposition to the court. In 1857, when the Matrimonial Causes Act was passed, a special court would be established to try cases of divorce, but at this time divorce was available only through an Act of Parliament—a very expensive procedure and used but rarely—or, in special cases like Effie's, through the ecclesiastical courts, which decided whether in fact a marriage had ever been legitimately contracted. Plaintiffs and defendants did not make appearances in the courtroom but gave their testimony privately to the proctors who then presented the depositions to the court. This procedure did away with the pain and shame of having to tell one's wretched story in public, although it did away with courtroom drama, too. Effie made her deposition and was examined by court-appointed doctors (Queen Victoria's accoucheur, Dr. Locock, was one of them), then returned to Scotland to wait. Ruskin, in Switzerland, helped matters along by submitting a document that acknowledged certain basic facts of the situation, such as that the marriage had not been consummated and that he believed his wife still to be a virgin. On July 20, Effie received a letter pronouncing her "free from all bonds of matrimony." Legally, the marriage never existed. It had been contracted on false grounds, because, according to the official Decree of Nullity, "John Ruskin was incapable of consummating the same by reason of incurable impotency."[53]

Ruskin resented the charge of impotence. The virility which he had not chosen to exercise in his marriage he had offered to prove in court. For the rest, he was unconcerned. He considered his behavior in his marriage foolish but guiltless, and the foolishness lay in having married Effie in the first place. She was a spoiled and trivial woman who grew to hate him because he refused to accommodate her petty social goals. He was certain that her behavior had gotten worse in the six months preceding her departure because she had conceived a passion for someone whom she thought she might marry, if she could get a divorce from him. What kind of shocking behavior? Well, for example, when he was drawing, she did not come and sit beside him but went about her business and then complained that he left her alone all the time. But all this troubled him really very little. His domestic calamities were a hundred times less important to him than Turner's death and the destruction of certain thirteenth-century buildings in Italy; those had been the *real* sorrows of recent years. Finally, he cared much more about Millais than he did about Effie. He only hoped for Millais's sake that the artist did not marry her, as Ruskin feared he would do from a false sense of chivalry. It never occurred to him that he might lose Millais's friendship.[54]

The Ruskins returned from abroad in October and Ruskin did the final sittings for his portrait, which was finished, at last, in the following month. It was displayed for a while in Millais's studio before being sent to the Ruskins at Denmark Hill. Mr. Ruskin paid Millais £350 for it. Like everyone else who saw it, the Ruskins thought it a marvelous painting, although John jokingly objected to the figure blocking the landscape and thought Millais had falsely given him a squint, and his parents thought he looked a little too yellow and bored. But the Eastlakes proclaimed it worthy of Van Eyck.

John Ruskin wrote to thank Millais and requested his new address, because, as he said, he would surely want to write to him often. Millais didn't answer. Ruskin wrote again, "Why don't you answer my letter—it is tiresome of you and makes me uneasy." The artist responded with his address but added, "I can scarcely see how you conceive it possible that I can desire to continue on terms of intimacy with you. Indeed I concluded that after the finishing of your portrait, you yourself would have seen the necessity of abstaining from further intercourse."[55] Ruskin was astonished—and hurt. He wrote a formal reply to Millais. He said he took Millais's disinclination to continue their friendship to mean one of two things: that Millais believed he had had an unfriendly purpose in inviting him to the Highlands or that Millais himself had cause to feel guilty about his behavior. He thanked Millais for this final lesson in human folly and ingratitude.

Millais wanted to see Effie in July, as soon as she received her decree of annulment, but she, with her anxious sense of propriety and her desire not to give people food for gossip, refused to see him until the following spring. Effie said she was reluctant to marry again. She said she was particularly reluctant to marry Millais, who had been so unfairly involved in the ugly business. Nevertheless they quickly reached an understanding and were married in early July of 1855.

The wedding took place in the home of the bride's parents in Perth at two o'clock in the afternoon. The new minister of Kinnoull, Mr. Anderson, presided. The bridesmaids were Effie's two little sisters and her cousin, Eliza Jameson. The room was *not* the one she had been married in before. After the ceremony, the couple was taken by carriage to the Glasgow train. The curtains of the carriage were drawn so no one could see in. This was useful, since the bridegroom was upset.

It was all like a dream, he said. Before the ceremony he'd been feeling feverish and out of sorts, with an exaggerated sensation of going to an evening party at the age of fifteen. His brain and soul were exhausted with dwelling on unpleasant possibilities. When they had signed the wedding contract, Millais wanted to throw down his pen. He felt he was playing a part in a farce. By the time they got onto the train, it was clear that the excitement had been too much for him. Instead of getting the comfort brides may expect to enjoy at such moments, Effie had to give her new husband all her sympathy. He cried dreadfully. He said he didn't know how he had gotten through it. He said it had added ten years to his life. Effie bathed his face in eau de cologne, held his head, opened a window. Eventually, he seemed a little better, but his dread is understandable. For all the romance and melodrama he had been involved in, he knew no more about women and sex than Ruskin had when he got married. And look what happened to Ruskin!

But within two months of the wedding Effie was pregnant. They had rented a house next door to Effie's parents in Perth and lived there for the first two years of their married life. Eventually, they would have eight children—four boys and four girls. Eventually, he would become Sir John Everett Millais and president of the Royal Academy. Their marriage would seem to be happy, except that when they travelled in Italy, Everett (for so Effie called him, to distinguish him from her first husband John) was never enthusiastic enough to suit Effie, who remained an Italophile. They would have built for themselves a sumptuous neo-Renaissance mansion opposite Kensington Gardens. He would be making £25,000 per year. From his deathbed, he would even prevail upon the queen to receive his wife at court again. But although he was a commercial and popular success, critics no longer thought so highly of his work as they once had. The meticulous Pre-Raphaelite had become sloppy and hasty, as well as sentimental, giving visual form to the domestic pieties of his time. The talent which had once been used to paint the foam on the rushing water at Glenfinlas now painted soap bubbles delighting a little girl, and the painting *Bubbles*—to Millais's own horror it is true—was used as an advertisement for Pears soap.

Ruskin continued to praise Millais's work in the Academy showings of 1855 and 1856, thus proving to most people his disinterestedness and lack of petty malice. However, when he began attacking Millais in 1857, his disapproval had all the more weight. Millais himself felt it couldn't be connected with their personal entanglement. Other critics, whether or not following Ruskin's lead, have dated Millais's decline from 1857, the year he exhibited *Sir Isumbras at the Ford*, and this date follows so closely upon his marriage that it has been hard for people, who, as Millais said, will always be unkind if they can, to resist the deduction that Effie was responsible for her husband's betrayal of his talent. One wicked wit went so far as to suggest that if Ruskin had stayed married to Effie, he would have written *Bubbles*. But it may be useful to think of George Eliot's reminder that there were "spots of commonness" in Lydgate which made him susceptible to Rosamund's trivialization and which explain why his wife was not wholly to blame (if blame is relevant) for his ending up a fashionable doctor and abandoning the high dedication of his youth. My own guess is that just as it took Ruskin's insistence as well as Millais's talent to finish the Glenfinlas portrait, it probably took two—or maybe even three—to paint *Bubbles*.

HARRIET

TAYLOR

and

JOHN

STUART

MILL

1830–1858

Prelude:
Carlyle and J. S. Mill's Maid

For five months during his first winter in London, Carlyle had been working on his history of the French Revolution. He wrote in a state of semi-possession. He read obsessively, filled his mind with the subject, then wrote it out at a dash, destroying his notes as he went along. There were, of course, no typewriters, no carbon papers, and no Xerox machines.

On the face of it, Carlyle's good friend John Stuart Mill would have seemed the more likely person to take up the subject of the French Revolution. Germany had been Carlyle's province intellectually; Mill was the expert on France. But Mill ceded the project to Carlyle, helping him with references and lending him books. When Carlyle finished the first volume of his ambitious work, he sent the manuscript to John Stuart Mill for comment.

On March 6, 1835, Mill arrived in the Carlyles' parlor white-faced and in a state of horrible agitation. They knew before he said a word that something was wrong, and when he asked Mrs. Carlyle to go down to his carriage to talk to his friend Mrs. Taylor, Mrs. Carlyle thought she knew what it was. "Gracious Providence," she whispered to her husband before running downstairs. "He has gone off with Mrs. Taylor!"

In the carriage, Mrs. Taylor, as distraught as Mill, could only say over and over, "You will never forgive him." Mrs. Carlyle continued to believe that they had finally decided to elope. So horrid was this prospect and so thoroughly did the Carlyles expect it, that it was, momentarily, a relief to hear the catastrophe Mill had in fact come to announce.

Mill's maid, cleaning up, seeing the pile of papers in his parlor, had taken them for scrap and burned the lot. The first volume of the *French Revolution* was entirely gone.

How banal are the plots we impose on others' lives. Or, how much more inventive is the subconscious mind than the conscious mind. Who in 1835 did not think it likely that John Mill would elope with Mrs. Taylor? Who would have imagined that he could have burned the only copy of his friend's masterpiece?

Five months of work had to be repeated, and under what a fog of discouragement! If the Carlyles had not forgiven Mill, it would not be hard to understand. But the man was so upset on that first terrible evening that the Carlyles had to spend hours cheering *him* up, making light of the loss, in fear he would harm himself out of remorse and despair. As time went on, instead of blaming Mill, the Carlyles seem to have transferred their irritation to the innocent Mrs. Taylor, constructing the fantasy that the manuscript had been burned in her possession, even suspecting that she had done it deliberately.

Living Reasonably

Beautiful nineteen-year-old Harriet Hardy was married in London in 1826 to John Taylor, prosperous junior partner in a firm of wholesale druggists. He was ten years older than Harriet. His family, like hers, was Unitarian. It was a suitable match. The couple seemed happy. John Taylor seemed to have a lot to offer quite apart from his wealth. Clever, good-natured, and hospitable, he took an interest in radical politics, helped found London University, and was one of the original members of the Reform Club. He made a habit of welcoming political refugees from the Continent. He adored his dark-eyed and lively wife and indulged her in every way. He was not so brilliant in conversation as she—not so witty or daring—but he didn't object to the way Harriet charmed and impressed everyone. In fact, he enjoyed it. There was none of the bully in John Taylor. He felt that Harriet was exactly the kind of wife a man could be proud of—attractive, cultivated, high-spirited.

In the first four years of their marriage, they had two children, both boys. (A daughter would follow in 1831.) John Taylor continued to be completely satisfied with Harriet, but she became increasingly dissatisfied with him. When the initial excitement of being married wore off, when the pleasure of being treated as a full-fledged adult grew thin, she realized that the man she was married to did not really interest her. Even though he was a man, she was smarter than he was; her mind moved more quickly and was more widely informed. When he came home at night, she was not particularly happy to see him. She felt intruded upon by his preoccupations, his jokes, his reports of the day's business. She felt intruded upon in more intimate ways, too. Since she never really felt like making love with him, his desire to make love to her came to seem like a demand. She complied at first resignedly, but then with more and more resentment. The very fact that he kept imposing himself on her in this way, which seemed so aggressive and brutal—the Victorian word was "inconsiderate"—strengthened her distaste for him.[1]

In the last century, women were forced to be inventive when they realized they had come to find the men they had married distasteful. Divorce for incompatibility did not exist. Even a separation was hard to effect, since a woman had no legal right to property apart from her husband and could finance no arrangement herself. With a likelihood of finding herself joined for life to someone whose mind, body, or both disgusted her, a woman nonetheless owed her husband "conjugal rights." She had to submit to what must be the most offensive of frequently recurring human activities—sex without affection, sex against the will. Mill, in *The Subjection of Women* (inspired, at least in part, by Harriet's marital experiences), would call it "the lowest degradation of a human being, that of being made the instrument of an animal function contrary to her inclinations." To escape this, a woman could produce a stream of excuses: headaches, infirmities, female complaints, religious scruples. She could stay almost constantly pregnant or nursing and could invoke the belief that sexual activity was dangerous at such times. If she were very daring, and unusually sophisticated, she might solace herself with a lover, although it seems doubtful that a woman whose first experience with sex was unpleasant would turn to sex for relief. If she were desperate, utterly amoral, and perhaps a bit demented, she might go so far as to kill her husband. Mary S. Hartman's fascinating book *Victorian Murderesses* records the stories of middle-class women driven by the stringencies of family life to kill people close to them. A recurrent theme in these histories is the woman's disgust at having to submit to her husband's sexual advances—a disgust which occasionally leads to radical insights.[2] Had these "lady killers" been intellectuals, they might have analyzed their rage and made it the force behind useful activity. As it was, they acted inarticulately and unself-consciously and produced nothing but harm to themselves and others.

Harriet Taylor was an intellectual. When she realized, after four years of marriage, that her husband was in various ways distasteful to her, she went to consult her minister. She told him that her husband was not her intellectual equal. She said she was bored. She did not mention that she disliked sex with him, perhaps out of modesty, perhaps because she assumed that sex was universally disagreeable. But she continued to think about Taylor's irritating assumption that he had the right to make love to her whenever he wanted to. Such brutishness in an otherwise kind and thoughtful man made Harriet, when she was quite young, into a severe critic of marriage, which she saw as a sexual contract in which one of the parties, the necessarily virginal woman, could have no idea of what she was committing herself to. Legally, it was outrageous. In no other contract could such a condition be possible—that one of the signers be ignorant of what the contract involved.[3]

You can judge, by her minister's response to her complaints, the enlightened nature of the Unitarian circle in which Harriet Taylor moved. This remarkable man, William Johnson Fox, editor of the *Monthly Repository*, later a friend of Charles Dickens and a drama critic, did not berate her or counsel submission; he did not remind her of her duty to her husband; instead he took absolutely seriously her desire for intellectual companionship and offered to introduce her to John Stuart Mill. Not only was Mill unquestionably brilliant, he also shared—and there were few men who did—Mrs. Taylor's concern for equal rights for women. So, in a sense, feminism brought them together.[4]

When they met, at a dinner party at Mrs. Taylor's house, with Fox and Harriet Martineau among the other guests, Mill was twenty-four, a year older than she, unattached and attractive. He might have seemed in need of some cheering up himself. His father had dedicated him to Reform as others dedicate sons to the Church. James Mill had supervised his son's education personally, in an effort to prove how much time is wasted by conventional methods. Consequently, Mill knew Greek by the age of three, Latin slightly later, and at the age at which most children have little more on their minds than mastering the bicycle, he was in the habit of reading books and summarizing their arguments aloud for his father as they took their daily walk. He was trained to argue both sides of every question and taught that you had no right to a belief unless you understood the arguments for its opposite. His mind was made into a fine machine—a logic engine—to be put in the service of radical thought and practical reform. But four years before Mill met Mrs. Taylor, the machine had broken down.

> It occurred to me to put the question directly to myself: "Suppose that all your objects in life were realized; that all the changes in institutions and opinions which you are looking forward to, could be completely effected at this very instant: would this be a great joy and happiness to you?" And an irrepressible self-consciousness distinctly answered, "No!" At this my heart sank within me: the whole foundation on which my life was constructed fell down. All my happiness was to have been found in the continual pursuit of this end. The end had ceased to charm, and how could there ever again be any interest in the means? I seemed to have nothing left to live for.[5]

He was a well-equipped ship with a rudder but no sail; he was without desire, engulfed by "a drowsy, stifled, unimpassioned grief." The borrowing of Coleridge's words to describe his depression was significant, for utilitarianism provided no vocabulary for emotional states beyond the crudely quantitative "greatest happiness of the greatest number." That was part of the problem.

Mill's portrait of his emotional makeup and development in his autobiography is perhaps familiar: trained too early and too rigorously in logical analysis, he became unhealthily deficient in feeling. He began to believe—quite in opposition to orthodox utilitarianism —that cultivating the inner person was just as important as bettering a person's living conditions or improving the laws that shaped the outward circumstances of his life. Happily for children everywhere, Mill decided that his mental breakdown was the result of his relentless education and that there was more to life than was dreamed of in his father's philosophy. In the late 1820s, to cure his depression, he began to take doses of Wordsworth like doses of medicine. Poetry seemed "the very culture of the feelings" which he was in quest of, because, without feelings, the logic machine couldn't work, as he himself had discovered. Thought could provide goals, and means, but only emotion could provide the motive, the power, the desire to achieve those goals. Fortunately, the animating power of poetry could be embodied in people.

In 1831 Carlyle descended upon London from the isolation of Craigenputtock, determined to make a place for himself in the literary world, and one of the people he sought out was young John Stuart Mill, whose essay "The Spirit of the Age," published in the *Examiner*, had so impressed him. Because Mill was not satisfied with the way things were, because he talked in terms of historic cycles of decay and change, as did Carlyle himself, Carlyle concluded that Mill shared his views and was ready to submit himself in discipleship. The two men met at the home of Mrs. Austin, whose friends included both radicals and romantics, pragmatic Benthamites like Mill and idealists like Carlyle. They immediately recognized in each other equivalent brilliance and were buoyed up by the meeting. Intellectually, they were as far apart as men could be, but, at the time, only Mill realized that, and he did not particularly care. He regarded Carlyle's ideas as hazy metaphysics, but he was fascinated by his forceful, passionate personality. He made Mill feel like a man of straw. "I felt that he was a poet, and that I was not; that he was a man of intuition, which I was not; and that as such, he not only saw things long before me, which I could only when they were pointed out to me hobble after and prove, but that it was highly probable he could see many things which were not visible to me even after they were pointed out."[6] He found in Carlyle a person of feeling such as he sought. He found what he wanted even more perfectly embodied in Harriet Taylor.

Greater than himself, greater than Carlyle—in an act of willed belief he made her transcend the everlasting dualism of thought and feeling by being perfect in both. "I had always wished for a friend whom I could admire wholly, without reservation and restriction, and I had now found one. To render this possible, it was necessary that the object of my admiration should be of a type different from my own; should be a character preeminently of feeling, combined however as I had not in any other instance known it to be, with a vigorous and bold speculative intellect."[7] He was too wary of the notion of innate differences, too much opposed to sexual stereotypes, to present the woman he loved, even to think of her, as playing feminine emotion to his masculine reason, and so, with a kind of rhetorical flourish which he wholly believed, he made Harriet as great a thinker as she was a "poet."

There are other ways of explaining why Mill reacted to Mrs. Taylor with such an explosion of feeling—Carlyle's, for example. "That man, who up to that time, had never looked a female creature, even a cow, in the face, found himself opposite those great dark eyes, that were flashing unutterable things, while he was discoursing the unutterable concernin' all sorts o' high topics."[8] Ruskin would say that the great flaw of his education was its failure to provide him with an object of love, with the result that love, when it came, came with a force he had no way of controlling. The same could be said of Mill. It could also be said that his father had never allowed him a mother, and he found a way of getting himself one, however belatedly, and against whatever odds.

By 1832, Mill and Mrs. Taylor were deeply involved, seeing each other daily, exchanging fervent letters. The *Monthly Repository* had helped to unite them, for Harriet Taylor had begun to write reviews and articles for it, and Mill worked on them with her, talking over the ideas, editing the prose. He accepted her suggestions, developed her ideas, told her with complete sincerity that she was as great a thinker as he was. It was the ideal companionship she had longed for when she went to complain to Fox about her discomfort in marriage.

You could see how they complemented each other by the way they looked. What people noticed first about Harriet were her eyes—flashing—and a suggestion in her body of mobility, whereas his features, variously described as chiselled and classical, expressed an inner rigidity. He shook hands from the shoulder. He spoke carefully. Give him facts, and he would sift them, weigh them, articulate possible interpretations, reach a conclusion. Where he was careful, she was daring. Where he was disinterested and balanced, she was intuitive, partial, and sure of herself. She concerned herself with goals and assumptions; he concerned himself with arguments. She was quick to judge and to generalize, and because he was not, he valued her intellectual style as bold and vigorous where another person, more like her, might have found her hasty and simplistic.

Together they read poetry, particularly Harriet's favorite, Shelley. Naturally they despised the cynical Byron. Harriet's tastes were ardent, romantic; her responses to beauty intense. She took Mill to see pictures and sculpture, and taught him to respond to them for the sake of their beauty, rather than looking in them for some "meaning" or utility. Mill's intellectual mentor, Jeremy Bentham, had been of the opinion that, if the quantity of pleasure it gave was the same, pushpin (for which read "Pac-man") was as good as poetry. Mill now felt as though another world were being opened up to him. This was what he'd misssed in those arid years: beauty, emotion, passionate response. Harriet seemed to care about everything, approaching ideas with passion and not the calm logic he had been trained to exercise. He liked that about her. In him, some crucial element seemed missing, so that he pursued the good and true conscientiously, but without drawing upon his deepest vitality. He admired people who were spontaneous and enthusiastic, who believed what they believed with emotion, not just as the inevitable result of a logical train of thought. For this reason he adored the company of Harriet Taylor and never ceased to think of her as a better human being than himself. His life, which had seemed to him formless and purposeless, began to take shape and cohere around Harriet.

At Harriet's request, they exchanged position papers on marriage, "the subject which, of all connected with human Institutions, is nearest to her happiness."[9] Harriet spilled out all the bitterness she had stored up in six years as a wife. "Women are educated for one single object, to gain their living by marrying—(some poor souls get it without the churchgoing. It's the same way—they do not appear to be a bit worse than their honored sisters)." "One observes very few marriages where there is any real sympathy or enjoyment or companionship between the parties." And, she said,

Whether nature made a difference in the nature of men and women or not, it seems now that all men, with the exception of a few lofty minded, are sensualists more or less—women on the contrary are quite exempt from this trait.[10]

Attempting to write philosophy, Harriet was writing the story of her life. Marriage appeared to her no more than the transfer of a sexual commodity, with men getting all the pleasure and women getting all the "disagreeables and pains." She heartily recommended that divorce be possible at will.

What Mill wrote for Mrs. Taylor was a closely reasoned argument against the indissolubility of marriage which, characteristically, stated the case against divorce as persuasively as the case for it. I quote some of it, because I think it's a remarkable piece of common sense and shows the temper of the man.

> Most persons have but a very moderate capacity of happiness; but no person ever finds this out without experience, very few even with experience: and most persons are constantly wreaking that discontent which has its source internally, upon outward things. Expecting therefore in marriage a far greater degree of happiness than they commonly find: and knowing not that the fault is in their own scanty capabilities of happiness—they fancy they should have been happier with some one else: or at all events the disappointment becomes associated in their minds with the being in whom they had placed their hopes—and so they dislike one another for a time—and during that time they would feel inclined to separate: but if they remain united, the feeling of disappointment after a time goes off, and they pass their lives together with fully as much happiness as they could find either singly or in any other union, without having undergone the wearing of repeated and unsuccessful experiments.[11]

In his argument in favor of divorce, Mill assumes that happiness is unlikely to be found in a first choice, made when people are young and inexperienced and too much under the influence of their parents. Indeed, at any time of life, the statistical chances of finding happiness in marriage are slim. "Marriage is really, what it has been sometimes called, a lottery: and whoever is in a state of mind to calculate the chances calmly and value them correctly, is not at all likely to purchase a ticket. Those who marry after taking great pains about the matter, generally do but buy their disappointment dearer."[12] Therefore, assuming there are no children involved, we ought to be free to change partners until we find one who suits us.

Mill saw that the problem of the marriage laws was inextricably tied with the position of women. They did not regulate a union of equals, but of master and slave, protector and dependent. Bad as they were, they were better than a state of nature in which man, relying upon his physical superiority, could simply pick up a woman and drop her when he chose. Whereas Harriet saw the marriage contract as binding essentially upon the wife, requiring her to supply sexual favors on demand, Mill saw it binding essentially upon the husband, requiring him to stay with his wife even after his appetite for her is sated and he wishes to wander to fresher sexual fields. The marriage laws, he said, were shaped *"by* sensualists, *for* sensualists, and *to bind* sensualists," and the most important thing shared by Mill's essay and Mrs. Taylor's, after their belief in marriage as a contract between equals which should be breakable like any other contract, is their contempt for sensuality. If most people married for the right reasons, for intellectual and emotional companionship, rather than for reasons of physical desire, there would be no reason why law should have to set limits on the freedom of uniting and separating.

To understand the story of Mill's affair with Harriet Taylor one must appreciate the disgust for sex which marriage had left her with, the low estimation of sexual activity which they shared, and their conviction that in each other they had found the highest companionship of which human beings were capable, a love compounded only of spirit and intellect, with no earthly dross, a love at the high end of the platonic ladder—the greatest good life had to offer.

Poor John Taylor tried to act like a man of reason. He believed his wife's assurances that her relationship with Mill was entirely innocent, founded on an intimacy of intellect alone. Still, he had cause for complaint, for if she was not sleeping with Mill, neither was she sleeping with her husband, boasting in later years that almost from the moment of meeting Mill she had been no more than a *seelen-freundin,* a soul mate, to the two men in her life. She told her husband with a brutal frankness she no doubt considered philosophic candor that she had found with Mill a companionship she had been missing with him and that she loved Mill more than she loved him.

Once, he asked her to "renounce sight" of Mill, and she agreed to do so. She wrote Mill a farewell letter, and he wrote back a heartbroken letter of compliance in French, a language which seemed to him more appropriate than English for discussing matters of the heart. But the solution was to be neither so dramatic nor so simple—and certainly not quick. Harriet found that she could not do without her friend, and her husband could not bear to make her unhappy. Gradually things returned to the way they had been, with Mill in the role of sanctioned platonic lover. He was at the Taylors' house almost every night of the week. He relinquished Wednesday, because that was the night the Taylors received company and he would then have to share Harriet with others. On the other nights, Mr. Taylor frequently went to his club in order to get out of their way.

In this situation, the husband about whom so little is known probably gave the most and got the least of the three. Insofar as he comes across through his letters, he is always puzzled, always trying to understand his wife's behavior and delicacies of sensibility. Harriet gave him to understand pretty clearly that she and John Mill were made of finer stuff than he was, that their thinking was very advanced indeed, and that a junior partner in a wholesale drug firm, however prosperous, would have to run hard to keep up with them. So he ran and ran. And the men in his club along with many others laughed at him, not appreciating the fine distinctions of his wife's behavior as he had been trained to do.

At last, Taylor reached the point of preferring to lose Harriet rather than enduring the humiliation of her liaison with Mill—however innocent. He made an ultimatum. If Harriet would not end her friendship with Mill, he would like a separation. Harriet agreed to the separation. She would go alone to Paris for six months. She would decide whether to spend her future with her husband, with Mill, or perhaps by herself in Paris. This was the moment of ultimate decision. If ever Harriet were to leave her husband and take the revolutionary step of living with Mill, she would have done it in 1833. It would have been daring, but Harriet Taylor and John Mill were daring people. They endorsed Robert Owen's radical definition of chastity as sexual intercourse with affection, prostitution as sexual intercourse without it. They did not, in thinking about sexual conduct, "consider the ordinances of society binding on a subject so entirely personal."[13]

Mill was considerably more reluctant than Mrs. Taylor to commit an unforgivable social sin. "What ought to be so much easier to me than her, is in reality more difficult—costs harder struggle—to part company with the opinion of the world, and with my former modes of doing good in it."[14] Farewell to reputation, farewell to all influence if he went off publicly with Harriet. As unworthy a goal as living for reform seemed to him in 1826, living for love seemed equally unworthy in 1833. He would be reduced to being "obscure and insignificant." Recklessly, he confessed his fear to Harriet. "Good heaven," she replied. "Have you at last arrived at fearing to be *'obscure & insignificant'*! What *can* I say to that but 'by all means pursue your brilliant and important career'. Am *I* one to choose to be the cause that the person I love feels himself reduced to 'obscure & insignificant'! Good God what has the love of two equals to do with making obscure & insignificant."[15] She called his reluctance to destroy his own career little more than "common place vanity." No wonder this imperious woman made Mill feel that at last he was alive. Her outrage is wholly silly—and wholly irresistible—to anyone who responds, as Mill did, to pure energy and passion.

Harriet thought she could bring herself to risk the scandal of running off with Mill, but would he, after all, be any better than her husband? Upon arriving in Paris, she felt a burst of gratitude and affection for Mr. Taylor, who, considering his limitations, was behaving remarkably well. (He was, of course, paying for everything.) Were she and Mill really suited? They had spent so little time together, and, close as they had been, were so restrained in their dealings. Not long after she went to Paris, Mill joined her there—breaking his promise to Carlyle to spend his vacation with him in Craigenputtock. It was Duty, he assured Carlyle, to "a person who of all persons alive I am under the greatest obligation." They spent two weeks together in perfect companionship. "We never could have been so near, so perfectly intimate, in any former circumstances—we never could have been together as we have been in innumerable smaller relations and concerns—we never should have spoken of all things, in all frames of mind with so much freedom and unreserve." It was probably at this time that a French friend of the Carlyles saw Mill and Mrs. Taylor eating grapes off the same bunch "like love birds." The result of this fortnight was that Harriet's doubts were put to rest. She was convinced they could live together happily, were in fact more suited to "that perfect than for this imperfect companionship."[16]

The discovery was perhaps academic, since the barrier to their spending their lives together—Harriet's husband—still existed and still *was* a barrier. Harriet wrote to him frequently, letters which expressed the affection she insisted she had always felt for him. She got carried away as she wrote. She was more affectionate, more exuberant than she could bring herself to be in his presence. Mr. Taylor was delighted with her letters and believed he had won her back. Tolerance had been the right strategy; absence had made the heart grow fonder. Mill was forced to explain it all to the bewildered Reverend Fox, who was trying to keep track of this domestic *pas de trois* from London. "Because her letters to Mr. Taylor express the strong affection she has always felt, and he is no longer seeing, every day, proof of her far stronger feeling for another, he thinks the affection has *come back*—he might have seen it quite as plainly before; only he refused to believe it. *I* have seen it, and felt its immense power over her. . . . Her affection for him, which has always been the principle, is now the sole obstacle to our being together—for the present there seems absolutely no prospect of that obstacle's being got over. She believes—& she knows him better than any of us can—that it would be the breaking up of his whole future life—*that* she is determined never to be the cause of."[17] Mill was not the person to sweep her off. Taylor was not the person to coerce her. If any of the three was capable of extreme action, it was Harriet, and it was probably not in her interests to act extremely. The situation was rich with material for thought as it was!

The triangle is a peculiarly stable arrangement, and Harriet Taylor was not unusual in finding deep satisfaction in being the apex between two men. Nor was she unique in thinking that her husband's life would go to pieces if she left him. But rarely has so much speculative care, so much seeming reason, gone into deliberations about the conduct that ought to follow upon a premise of passion. Systematically, philosophically, they considered whether Mrs. Taylor should leave her husband and live with Mill. Bringing to the drama of their own lives all the scrupulous consideration they devoted to theoretical problems of justice in society, Mrs. Taylor and Mill determined that nothing could justify so great an injury to Mr. Taylor except the clearest perception that it would not only guarantee their happiness but that either or both of them would be insupportably unhappy if they did not live together. Here is the Utilitarians' greatest happiness principle applied to personal ethics with a stoical twist: how is the greatest quantity of unhappiness to be avoided? These people of strong will and reason and not negligible passions decided at last that the least unhappiness would result from Harriet's staying with Taylor if she could continue to enjoy the company of Mill. It would frustrate and irritate all three of them but would create utter misery in no one. So persuasively did Harriet state the case to her husband that he agreed he had been selfish before and vowed to think less about himself and more about others in the future. He would allow her to see Mill if she would agree to keep up the appearance of marriage. In other words, after all the agonized thought and talk, they decided to continue exactly as they had been, with Taylor resigned to being no more than a "friend and companion" to his wife.

You have to hand it to Harriet. She had a solid husband against whose placidity her own wit could shine all the more dazzlingly. Out of an uncomfortable marriage in which she felt sexually oppressed she had constructed a situation in which she had her husband's support, both emotional and financial, without paying the sexual debt she so much loathed. She had the luxury of thinking she was sacrificing her happiness for his. She had one of the most brilliant men in London as her intimate and devoted friend, and she had him convinced she was making a sacrifice for his sake, too. She had the love of her three children, who adored her, no doubt, for the same reasons Mill did—for her clarity and firmness, combined with warmth and spontaneity. She was an excellent mother and, throughout all these complicated domestic maneuvers, retained the reputation of being an excellent mother. Precariously, she even had her respectability. This was evidently a woman of extraordinary talents, as John Mill always said.

Of course they were talked about, by no one more than that enthusiastic gossip Thomas Carlyle, who considered himself, in those years, a good friend of Mill. But although the two men had corresponded since 1831, exchanging long letters on a more or less monthly basis, and although Mill had even agreed to visit Craigenputtock in 1833 (the visit which had to be cancelled in favor of Mrs. Taylor and Paris), he had told Carlyle nothing about Mrs. Taylor, which made both the Carlyles all the more shocked when they moved to London in 1834 and heard about the matter. Carlyle reported to his brother:

> Mrs. Austin had a tragical story of [Mill's] having fallen *desperately in love* with some young philosophic beauty (yet with the innocence of two sucking doves), and being lost to all his friends and to himself.

And Jane less graciously reported that "a young Mrs. Taylor, 'tho encumbered with a husband and children, has ogled John Mill successfully so that he was desperately in love."[18]

When they were introduced to Mrs. Taylor, both Carlyles found her fascinating. "She is a living romance heroine, of the clearest insight, of the royalest volition, very interesting, of questionable destiny." Jane paid a call on her and they dined at her house, in the company also of W. J. Fox and John Taylor, "an obtuse, most joyous natured man, the pink of social hospitality." But Platonica—as Carlyle took to calling Mrs. Taylor—did not wear well. Her manner was a little too regal for the Carlyles. She affected a "sultana highmindedness" they did not care for, along with a "girlish petulance." They did not approve the liberal politics of Mrs. Taylor and her friends, whom Carlyle called snidely "friends of the species." "Jane and I often say: 'Before all mortals, beware of a friend of the species!' Most of these people are very indignant at marriage and the like; and frequently are obliged to divorce their wives, or be divorced: for though the *world* is already blooming (or is one day to do it) in everlasting 'happiness of the greatest number,' these people's own *houses* (I always find) are little Hells of improvidence, discord, unreason."[19]

Gradually they came to worry about their friend Mill and to distrust Platonica, "a dangerous looking woman," said Jane now, "engrossed with a dangerous passion," between whom and herself no "useful relation" could grow. When the terrible accidental burning of the manuscript occurred, the Carlyles seem to have transferred any irritation they might reasonably have felt against Mill to Mrs. Taylor. She was ruining Mill's life, one of the clearest signs of which, in Jane's estimation, was that his intellect was failing in its strongest point—his "implicit admiration and subjection" to her husband. Nevertheless, in one point of friendship they never wavered; perhaps the more easily because of the nature of their own relationship, they never doubted that Mill's relationship with Mrs. Taylor was technically innocent.

> Is it not strange, this pining away into dessication and nonentity of our poor Mill, if it be so, as his friends all say, that his charmer is the cause of it? I have not seen any riddle of human life which I could so ill form a theory of. They are innocent says Charity: they are guilty says Scandal: then why in the name of wonder are they dying broken-hearted? One thing only is painfully clear to me, that poor Mill is in a bad way.[20]

Poor Mill was in fact consumptive, and a trip to the Continent would later miraculously arrest the disease. But Thomas Carlyle, out of an inability to comprehend a man's devotion to a woman as anything but besotted and comic infatuation, out of jealousy because Mrs. Taylor had secured the very friend *he* had wanted, and partly out of congenital malice, which colored almost all his observations about his contemporaries, contributed to the popular version of Mill's romance with Mrs. Taylor the tale of a naïve philosopher ruined by a *femme fatale*.

None behave with a greater appearance of guilt than people who are convinced of their own virtue. Mill and Mrs. Taylor tried to go about London together openly, but they caused too many shocks. John Roebuck, for example, watched them arrive at a dinner party at the home of Charles Buller's mother. Mill entered with Mrs. Taylor on his arm. "The manner of the lady, the evident devotion of the gentleman, soon attracted universal attention, and a suppressed titter went round the room."[21] Roebuck, who was one of Mill's closest friends, went to his office the next day to beg him to relinquish his compromising entanglement. Mill refused ever to speak to him again. Mill's father, the old Utilitarian, told his son plainly that he was coveting another man's wife, which was as bad as coveting his goods. John Mill replied that his feelings for Mrs. Taylor were no different from what they would be for a competent man, and no more was ever said within his family about his closest friend.

John Taylor once again rescued the situation by taking a house for Harriet in the country, where she might see Mill in privacy, and from which Mr. Taylor could more easily absent himself than from his London home. In as much secrecy as could be mustered, Mill regularly went out to Kingston or Walton and spent weekends with Mrs. Taylor. In secrecy they travelled together abroad, usually in search of health, which was failing in both of them. Sometimes Mr. Taylor would escort his wife as far as Paris, where he would turn her over to the protection of Mr. Mill. On one trip, in 1836, they were accompanied by Harriet's children and Mill's young brothers. The youngsters were left in Switzerland while Mill and Mrs. Taylor continued on to Italy, spending two months on the bay of Genoa. In his autobiography, in a passage heavily worked over by Harriet and written at her suggestion, Mill said of those years, "I . . . was greatly indebted to the strength of character which enabled her to disregard the false interpretations liable to be put on the frequency of my visits to her while generally living apart from Mr. Taylor, and on our occasionally travelling together, though in all other respects our conduct during those years gave not the slightest ground for any other supposition than the true one, that our relation to each other at that time was one of strong affection and confidential intimacy only."[22]

In their own time, their innocence was not self-evident, and scandal led Mill and Mrs. Taylor to withdraw almost completely from society throughout the 1840s. In that difficult decade, they worked together closely on the *Principles of Political Economy* and other of Mill's writing. Mrs. Taylor had stopped writing, finding it more satisfying to work with—and through—Mill. He was so grateful for her help with the *Principles of Political Economy* that he wanted to include in the book a public acknowledgment:

To
MRS. JOHN TAYLOR
as the most eminently qualified
of all persons known to the author
either to originate or to appreciate
speculations on social improvement
this attempt to explain and diffuse ideas
many of which were first learned from herself,
is
with the highest respect and regard
dedicated.[23]

It was perhaps exaggerated; it was certainly indiscreet. Harriet consulted with her husband about whether or not to accept the dedication and was surprised to encounter one of his rare bursts of irritation. John Taylor found dedications generally in bad taste but this one betrayed a want of taste and tact which he could not have believed possible. "It is not only 'a few common people' who will make vulgar remarks, but all who know any of us— The dedication will revive recollections now forgotten and will create observations and talk that cannot but be extremely unpleasant to me." It was never pleasant to differ from Harriet, and he regretted the vexation his opinion caused her (she wanted to accept the dedication), but this infraction was so serious he was willing to risk her displeasure. For all that, the dedication was inserted into all copies given to friends.[24]

In December of 1848, Harriet decided to go to the south of France for the winter, partly for her health, but partly to avoid her brother, with whom she did not get along, who was visiting London from Australia. Mr. Taylor was very sorry when he heard her plans. He was not feeling well himself and wished to have her less drastically away from him. But Harriet didn't waver. "I can assure you I do not do it for my pleasure, but exceedingly the contrary, & only after the *most* anxious thought— Indeed I am half killed by *intense anxiety*. The near relationships to persons of the most opposite principles to my own produces excessive embarrassments." She meant her brother. If she stayed she would be sure to get into difficulties about him which she hadn't the strength to bear. "Your saying that you are sorry I am going has given me ever since I read your note so *intense* a headache, that I can scarcely see to write— However it is only one of the vexations I have to bear and perhaps everybody has."[25]

Harriet felt everything she did was rationally justified, so that when, the following March in Pau, she received a letter from her husband saying that he was sick and asking her to come home to him, she declined to do so on the grounds that Mr. Mill was coming to Europe in the middle of April for *his* health and she had promised to meet him. Nothing but a "feeling of right," she said, would keep her from returning home immediately. She was quite certain that her obligation to Mill, who was suffering from a loss of vision and inability to write, was greater than her obligation to her husband, who was in fact dying of cancer, although she could not have known it. When she finally returned home, he was close to death. For two months she nursed him, attending him constantly. "There is nothing on earth I would not do for him and there is nothing on earth which *can* be done."[26] Perhaps she felt for once that she had not treated him uniformly well. But she had always been fond of him and he of her. In their way, they were platonic lovers, too. In July of 1849 he died, leaving her all his property.

The next day Mill and Mrs. Taylor began to discuss whether Mill should appear at the funeral. She wrote:

My *first* impression about your coming was a feeling of "better not" grounded on the sort of distance which of late existed. But now on much consideration it seems to me in the first place that coming is certainly thought a mark of respect? Is it not? and that therefore your not doing so will be a *manque* of that. Then again the public in some degree and *his* public too have heard . . . of our intimacy. . . . Does not therefore *absence* seem much more noticeable than coming? On the other hand nothing is more true of common world than "out of sight out of mind."[27]

It is typical of how the best in them sometimes slid over into being the worst. Is this an example of the examined life? Or is it an example of the absence of something spontaneous which lends grace to action, whatever action is taken?

Daring in her thought, Harriet was in some ways deeply conventional in behavior. Two years, the conventional period of mourning, elapsed after John Taylor's death before Harriet agreed, conventionally, to become Mrs. Mill. That marriage was the course for them was not completely obvious. They wanted to live together, to end the perpetual coming and going which aggravated every minor difference between them. Marriage, however, had dismal associations for Harriet, and both of them disliked the institution, believing it legalized an essentially immoral transfer of all power and property to the man. As they moved closer to marriage in 1852, Mill produced a remarkable document disclaiming the rights which would be conferred on him as a husband.

Being about, if I am so happy as to obtain her consent, to enter into the marriage relation with the only woman I have ever known, with whom I would have entered into that state; and the whole character of the marriage relation as constituted by law being such as both she and I entirely and conscientiously disapprove, for this amongst other reasons, that it confers upon one of the parties to the contract, legal power and control over the person, property, and freedom of action of the other party, independent of her own wishes and will; I, having no means of legally divesting myself of these odious powers . . . feel it my duty to put on record a formal protest against the existing law of marriage, in so far as conferring such powers; and a solemn promise never in any case or under any circumstances to use them. And in the event of marriage between Mrs. Taylor and me I declare it to be my will and intention, and the condition of the engagement between us, that she retains in all respects whatever the same absolute freedom of action, and freedom of disposal of herself and of all that does or may at any time belong to her, as if no such marriage had taken place; and I absolutely disclaim and repudiate all pretension to have acquired any *rights* whatever by virtue of such marriage.[28]

Harriet would have understood that by these dry and graceless sentences Mill repudiated not only property rights conferred on him by marriage but the sexual rights which had made her first marriage such a source of misery. Any sexual activity between them would not be a matter of rights and debts.

They were married quietly at a registry office outside London, with two of Harriet's children the only witnesses. Mill signed the registry with his customary signature, "J S Mill," only to be told that his full name was required, necessitating that he squeeze in the omitted letters and making his signature look in the end rather silly. The incident preyed on his mind so much that it is hard not to take it seriously. Sometime later he formally wrote to his wife explaining the mistake. The letter itself served, it would seem, a quasi-legal function, as they were living together at the time he wrote it. He begged her to re-marry him so that no one could doubt the propriety of their marriage. As an administrator and legislative reformer, he had great respect for the letter of the law, and he was so worried about being married that he was worried he wasn't married at all.

Mill had seemed a man entirely without anger. According to his friend and biographer, the logician Alexander Bain, he never got into a rage, and all hatred and abuse was, in Bain's strange phrase, "crucified" in him.[29] His strongest sign of emotion in controversy was the chuckle. But now, upon his marriage, he started lashing out at some of the people he had been closest to, not on his own account, to be sure, but on Harriet's. Until the day of his wedding, Mill had continued to live with his mother and two of his sisters, yet he broke with them completely because they did not immediately pay a call upon Harriet when he announced his engagement. His anger was as unreasonable and as unreasoning as the sudden movement of long-lying magma in the eruption of a volcano. It devastated the devoted ladies in Kensington, who had never been anything but proud of and compliant to the man who had been beloved head of their family since James Mill's death. In twenty years of friendship, Mill and Mrs. Taylor had lived a furtive existence, hiding their meetings, misleading people about their travel plans, enduring malicious gossip. Perhaps the anger had pooled, waiting for expression until they achieved the respectability of marriage. The reasonable man who could not get angry, the man unschooled in the expression of emotions, was now swept away by anger as years before he had been swept away by love—so much so that in his anger as in his love he seems like a bad actor trying to play a lover, trying to play an angry man.

One of the people who was surprised by Mill and Mrs. Taylor's decision to marry was Mill's younger brother, George, who was engaged in the silk trade in Madeira. He admired his eldest brother and the woman he had heard about. He admired their principles, which he thought included a cavalier disregard for the forms of society. He did not see what two such people, who scorned conventional institutions, had to gain from marriage. They had enjoyed each other's companionship for many years without being married. (George Eliot would encounter the same disappointed response from free-thinking friends when, after her unconventional liaison with Lewes was ended at last by his death, she married J. W. Cross.)

A month after his marriage, Mill wrote to his brother without announcing the change in his life. George heard the news eventually from his mother and sisters in London and politely wrote a note to his new sister-in-law and one to her son Haji. He mentioned his surprise. He said he didn't understand why they had done something so at variance with their principles. He didn't know what changes, if any, their union would make in their mode of life, but he wished them well. In light of the document Mill wrote disclaiming his rights as a husband, George's befuddlement may seem understandable. But no ambivalence about the institution of marriage showed in Mill's savage reply to his brother.

I have long ceased to be surprised at any want of good sense or good manners in what proceeds from you—you appear to be too thoughtless or too ignorant to be capable of either—but such want of good feeling, together with such arrogant assumption, as are shown in your letters to my wife and to Haji I was not prepared for. . . . You were "surprised," truly, at our marriage and do not "know enough of the circumstances to be able to form an opinion on the subject." Who asks you to form an opinion? An opinion on what? Do men usually when they marry consult the opinion of a brother twenty years younger than themselves? or at my age, of any brother or person at all? But though you form no "opinion" you presume to catechize Haji respecting his mother, and to call her to account before your tribunal for the conformity between her conduct and her principles.[30]

Either Mill is firing a cannon to kill a mosquito, or there is more involved here than might at first appear. I would suggest there *is* a buried issue, nothing less than the meaning Mill wished to be drawn from the story of his relations with Harriet, the meaning of the story of his life.

It requires little reading between the lines to see that George assumed that their relationship had always been sexual. He admired them as sexual radicals—on the lines of Shelley—a hero and heroine of free love, flouting marriage, flouting conventional sanctions. Nothing could have been further from the moral Mill and Harriet wished to be drawn from their story. They had no desire to be seen as people who believed in acting on passion. Why, but for their rational concern for John Taylor's feelings, would they have deprived themselves of the pleasure of each other's company for all those years? They did not want to be viewed as the philosophic heirs of Shelley, with his absurd and childish romanticism, but as advanced in a manner more distinctly modern, with a greater emphasis on restraint, moral fiber, progress through self-discipline, a manner, if I may say so, more Victorian. Like a hardworking but not very bright schoolboy, George Mill had studied his lessons but had come up with the wrong interpretation, turning a complex and subtle meaning into a vulgar and simplistic one, and Mill came down on him with the frustrated anger of the teacher whose point has not gotten across.

Mr. and Mrs. Mill believed that their personal history proved something the world greatly needed proven: that rationality could be a more important bond between men and women than sensuality; that sex was less important in love than intellectual companionship; that sex could be done without altogether. When Mill began writing his autobiography, Harriet requested that he include a history of their relationship from 1830 until their marriage, focussing on the strong affection between them, the intimacy of their friendship, and the absence of impropriety. "It seems to me an edifying picture for those wretches who cannot conceive friendship but in sex—nor believe that expediency and the consideration for the feelings of others can conquer sensuality."[31]

Mill obeyed her instructions with the scrupulousness he always devoted to her wishes and wrote,

> We disdained, as every person not a slave of his animal appetites must do, the abject notion that the strongest and tenderest friendship cannot exist between a man and a woman without a sensual relation, or that any impulses of that lower character cannot be put aside when regard for the feelings of others, or even when only prudence and personal dignity require it. Certain it is that our life, during those years, would have borne the strictest scrutiny, and though for the sake of others we not only made this sacrifice but the much greater one of not living together, we did not feel under an obligation of sacrificing that intimate friendship and frequent companionship which was the chief good of life and the principal object in it, to me and . . . I may also say to her.[32]

The phrase "during those years" might suggest that in later years Mr. and Mrs. Mill did *not* abstain from sex. The reference to abstinence as a "sacrifice" argues even more persuasively against the chastity of their relationship after marriage. Yet most modern scholars have assumed that the Mills' marriage was never consummated. These scholars cite a habit of abstinence which they think would have been deeply ingrained by the time the Mills married, in their late forties. They also cite Harriet's back problems, stemming from a carriage accident in 1842, which left her an invalid, virtually unable to walk. Alexander Bain, the only one of Mill's biographers who knew him personally, believed that "in the so-called sensual feelings, he was below average," not a good representative of humanity. "He made light of the difficulties of controlling the sexual appetite." The only documentary glimpse we have into John Mill's buried life suggests sensuality efficiently repressed. It is provided by a dream of 1857 in which Mill longs to find in one woman both friend and "Magdalene," is rebuked for the thought by a woman who sounds very much like Harriet, and retreats into dowdy abstractions about the nature of the good.[33] None of this is conclusive. I myself would like to think that the marriage was consummated. I would like to think it was lust fueling Mill's hyperbolic attachment to Platonica. But there is no evidence, one way or the other—no smoking pistol. What can be said with certainty is that sex was not the binding element in Harriet's attachment to John and John would not have approved its playing any part in his attachment to her.

In John Mill's mind as in Harriet's, sex was hopelessly associated with an unjust arrangement of power: it gave men pleasure at women's expense. Like most Victorian feminists, Mill saw women as the victims of male sexuality and looked forward to an age of diminished sexual activity as an advance. He felt—again like most feminists— that he was addressing himself to an over-sexed and self-indulgent age. (When Josephine Butler led her great campaign against the double standard, her demand was not that women be given the same sexual freedom as men but that men conform to the standard of sexual purity applied to women.)[34] Victorian feminism generally was opposed to birth control because it would remove one of women's few defenses against sex—the fear of pregnancy—and would make them vulnerable to male sexuality more of the time.

For Mill the goal of equality between men and women and the goal of conquering sensuality were connected. But since his time, mainstream feminism has tended to valorize sexual fulfillment. Now, when so many of Mill's ideas about women and marriage are accepted, it is hard to resist the impulse to present his relationship with Mrs. Mill as prefiguring a contemporary feminist ideal of a heterosexual relationship in which "sex and intellect, family and work, are blended."[35] Alice Rossi, in presenting the Mills' as an ideal marriage, frankly acknowledges that hers is an exercise in retrospective utopianism, an attempt to find in the past models that, as a feminist who values heterosexual relationships, she would like to find in the present. But the fit is not a good one. The Mills are not such a perfect blend. Moreover, they would not have approved this vision of themselves—any more than they approved George Mill's.

Ironically, as Mill tried to use his life to prove the truth of his theories (how sensuality could be transcended in a rational relationship between a man and a woman; the nature of a marriage of equals), his enemies used it to discredit him. In 1883, when a young Viennese woman expressed admiration for Mill's ideas about marriage, her fiancé hastened to set her straight.

> This is altogether a topic on which one does not find Mill quite human. His autobiography is so prudish or so unearthy that one would never learn from it that humanity is divided between men and women, and that this difference is the most important one. His relationship to his own wife strikes one as inhuman, too. He marries her late in life, has no children from her, the question of love as we know it is never mentioned. . . . In all his writings it never appears that the woman is different from the man, which is not to say she is something less, if anything the opposite. For example he finds an analogy for the oppression of women in that of the Negro. Any girl, even without a vote and legal rights, whose hand is kissed by a man willing to risk his all for her love, could have put him right on this.

Freud (for it was he) concluded sternly, "The position of woman cannot be other than what it is: to be an adored sweetheart in youth, and a beloved wife in maturity."[36] As he was in the dominant nineteenth-century scientific tradition in his biological determinism about women, Freud was in the majority, too, in using Mill's relationship with his wife—"inhuman," "unearthy"—as a way of attacking the credibility of his theories about women. Late-nineteenth-century critics of Mill hinted more or less snidely at the sexlessness of his life or the absence of masculinity in his nature. "For though he could not be argued down by reason even after he was dead," writes Mill's biographer Michael St. John Packe, "it could be asserted that he was more a woman than a man, and as a woman, need not be listened to."[37]

It seems appropriate that in trying to imagine the married life of those intensely mental creatures Mr. and Mrs. Mill, so gloriously wrapped up in their experiment of living reasonably, we are strongly drawn to trace conflicting ideas about them—ours, theirs, others'. And it appears to me that their idea of the point and shape of their life together was no less a fiction—and no more convincing a fiction— than George Mill's or Freud's or Alice Rossi's or mine. They cling to each other in London drawing rooms devoted to enlightened discussion. They stroll through Parisian streets discussing the ethics of their behavior. They exhibit supremely, deliciously, that exclusive preference for each other's company to which we generally give the name *love*. They remain devoted to each other for twenty years, waiting for the chance to marry. Like the lovers in *A Midsummer Night's Dream*, like lovers everywhere with a respect for the life of the mind, they dote on each other and congratulate themselves on their Reason.

A Marriage of Equals

They took a secluded house on a twenty-year lease in Blackheath Park, about eight miles outside London. Every day a little after nine Mill left for his office, walking the half mile from his house to the railway station and then the hefty distance from Charing Cross to Leadenhall Street, where he had worked, in India House, from the age of seventeen and would continue to work until the government of India was removed from the hands of the East India Company. Until he was fifty-two, his job, like his father's before him, was to read dispatches from the company's agents in India and to draft replies, in effect instructing them, from halfway around the world, how to run a country he had never seen. He did it well. His services were appreciated by the company, and he was making £1,200 per year at the time of his marriage. He considered his job the perfect way for a writer like himself to make a living. Intellectual enough not to be drudgery, his office duties were a kind of relaxation after the demands of philosophic thinking and writing. Had he tried to make a living from his pen alone, he would have had to compromise his opinions or work himself to a frazzle. As it was, he sacrificed only his leisure to travel and freedom to live in the country. It was worth it.

Governing India did not occupy his entire day, and what time he had left before returning home for six o'clock tea was spent on his own writing and correspondence or entertaining friends, like George Grote, who was writing his classic history of Greece, and Alexander Bain. Sometimes Grote and Bain would walk with Mill back to Charing Cross Station, but after his marriage, they never accompanied him farther. They were Mill's friends, to be seen on his time, on his turf. Only friends of both the Mills were invited to Blackheath, and there were few such people—W. J. Fox, who had brought them together, and the Italian patriot Giuseppe Mazzini, in exile in London, who had entered their life by way of John Taylor. These and two foreign scholars—Theodor Gomperz from Austria and Pasquale Villari from Italy—were the only people genuinely welcomed at Blackheath in the seven years the Mills lived there, not in total seclusion, because Harriet's son was there for all but the last two years and her daughter Helen lived with them the whole time.

Mill's friends, who had hoped that his marriage would mark his re-entry into social life, were disappointed. He lived in even greater retirement after his marriage than before. Neither he nor Harriet had any difficulty giving up the tepid pleasures of society, for they found each other absolutely fascinating. Both had been made lonely by exceptional intelligence, and they rejoiced in each other like two giants, two midgets, or any two people who have feared their oddness would prevent them from ever knowing close companionship. They were a happy couple, discussing everything, sharing everything. Most important, they shared his work—or what posterity calls his work, despite Mill's insistence that virtually everything published in his name was Harriet's as much as his.

Mill believed that when two people together probe every subject of interest, when they hold all thoughts and speculations in common, whatever writings may result are joint products. The one who has contributed the least to composition may have contributed the most to thought. It is of little consequence which of them holds the pen. In that sense, "not only during the years of our married life, but during many years of confidential friendship which preceded it, all my published writings are as much my wife's work as mine."[38] *The System of Logic*, published in 1843 and the basis of Mill's fame, owed little to Harriet except felicities of composition, but after that, everything we call John Mill's was a joint production: *Principles of Political Economy, On Liberty, The Autobiography, The Subjection of Women*, the essays on religion. Some of these works were published only after Harriet was dead, but they had been discussed, drafted, planned, in some cases dictated by her, long before their actual publication.

Harriet's co-authorship of Mill's work has proved a hard fact to swallow, and for many years after the claims of joint production were made in Mill's autobiography, commentators labored mightily to prove that Mill was mistaken and to provide reasons why he might have been mistaken about a subject (the authorship of his works) on which he ought to have been the expert. Alice Rossi has examined a century's worth of resistance to the idea that Harriet could have collaborated with so clear, logical, and forceful a mind as Mill's and concludes that it is sexist: Harriet provokes hostility from Mill scholars because, being brilliant and aggressive, she does not conform to their standard of femininity. Moreover, various kinds of political bias have affected assessments of Harriet's role in Mill's career. Unitarians in the nineteenth century—Harriet's friends—were enthusiastic about her influence on Mill, whereas the Utilitarians, who saw her as removing Mill from their orbit, tended to be harsh on her; later, Harold Laski downplayed the importance of Harriet's role in Mill's thinking because he did not want Mill's socialism to appear the result of a mere woman's influence. "Though it is couched in terms of detached scholarship one senses in Mill scholars an unwitting desire to reject Harriet Taylor as capable of contributing in any significant way to the vigor of Mill's analysis of political and social issues unless it included some tinge of sentiment or political thought the scholar disapproved of, in which case this disliked element was seen as Harriet's influence."[39] More recently, every serious scholar of Mill's life and work has believed what Mill says about Harriet's share in his intellectual life. "In so far as Mill's influence, theoretic or applied, has been of advantage to the progress of the western world, or indeed of humanity at large," says Packe, "the credit should rest upon his wife at least as much as himself."[40]

Consider, for example, the enormously influential *Principles of Political Economy*, begun in 1845 and ready for the press by the end of 1847, when Harriet was still married to John Taylor. Mrs. Taylor read and commented on every paragraph. She thought that the first draft lacked a chapter on the future of the working class, and Mill accordingly wrote one to her specifications. She helped him, too, with the proofs, with arranging for the binding, and in negotiating a contract with the publisher. When the time came for a second edition, Harriet wanted even more than the insertion of a new chapter. She wanted Mill to change his mind on a long-held, well-thought-out, and important opinion—his belief in capitalism as the most desirable system of ownership.

In the first edition, Mill had grounded his opposition to socialism and communism (little distinction was then made between the two) in the conviction that men worked best when they worked in their own interests and in the hopes of accumulating, by their own efforts, rewards. He feared that when subsistence was guaranteed, motivation to work would disappear. He argued that people who had never known freedom from anxiety about the means of subsistence are apt to over-rate it as a source of pleasure. Under socialism, "labour would be devoid of its chief sweetener, the thought that every effort tells perceptibly on the labourer's own interests or those of someone with whom he identifies himself."[41] Re-reading this paragraph, Harriet objected strongly and totally. Perhaps the revolutionary events of 1848 had helped to change her mind. Perhaps the Chartists had made her more optimistic about the ability of the working class to direct its own economic and political life. Whatever the reason, she now believed it was of the first importance to guarantee people a living and to remove their anxieties about subsistence.

Mill was astonished. The paragraph she objected to had been inserted at her suggestion and in her very words. Moreover, he considered it the strongest part of the argument. If it were removed, the most cogent objection to socialism would disappear and he would have to turn around and embrace it. Nevertheless, he neither pressed Harriet for an explanation of her change of mind nor attempted to re-argue his earlier position. Placidly, he accepted the correction. "This is probably only the progress we have always been making, and by thinking sufficiently I should probably come to think the same—as is almost always the case, I believe always when we think long enough."[42] His complex portrait of some weaknesses of socialism was replaced by bland pieties in its favor: "There would be an end to all anxiety concerning the means of subsistence; and this would be much gained for human happiness."[43] And so there entered into the *Political Economy* a utopianism much more typical of Mrs. Taylor than of Mill and an endorsement of socialism which had enormous impact through the decades, making a little bit of England what it is today because Harriet Taylor changed her mind in 1849.

The man who had been trained to think for himself from the age of five informed Mrs. Taylor that he would change any opinion if she asked him to "even if there were no other reason than the certainty I feel that I never should continue of an opinion different from yours on a subject which you have fully considered."[44] He thought himself fit only to interpret, to set down what others believed, insisting again and again, in his private diary as well as his letters and autobiography, that Mrs. Taylor was the source of any wisdom he had and he merely her mouthpiece. "What would be the use of my outliving you!" he wrote to her. "I could write nothing worth keeping alive except with your prompting."[45] She was his audience and his source; he wrote from her and for her. On his own he seemed unable to decide whether one thing was more worth doing than another, so she set him topics. In the production of some of his most important works, he took the position of a schoolboy fulfilling an assignment. "I want my angel to tell me what should be the next essay written. I have done all I can for the subject she last gave me."[46] And,

I finished the 'Nature' on Sunday as I expected. I am quite puzzled what to attempt next—I will just copy the list of subjects we made out in the confused order in which we put them down. Differences of character (nation, race, age, sex, temperament). Love. Education of tastes. Religion de l'avenir. Plato. Slander.

Foundation of morals. Utility of religion. Socialism. Liberty. Doctrine that causation is will.[47]

Practically all Mill's later work may be seen in that shorthand list of ideas. Where he began did not much matter, so long as he began, and Harriet was happy enough to tell him what to do. She was the executive. She made decisions. Unhampered by the subtleties and nuances of thought which sometimes impeded Mill, unafraid of inconsistency, she cut crudely, perhaps, but emphatically and practically to important matters. In this case, she selected religion from the welter of possible subjects. "About the essays, dear, would not religion, the Utility of Religion, be one of the subjects you have most to say on?" He could (she suggested) account for the nearly universal existence of some kind of religion; could show how religion and poetry fill the same wants, the need for consolation, the craving for higher objects; could suggest how all this must be superseded by a morality deriving its authority from the approval of people we respect rather than from hope of reward in an afterlife. It was fairly standard positivist stuff, but Mill responded ecstatically. "Your program of an essay on religion is beautiful, but it requires you to fill it up—I can try, but a few paragraphs will bring me to the end of all I have got to say on the subject."[48] Nevertheless, he wrote the essay which was posthumously published as "The Utility of Religion."

Almost everyone who talked to Mill agreed that his mind was one of the amazing phenomena of the age, so clear, so productive, so just, so inexorable. (In fact, his skull is reported to have the largest brain size known to science.) But it had a defect which Mill alone perceived. It initiated nothing. He was like an automaton which functioned perfectly when set on course, but could not set its own course or turn itself on. So Harriet, spontaneous, imperious, intellectually passionate, without self-doubt, put the logic machine into motion. She was his starter button. She was "Feeling," mysteriously energizing, required to mobilize "Thought." She served as the part of himself that cared. She might change her mind. She might advocate capitalism one year and socialism the next. But she always cared. When she died he would say that the spring of his life was broken, and the metaphor was absolutely right. She wound him up. She set him off.

Sharing interests and a general dedication to human improvement, but differing so much in the ways their minds worked, they were a perfect intellectual team.

The world does not take kindly to a successful collaboration between a married couple. When John Lennon insisted on making records with Yoko Ono, he was accused of deifying an inferior artist, and she was accused of destroying a great artistic unit. Alice Rossi's feminist explanation of the hostility Harriet Taylor evoked might account for some of the passion aroused by Yoko Ono, too. But cases exist in which men are resented for intruding on women's careers. Opera-lovers will perhaps recall the initial resistance to Joan Sutherland's demand that her husband, Richard Bonynge, conduct whenever she sang, and—at the other end of the cultural spectrum—the resistance to Barbra Streisand's elevation of her lover from hairdresser to producer. What is at work here seems to be a collective jealousy. The public, whose relationship with any celebrity (writer, philosopher, or film star) is partly erotic, resents another person's coming between it and the object of its attention, and any artist who insists on giving more credit to a loved one than the public thinks is appropriate risks bringing down upon him or her the public's wrath.

Such was the tactical blunder John Stuart Mill committed in writing his autobiography. His purpose, when he decided three years after his marriage to write the story of his life, was to fix in words for posterity the record of his debt to "one whose intellect is as much profounder than mine as her heart is nobler." At the time he was suffering badly from consumption. He thought he was dying. It was his last chance to make the world see and appreciate Harriet as he saw and appreciated her. Most autobiographies are written as a defense of self; Mill's was written as a defense of his wife. Usually read as a conversion story or political testament, *The Autobiography of John Stuart Mill* seems instead a monument in the annals of Victorian domesticity. It demands comparison with a narrative like *David Copperfield*, which asks in its opening sentence whether David will turn out to be the hero of his own life and makes it clear by the end that he has not, that his wife plays that role.

Attempting to win recognition for Harriet, Mill overstated the case and evoked only disbelief and scorn. Alexander Bain believed that if

Mill had scrupulously listed the ways in which his wife collaborated with him, he would have been believed and Harriet respected. Unfortunately, "he outraged all reasonable credibility in describing her matchless genius, without being able to supply any corroborating testimony."[49] Reading proof of *The Autobiography* in 1873, Bain begged Helen Taylor, Mill's executor, to remove some of the more fulsome references to her mother. The incredulous world, he said, would be startled enough by what remained. Bain had in mind passages like the following, in which Mill describes Harriet Taylor as she was in 1832, and which her daughter allowed to stand:

> I have often compared her, as she was at this time, to Shelley: but in thought and intellect, Shelley, so far as his powers were developed in his short life, was but a child compared with what she ultimately became. Alike in the highest regions of speculation and in the smaller practical concerns of daily life, her mind was the same perfect instrument, piercing to the very heart and marrow of the matter; always seizing the essential idea or principle.[50]

Bain also found distressing the assertion that James Mill, in his impact on progressive thought, had no equal among men and but one among women. Nor did he like the passage about Carlyle which ends with Mill calling Harriet "one greatly the superior of us both—who was more a poet than he, and more a thinker than I—whose mind and nature included his, and infinitely more."

It is possible to create a context in which such passages seem less glaring. Mill over-estimated Harriet's mental qualities, I have suggested, because they were so different from his own. Also, he tended to allegorize people, to make them Thinkers or Feelers, and to such a man the highest praise would naturally be to say that the eulogized one combined both virtues. Since Mill thought of poetry as a mode of feeling rather than a feat of writing, he did not perceive the ludicrousness of comparing Harriet to Shelley as a poet. He meant that she felt as deeply as Shelley did, not that her poems were as good as his. But the most outrageous of all Mill's hyperboles about Harriet fortunately did not make its way into his autobiography or present itself to the attention of that dry Scotsman, Alexander Bain: in 1855, writing from Italy, Mill sent New Year's greetings to "the only person living who is worthy to live."[51]

It is pointless to read Harriet's scraps of verse looking for a mute, inglorious Shelley. It is pointless to compare the fragmentary essays left us with the prose of Carlyle. Even her surviving letters—most of them were destroyed at her request—offer no convincing evidence of her genius. They are often confused, contradictory, bossy, intolerant of other people's faults but unaware of her own. Mill's contemporaries could see no resemblance between the genius described in the autobiography and the woman they knew. Some said that Mill was literally the only person in the least impressed with her. Some said she wasn't even bright. Some said she parroted back to Mill his own thoughts and words, and that was why he thought she was so brilliant. All agreed there was a great gap between the reality of the woman and John's vision of her, and his autobiography, insofar as it described Harriet, has generally been taken to represent the strength of his feelings rather than to portray accurately the object of them.

Of course he made her up, as we all make up the people we love. Bain called it an "extraordinary hallucination." Diana Trilling considered it evidence of neurosis.[52] But one person's hallucination or neurosis is another person's love, which is nothing if not an inspired and happy warping of one's perceptual mechanism in favor of the person perceived. Mill's delusion about Harriet is his love for her and, written all over his autobiography, it makes that book, sympathetically read, one of the most touching love stories of the nineteenth century. The more ordinary Harriet Taylor was in fact, the more impressive the spectacle of a man projecting upon the world the lineaments of an inner need.

If Mill's *Autobiography* fails to make us see the woman he saw, the chapters describing his childhood enable us to understand why he saw her that way. The blueprint for loving was drawn, and drawn powerfully, by his father, who at one level was teaching his son to think for himself but at another was training him in exactly the opposite behavior, drilling into him with every lesson the feel of domination, the surrender of will to a being stronger than himself.

How well Mill understood the experience of subjection would become clear in his sympathy for the subjection of women. His early experience led him to resent subjection but also to experience it as the most intense connection between two people. It seems therefore inevitable that Mill would be drawn to a woman who made lavish use of rebuke and reproach, someone stronger than himself, someone controlling, whom he endowed with all the qualities he felt himself to lack: deep feeling, intuitiveness, passion.

Mill may have been like most people in creating imaginatively the person he then fell in love with, but he differed in being able to present her to the world as both philosophically and politically significant. Philosophically, Harriet represented the cure for the spiritual emptiness of eighteenth-century rationalism. Politically, she represented the fate of intelligent women, under-utilized, under-respected, prevented from achieving what she might have if positions were determined by talent and not by an accident of birth. If circumstances had been encouraging, Harriet *could* have been a great artist. She *could* have been a great orator. Her knowledge of human nature and her cleverness about practical life "would, in times when such a *carrière* was open to women, have made her eminent among the rulers of the world."[58]

If the French Revolution allowed and the example of Napoleon encouraged men of humble birth to achieve high station (*la carrière ouverte aux talents*), one kind of chain on humanity had been broken and one form of slavery overthrown. But it remained for women to enjoy the same opening of opportunity brought to the base-born by the Revolution and, more remotely, to blacks by the Emancipation. (Mill would develop this analogy between women and other disadvantaged classes in *The Subjection of Women*.) In his exorbitant praise of his wife, Mill seems at times to be apologizing for the collective disadvantage of the female sex, assuming the collective guilt of the male. And if the outrageous statements about Mrs. Mill's genius are not quite a tactical maneuver, designed to suggest women's potential and their systematic discouragement, they may be calculated in a way that does not wholly represent the effusions of love. As one of the keenest students of power in modern times, Mill could not have been unaware that he was, in his dealings with Harriet, altering the usual allocation of power between the sexes. He must have realized it was unusual for a man of his stature to claim that he had merely written down what a woman had told him to write.

Mill believed that nothing is innate, that character is formed by circumstance, and that therefore no class, sex, or race is "naturally" superior to the other. Women provided his central example. Until little girls were brought up in exactly the same fashion as little boys, with the same expectations, the same encouragements, even the same toys, you could make no statement about what women were like. They would merely continue to turn themselves into the decorative and dependent creatures they have historically been rewarded for being. Feminism was in this way at the center of Mill's beliefs, and his conviction that, cultural circumstances apart, women could be men's equals in ability and accomplishment became for him a touchstone of philosophic worth.[54]

The nineteenth century's most important theorist of feminism was concerned not to reproduce in his own life the historical iniquities of his sex. He would not be the conventional husband, assuming his own dominance within the family, the ruler of a microcosmic state with Harriet as his subject—the situation which Dickens, in his role of apologist for the patriarchal family, idealized in his novels. In the Mill family, power would be shared, the reins held jointly. The Mills were embarked upon a great experiment, something new in the history of relations between men and women—a true marriage of equals. But so unusual was this situation that for Harriet to be anywhere near equal she had to be "more than equal." Think of it as a domestic case of affirmative action. To achieve equality, more power had to go to Harriet, in compensation for the inequality of their conditions.

Mill intended both the fact and the written portrait of their friendship—and later of their marriage—to be an *acte provocateur*. However, in attempting to perform a revolutionary act, setting up woman as ruler, he was tracing an ancient pattern more accessible to ordinary minds, the man besotted by love into yielding his rule to a woman, Hercules with a distaff, a figure of fun for centuries. What Mill saw as a daring political gesture seemed to others no more than a grievous case of uxuriousness. Bain's words emphasize the political infraction at the heart of the offensive spectacle, "Such a state of subjection to the will of another, as he candidly avows and glories in, cannot be received as a right state of things. It violates our sense of due proportion, in the relationship of human beings."[55] One wonders if a similar subjection of a woman's will to a man's would have violated Bain's sense of due proportion to the same degree. And if a woman wrote about her husband as extravagantly as Mill wrote about his wife, would she be so violently accused of hallucination about her husband's personal qualities? Nevertheless, Bain has a point. "Such a state of subjection . . . cannot be received as a right state of things." How splendid it would be if we could find in the Mills' marriage what they hoped we would find, an exemplary model. But in practice, Harriet made the decisions. Harriet ran the show. A female autocrat merely replaced the usual male.

In their daily life as in their collaboration, he obeyed her in all things. If he was willing to change his mind at her request on such issues as the relative merits of socialism and capitalism, the secret ballot, and capital punishment, he was certainly willing to drop Mrs. Grote and Mrs. Austin when Harriet asked him to. He had been close to them in his youth. He would see them again after Harriet's death. But she did not like them, and that was enough to keep Mill from them during her lifetime. When his mother's property was divided among her children at the time of her death, Mill thought to refuse his share since he had been on such bad terms with his mother and sisters since his marriage. But Harriet rebuked him. To refuse four or five hundred pounds was a species of vanity only a rich man could afford. Of course he should take the money. Of course. "As your feeling is so directly contrary, mine is wrong and I give it up entirely," he said.[56]

The pattern of rebuke and abdication repeats itself in the most minute of their household affairs. Once, in Harriet's absence, their neighbor informed Mill that rats were infesting their shared garden wall. Mill ventured to reply with a noncommittal, bland acknowledgment of receipt of the note and reported his action to Harriet. She was furious. Mill ought to have replied aggressively, throwing the rats back upon the neighbor, making them his responsibility. And so, in his next note, Mill did. He never knew how Harriet would react; that was part of her fascination. Expecting reproach, he was praised; expecting praise, he was rebuked. "Age cannot wither her nor custom stale her infinite variety," Shakespeare wrote of Cleopatra, who also had the gift of contrariness.

When they were apart, they questioned and instructed each other minutely on the state of their health. "How is it my darling," Mill inquired, "that you say you have broken the habit of expectoration? When you cough are you not obliged to swallow something if you do not spit it up?"[57] "I cannot but think," replied Harriet with her characteristic note of self-righteousness, "that if you tried as earnestly as I have done since October to avoid any expectoration that you would lose the habit altogether as I have done."[58] It was her idea that Mill was bothered by phlegm because he was in the habit of spitting, not that he was forced to spit because he was bothered by phlegm. Perhaps she was right.

The matter was not a small one, because Mill's spit was tinged with blood. He had tuberculosis, consumption, contracted in all likelihood (although Mill thought it was inherited) from his father, who had died of it, as had or would many of their friends and relatives. Within two years of their marriage the Mills were serially or concurrently so sick and treatment so imperative that the happiest and most self-sufficient of couples was forced to separate repeatedly in order to pursue individual health. First Harriet had to spend a winter in the milder climate of southern France while John, because of business, had to stay in London. Then his health deteriorated so badly that the East India Company gave him a medical leave to spend the winter of 1854–55 out of England. But at that time, Harriet was too fragile to undertake a journey abroad, and Mill was forced to leave her in the seaside town of Torquay, whose climate was the mildest to be found in England. That winter he sent her forty-nine letters, written a few pages a day, which make a volume in themselves. Theirs was the kind of intimacy that could be maintained—however frustratingly to them—at a distance, and they continued, as Mill toured Rome, Sicily, then Greece, to consult on their household and to conduct his career together.

She died first and a mere seven years after their marriage. But since

Harriet was to such an extent a character in his imagination, their marriage did not have to end with her passing. Mill proved to be a grave fetishist. Like Queen Victoria, who continued to set out Albert's shaving water after his death, he couldn't let go. Harriet had died in Avignon, on one of her yearly removals to the south of France in search of health. Mill bought a house overlooking the cemetery where she was buried and spent more and more time there every year. He hired an architect to design a tomb, for which Carrara marble was especially imported. The vast and perfect piece of stone which made its way slowly by ship to Marseille and then up the Rhone to Avignon proved big enough only for the covering slab, and more marble had to be ordered for the sides. When finished in March 1860, the tomb had cost about £1,500, or an entire year's salary for Mill.

He composed, to be cut into the marble, another series of hopelessly hyperbolic praises of Harriet, destined, like his autobiography, not to be believed. Mill never wrote worse than when his heart was most engaged. "Her Clear Powerful and Original Comprehensive Intellect." "As Earnest for the Public Good As She was Generous and Devoted to All who Surrounded Her." The phrases knock together bombastically. "Were there but a few hearts and intellects like hers, the earth would already have become the hoped-for Heaven."[59] The monument became a stopping place on the Victorian Grand Tour, and Marian Evans, travelling to Italy in 1861 with Mr. Lewes to do research for *Romola*, was touched by the way in which the vast marble surface seemed too small for the overflowing of Mill's devotion.[60]

Every day, when he was in Avignon, Mill spent an hour by the grave. Away, he did the work Harriet would have wanted him to do. She continued to guide his life. It was, in a sense, satisfactory. As with Petrarch and Laura, Dante and Beatrice, Auguste Comte and Clothilde de Vaux, the woman who had inspired great work as well as great love died into the condition of pure, disembodied inspiration. Moreover, to Mill's great comfort, Harriet had left a daughter, Helen Taylor, twenty-seven at the time of her mother's death. She would be Mill's companion for the rest of his life. "Surely no one ever before was so fortunate, as, after such a loss as mine, to draw another prize in the lottery of life—another companion, stimulator, adviser, and instructor of the rarest quality."[61] Whether she was "the inheritor of much of [Harriet's] wisdom, and of all her nobleness of character," as Mill claimed, we will not attempt to discover. Certainly she took Harriet's place in the way most necessary to Mill, by providing some-one outside himself whom he could obey.

One of Matthew Arnold's touchstones of greatness in poetry was Dante's line, *"In la sua volontade è nostra pace"*—in Thy will is our peace—a line whose beauty must reside as much in the reas-surance about divine protection it offered as in anything innately poetic. We have heard about the secularization of love in the nineteenth century, how love of God was replaced by love for a specific human being as the most exalting experience of life. It could also be said that with the "disappearance of God," serious thinkers, those with an essentially religious temperament but divorced from religion by the failure of faith, were bound to search for a personal, freely chosen authority to validate their lives, as T. H. Huxley would elevate in the place of God an abstraction called Fact.[62] The history of nineteenth-century thought is the record of various people's efforts to find substitute sources of authority. John Mill, brought up an atheist, trained to distrust any authority outside himself, a man who scorned in every way the notion of one person surrendering his will to another, nevertheless felt as one of the profoundest needs of his emotional life the need to do precisely that—to surrender the will. In imagining that being what some would call henpecked constituted a utopian marriage of equals, he created a delusion which he and his wife could happily share.[63] He invented a role for her which she liked both in theory (she liked the idea of equality) and in practice (she liked the feel of mastery). Her subject was willing. Mill's mind approved equality but his soul craved domination. He atoned for the subjection of women by the voluntary, even enthusiastic, subjection of one man and portrayed the result as a model marriage of equals.

CATHERINE
HOGARTH
and
CHARLES
DICKENS

1835 – 1858

Prelude:
The Carlyles and the
Magnetized Body

In the 1830s a new therapy called Mesmerism or Animal Magnetism became popular in England. (We call it hypnotism now.) It offered cures for the nervous problems which would seem increasingly to be the nineteenth century's characteristic form of illness. By manipulating the electric fluid field that was thought to exist between people, using certain movements of the hand called "passes," the operator could throw the subject into a magnetic sleep or trance. This was an odd state, resembling death as much as sleep, in which the subject could do things impossible for her to do in normal life, in which she might say things she would never say in normal life, and in which she was immensely susceptible to suggestion. (The operator was almost invariably male, the subject usually female.) Insomniacs could be made to sleep. A person prey to fears and horrors might be brought to speak of them—and so to exorcise them. Mesmerism's potential for good seemed great, yet many people worried about the possibilities for sexual abuse.

Charles Dickens was an early and enthusiastic amateur of mesmerism. England's leading mesmeric practitioner, Dr. John Elliotson, became a close friend. From Elliotson and Chauncey Hare Townshend, Dickens learned how to perform the mesmeric passes. His first subject, in 1841, was his wife, whom, in a few moments, he successfully threw into hysterics and then into a magnetic trance. Later, he practiced on other family and friends. In 1844–45, on a sabbatical from writing passed in Genoa, Dickens spent the best energies of three months in the mesmeric treatment of Madame de la Rue, the English-born and mildly disturbed wife of a Swiss banker who lived nearby.[1] Although he would never allow himself to *be* mesmerized, Dickens was fascinated by what the process revealed about the mind's secrets and by the curious way in which one personality seemed able to exercise influence over another.

Jane Carlyle would have none of it. She was sniffy about all fads and mass enthusiasms. One night in 1847, at Mrs. Buller's house, she and Mr. Carlyle witnessed a demonstration of magnetism. The magnetizer was a lower-class person who did not pronounce his *h*'s and who irritated Mrs. Carlyle by telling her that mesmerism depended on "moral and intellectual superiority."[2] Nevertheless, in a quarter of an hour, by gazing into the eyes of a Miss Bölte and by holding one of her hands, he succeeded in throwing her into a deep magnetic trance. She looked like a marble effigy: pale, cold, motionless. Her face had that beautiful expression seen only on the faces of the dead or the mesmerized. The mesmerist arranged Miss Bölte's arms and legs into unnatural positions which they could not have held ordinarily for a moment and left her like that for an hour. Mrs. Carlyle stepped up to the magnetized body and touched the arms. They felt horrible, stiff. With all her force she could not unbend them. Other people poked Miss Bölte's skin with a penknife, but she showed no signs of feeling anything.

The mesmerist was triumphant. "*Now* are you convinced?" he asked the Carlyles.

"Yes," said Carlyle. "There is no possibility of doubting that you have stiffened poor Miss Bölte into something very awful."

"Yes," Mrs. Carlyle agreed. "But then she wished to be magnetized; what I doubt is whether anyone could be reduced to that state without *the consent of their own volition*. I should like for instance to see anyone *magnetize me!*"

"You think I could not?"

"Yes. I defy you."

So Mrs. Carlyle gave him her hand, and he made some passes over it, and she thought to herself, "You must learn to sound your *h*'s, Sir, before you can produce any effect on a woman like *me!*" and then, to her horror, she felt her body seized from head to foot by a galvanic flash. Fortunately, she retained enough self-control to keep him from seeing her state, thus disproving his theory of power through superiority. For had it not taken superiority to keep him from seeing her response? At the same time, it was disturbing to learn that her theory of the need for a consenting will was also nonsense.

Paterfamilias

When he turned twenty-three, Charles Dickens, a young reporter for the *Morning Chronicle*, threw a birthday party for himself in his rooms in Furnival's Inn. He had good reason to feel like celebrating, for he was beginning to attract attention as the author of sketches of London life being published in the *Chronicle* and the *Monthly Magazine* under the pen name "Boz." Not long before, he had been jilted, because of his lack of "prospects," by Maria Beadnell, a woman he had loved desperately. Young Dickens would not, on the strength of his mounting fame, with the growing acclaim for "Sketches by Boz," renew his suit, but he could allow himself to gloat a little. He could offer himself a party. It was a Saturday night. There was dancing. His mother and his sisters presided, and the lovely and talented Fanny Dickens, one of his sisters, favored the company with her singing.

Among the guests was George Hogarth, also a journalist on the *Morning Chronicle*, and some of his family. Dickens particularly respected this older man who was an accomplished writer, a genial person, and had been, in his native Edinburgh, a friend and adviser to Sir Walter Scott. Dickens was the son of a navy pay clerk distinguished only by his inability to provide for his family. George Hogarth, by contrast, seemed confidently and even glamourously established in the literary world which Dickens aspired to enter. The young man was proud of his friendship and pleased to go to his colleague's house. The eldest of the Hogarths' children, twenty-year-old Catherine, particularly enjoyed Dickens's birthday party. She also liked the host. "Mr. Dickens improves very much upon acquaintance he is very gentlemanly and pleasant," she reported later to a Scottish relative.[3]

By the end of that spring, in the year 1835, Catherine Hogarth and Charles Dickens were engaged to be married. She was three years younger than he, pretty, with heavy-lidded blue eyes and fresh plump skin, good-natured and affectionate. He liked and esteemed her family. Although she did not elicit from him the passion that Maria Beadnell had, she seemed to suit him admirably. Dickens intended to make a place for himself in the world. He meant to live hard, and his pace was naturally fast. He wanted a wife and a family. His deeply passionate nature attached itself to his chosen mate. They were a team. She was "his better half," "the missis," "Mrs. D." In the early years of their marriage, he flung around those references to her with exuberant delight. He was evidently proud of her, and proud of himself for having acquired that dignifying satellite, a wife.

They were married in April 1836 and, in order to live as cheaply as possible, they decided to stay on in Dickens's chambers in Furnival's Inn, which were small, but tastefully furnished—the drawing room in rosewood and the dining room in mahogany. The household was lively and crowded, for Dickens's younger brother, Frederick, came to stay with them, as did Catherine's seventeen-year-old sister, Mary. Beloved, delightful Mary was as good a companion to Dickens as she was to her sister. The three of them went everywhere together, enjoyed all their amusements in common. Mary testified to what a happy young couple the Dickenses were. "She makes a most capital housekeeper and is as happy as the day is long—I think they are more devoted than ever since their marriage if that is possible."[4] They must have been having the fun that college students do when they leave their parental homes and move into a dormitory—the fun of being free and being young together. Not long after, already nostalgic, Dickens would write of those early days of marriage, "I shall never be so happy again as in those Chambers three Stories high— never if I roll in wealth and fame."[5]

Very quickly they started having children. Charles, Jr., their first, was born nine months after their wedding, in early January 1837, the year of Victoria's accession. Mary Hogarth and Charles's mother, Elizabeth Dickens, attended Catherine at her confinement. She recovered well, except that she proved unable to nurse the baby, which made her quite unhappy. Every time she looked at the baby she cried, imagining that if she did not nurse him, he would not love her. "Could she but forget this," Mary Hogarth wrote philosophically to her cousin in Scotland, "she has everything in this world to make her comfortable and happy—her husband is kindness itself to her and is constantly studying her comfort in everything—his literary career gets more and more prosperous every day and he is courted and flattered on every side by all the great folks of this great city—his time is so completely taken up that it is quite a favour for the Literary Gentlemen to get him to write for them."[6]

As Mary Hogarth noted, Dickens was, by 1837, a celebrity. Many people already recognized him as a literary genius. His inventiveness was astonishing. A world of delightful characters and incidents seemed to exist inside his mind, and he only needed time to put it all down on paper. In the year of Charley's birth, Dickens was writing, and publishing in serial parts as he wrote them, both *The Pickwick Papers* and *Oliver Twist*. No sooner did he finish *Pickwick* than he started on *Nicholas Nickleby*, which he wrote concurrently with *Oliver Twist*. In the history of literature, I can think of nothing comparable to this astonishing outpouring of invention—the sheer quantity of great work produced by Dickens in his twenties. By the time he was thirty, he had published, in addition to *Sketches by Boz*, *Pickwick*, *Oliver*, and *Nickleby*, *Barnaby Rudge* and *The Old Curiosity Shop*. For a time, he also edited a magazine, *Bentley's Miscellany*, and he wrote many occasional pieces to boot. He worked unrelentingly, turning out his copy for monthly, and then, with the later novels, for the even more grueling weekly publication schedule. The energy involved was immense, the sheer drudgery appalling. People do not work so hard unless they are driven. They cannot work so hard unless they are supported in the effort by those close to them.

Why is it that today, when ambitious young women who have postponed marriage in order to launch their careers finally look around for someone to marry, so few men seem to be available? Perhaps because ambitious men marry young. Marriage and career, family and work, which so often pull a woman in different directions, are much more likely to reinforce one another for a man. Dickens provides a good case in point. Professionally, his marriage helped him. His household was arranged for him. His needs for sex and companionship were satisfied. No time-consuming courtships, no fretting about rejections, no hunting around, no wasteful fantasizing. Most important, he had a reason to devote himself wholeheartedly to work. Not only was he working for his own advantage and to satisfy his own ambition, he was working for her, for them, for their children. The guilt a woman artist might feel in removing herself from her family in order to create is less likely to trouble a man, a man who imagines himself—as Dickens did—working *for* his family.

Dickens's children arrived in the world almost as regularly as his books. Charley was followed by Mamie in 1838, then by Kate in 1839 and Walter in 1841. (Between Charley and Mamie, Catherine had a miscarriage.) Not until after Walter's birth did Dickens begin to get ironic about more additions to his family. The first four, at any rate, made him very happy. He was deeply concerned about Catherine's health and safety during the deliveries. He enjoyed himself as a family man, the center of a growing circle of devoted people. He took satisfaction in how well he was able to provide for them. He moved his growing family from the small chambers in Furnival's Inn to a larger house in Doughty Street and then to an even larger and grander one in Devonshire Terrace near Regent's Park.

Regularly, he ended his novels with some image of domestic happiness, with a married pair happily generating children. The family, its population dividing and subdividing like bacteria in a Petri dish, was for Dickens the perfect emotional resolution of all discord. His early novels conclude as reliably with a domestic vignette as westerns used to end with a cowboy riding off alone into the sunset. This passage, near the end of *Barnaby Rudge*, may stand as typical:

It was not very long, you may be sure, before Joe Willet and Dolly Varden were made husband and wife, and with a handsome sum in the bank reopened the Maypole. It was not very long, you may be sure, before a red-faced little boy was seen staggering about the Maypole passage, and kicking up his heels on the green before the door. It was not very long, counting by years, before there was a red-faced little girl, another red-faced

little boy, and a whole troop of girls and boys: so that, go to
Chigwell when you would, there would surely be seen, either
in the village street or on the green, or frolicking in the farm-yard
. . . more small Joes and small Dollys than could easily be
counted.[7]

This sentimental strain in Dickens's work is hard for contemporary
readers to swallow. Northrop Frye dismissed the moments in Dickens's novels when he extols the values of hearth and home as "the
commercial." Since 1941 when Edmund Wilson created his striking
image of a dark, tormented Dickens, it has crossed the minds of
various readers that these domestic passages in Dickens are bad because his heart isn't in them, his deepest sympathies being anarchic
and rebellious. Resenting the family as a form of imprisonment, he is
forced—by internal compulsion and external encouragement—to
praise it. My own feeling, however, is that passages such as the one
from *Barnaby Rudge* were produced in complete sincerity. If such
passages fail, it is not because Dickens is insincere in describing the
happiness of being part of a family, but because he believes in it too
completely.

His own childhood had been marred by his father's improvidence,
by their imprisonment for debt (the family was companionably allowed to join the debtor in prison), and by his enforced labor in a
blacking (shoe polish) factory, for which he blamed his mother even
more than his father. When Dickens told his parents how miserable
he was in the factory, separated from the family, put to degrading
work with degrading companions, kept from all hope of advance-
ment, his father—consistently feckless—was willing to let him give
up the job and return to them. But his mother insisted they needed
the money, and she made him continue in exile and misery, supporting the parents who should have been supporting him. So Dickens
valued highly—perhaps too highly—the kind of family in which the
father worked and provided, the mother took care of the house and
children, and the children had nothing to do but enjoy themselves.
Dickens admired family life. It made him happy. There was nothing
hypocritical in his warblings about domesticity in his early novels. He
was singing the praises of what he had, what he respected. He and

Catherine were as devoted to each other as any young couple would be who, together, have made a life better than the ones they had known as children in their parents' houses. I emphasize their happiness because Dickens, in his later pain, denied that a time of happiness with Catherine had ever existed. In fairness to Catherine, I want to insist that it did exist.

In later years, Dickens would say that he and Catherine never had anything in common. He would present himself as a misunderstood genius, mismated with a dull and uncomprehending woman. And it may very well be true that with Catherine he missed out on an ideal intellectual companionship. How many clever people ever find it with their mates? But Dickens had close male friends—John Forster, the lawyer and writer; Daniel Maclise, the painter; and William Charles Macready, the tragedian—with each of whom he dined frequently and with each of whom, especially Forster, he shared the details of his professional life. He was devoted to male conviviality, and he did not complain in his early years, when he was minded to be content with his life, about the absence of ideal companionships.

In fact, he and Catherine shared a lot—above all, their children, but some non-domestic interests too. He tried out his work on her, and her extraordinary reaction to Sikes's murder of Nancy in *Oliver Twist* gave Dickens an early indication of what a great success this passage would be. When he was sent books to read, he sometimes passed them on to Catherine. He gave her Lady De Lancey's affecting narrative of her husband's death at the Battle of Waterloo, and Catherine sobbed over it while Dickens wrote a thank-you note to the author's brother, describing her reaction. Her grief gave him material for the letter and us some evidence that the young Mr. and Mrs. Dickens did more together than make and play with their children. As for Catherine, her pride in her talented husband comes through touchingly in an invitation to a distant cousin: "What pleasure it would give me to see you in my own house, and how proud I should be to make you acquainted with Charles. The fame of his talents are now known over all the world, but his kind affectionate heart is dearer to me than all."[8]

One tragedy marred the happiness of the Dickens's early years, but it was the kind of tragedy which tends to bring people together rather than to drive them apart. Catherine and Charles were both devoted to Catherine's sister, Mary Hogarth, who was in many ways the mascot of their establishment. In May 1837, not long after Charley's birth, Mr. and Mrs. Dickens and Mary went to the theater, enjoying a performance of *Is She His Wife?* They came home at about one at night. Mary went upstairs in her usual good health and high spirits and fell ill while undressing. She sank rapidly and died the next afternoon, in Dickens's arms. There had been no sign of illness, but she probably died of heart disease. Dickens was devastated. For the only time in his career, he was unable to work and missed his monthly deadlines. There was no June 1837 number for either *Pickwick* or *Oliver Twist*. He dreamed about Mary for months. Catherine had a miscarriage, which she and her husband thought was brought on by her distress, and Dickens had to take her away from the house they had shared with Mary to the quiet of Hampstead (then a country village) to recuperate. Both of them felt, almost superstitiously, that they had had too much happiness to last. Mary's death ended what was for both of them an idyllic period. Not that things started going badly after her death, but (one turns events into such milestones) it marked a peak of happiness which could never be matched.

Some people have found Dickens's attachment to his young sister-in-law unnatural. It seems to me rather a measure of how fiercely attached he was to those close to him, of whom Mary was the closest after Catherine and the first to die. Because of her youth and her beauty, her death was particularly shocking and cruel. As he did everything early, Dickens confronted death early, learning at the age of twenty-five the rending grief of having something you love taken away from you irrevocably, something which no amount of effort, no genius, no success can restore. The death of young people became—along with family happiness, frequently highlighting it—a subject which Dickens claimed in literature as distinctively his.

In June of 1841, when Dickens was twenty-nine, he made a trip to Scotland—quite an event for this child of London who tended to stay close to home. As it turned out, it was a dry run for the triumphal tour of America he would make in the following year. Catherine accompanied him. She had been born in Edinburgh and was revisiting it for the first time since her childhood. In her native city, her husband was honored with a huge testimonial dinner. Accompanied by one hundred and fifty ladies, Catherine came into the gallery after the banquet to hear the speeches. John Wilson, a *Blackwood's Magazine* writer who was a respected literary figure in Edinburgh, made the principal address, calling Dickens the greatest writer then alive, a writer who had earned his popularity by his almost divine insight into the workings of the human heart. The only flaw in Dickens's work (Wilson said rather gratuitously) was his failure to portray the female character in all its fullness and complexity. But who besides Shakespeare had been able to do that?[9] Mrs. Dickens had the pleasure of hearing her own health proposed by the sculptor Angus Fletcher, who gracefully said that Dickens owed much of his distinction to having chosen a Scotswoman as his partner in life. If this was a great moment for Dickens—the first public tribute to the extraordinary extent of his popularity—it must have been a great moment for Catherine, too, so warmly and pointedly included in her husband's apotheosis.

They went from one dinner to another. Everyone wanted to entertain the most popular writer then alive, and his wife. It was Dickens's first experience of lionization, and his reaction was to miss his home and his small circle of friends. To his best friend, John Forster, he wrote, "The moral of all this is, that there is no place like home; and I thank God most heartily for having given me a quiet spirit and a heart that won't hold many people."[10] He longed for his house in Devonshire Terrace, and for Broadstairs, the seaside town where he and Catherine took the children every summer. He wanted to play battledore and shuttlecock and to have an informal and raucous dinner with Forster, Maclise, and Macready, his chums. "The only thing I felt at the Edinburgh dinner (and I felt it very strongly) was, that except Kate there was nobody there I cared for."[11]

It was not the desire to be lionized that drew Dickens to America. He wanted new experience, and he hoped to see a perfectly classless, democratic society—the republic of his dreams. Certainly he needed a rest from writing. He had been on a daily production schedule for five years and had completed five major novels. Perhaps he would find new material in America. There were any number of reasons to go. When he first mentioned his idea to Catherine, she was distraught. She could not bear to think of being separated from him for months, nor could she bear the thought of being separated from her children, if she accompanied him. Whenever he mentioned America, she cried. Dickens took her distress quite seriously and consulted Macready about the advisability of taking the children along with them. (Macready had children and had twice been to America, so he seemed the right person to ask.) Macready advised strongly against taking the children, suggesting instead that he and Mrs. Macready would look after them in the Dickenses' absence. Gradually a plan developed which satisfied Catherine. Their house in Devonshire Terrace would be rented out and a smaller place for the children and their nurses taken in Osnaburgh Street near the Macreadys. Frederick Dickens would stay with the children, and they would visit the Macreadys daily. From the moment these plans were made, Catherine cheered up and joined her husband in excited preparations for their trip. She had the excellent idea of asking Maclise to make her a drawing of the four children, and this sacred object (exactly as a photograph of loved ones would be today) was a real source of comfort to her in her travels.

They left from Liverpool by steamer in January 1842. It was not a good time of year for a crossing, and they could expect rough weather. But they were both excited and happy. Forster saw them off and reported to Maclise on Catherine's cheerfulness. "She deserves to be what you know she is so emphatically called—the Beloved."[12] For four and a half months of hard travelling, Catherine and her maid, Anne Brown, were Dickens's only companions. Although she was not trained to physical daring, was easily frightened, and must have had a harder time than Dickens in adjusting to the discomforts and trials of travel, Catherine rose to the occasion splendidly.

The boat was crowded, the crossing dreadful, and almost all the passengers were sick. Even Dickens. "We were eighteen days on our passage," Catherine later wrote to Dickens's sister Fanny, "and experienced all the horrors of a storm at sea, which raged frightfully for a whole night, and broke all our paddle-boxes and the life-boat to pieces. I was nearly distracted with terror, and don't know what I should have done had it not been for the great kindness and composure of my dear Charles."[13] All through that dreadful night, they expected to die at any moment. The smokestack seemed about to blow off, and if it had, the vulnerable ship inevitably would have caught fire and burned completely. Charles and Catherine Dickens thought a great deal about their children, whom they expected never to see again. Charles must have been pleased with himself—if one can be pleased on the verge of death—for having had the forethought to take out a special insurance policy to cover him on his travels. At least the children would be provided for. However, towards morning the storm abated and their lives were spared.

By the time Catherine wrote her description of the storm to Fanny Burnett, they were safely on land and already beginning to see how it was possible to be killed with kindness. People everywhere seemed to worship Dickens, and their days were a perpetual round of dinners, visits, and receptions. (Catherine foreswore trying to describe to Fanny the manner and customs of the people "and so on, as my powers of description are not great, and you will have it some day or other so much the better from Charles.")[14] In the annals of contemporary literary celebrity, there is nothing to which one can compare Dickens's reception in America in 1842. The welcome was so extreme as to be more of a torture than a pleasure to the object of all praises, invitations, requests, demands. Even with his immense energy and intense enjoyment of toasting and jovial dinners, Dickens found his American reception exhausting and ultimately dismaying. He complained that his very coat was being torn to shreds by people reaching to touch him, or to grab some cloth as a souvenir. If he answered all the requests for locks of his hair, he would be totally bald. For celebrity to compare with this, one must think of rock stars, not writers. The mobs who oppressed The Beatles on their first trip to America or the stampeding crowd at The Who's concert in Ohio provide analogies to the horrible force of popular fame which Dickens brought down on himself in America. In Boston and New York, he and Catherine daily received and shook hands with hundreds of people. Dickens described them as a kind of Queen Victoria and Albert, holding levees wherever they went. And wherever they went, wherever they received admirers, the framed portrait of their children by Maclise was set up beside them. The American literary establishment (as opposed to the crowds) scrutinized them more genteelly, and Mr. and Mrs. Dickens passed the test. Everyone noted Dickens's youth, his lovely long hair, and the mobility of his features. Even those who were shocked by a certain lower-class Cockney manner were dazzled by his brilliance and wit. Catherine was equally admired, for her unassuming manners, her evident sweetness, and her good-natured appreciation of everything done for her.

As they left the East behind, the physical going got rougher. There were fewer mobs, fortunately, but the terrors of nature took the place of the terrors of people in groups. Anne Brown, the maid, tripped on a patch of pavement and fell flat, but didn't hurt herself. "I say nothing of Kate's troubles," Dickens reported to Forster, "but you recollect her propensity? She falls into, or out of, every coach or boat we enter; scrapes the skin off her legs; brings great sores and swellings on her feet; chips large fragments out of her ankle-bones; and makes herself blue with bruises. She really has, however, since we got over the first trial of being among circumstances so new and so fatiguing, made a *most admirable* traveller in every respect. She has never screamed or expressed alarm under circumstances that would have fully justified her in doing so, even in my eyes; has never given way to despondency or fatigue, though we have now been travelling incessantly, through a very rough country, for more than a month ...; has always accommodated herself, well and cheerfully to everything; and has pleased me very much, and proved herself perfectly game."[15] The first part of this report has been cited extensively to prove that Catherine Dickens was unusually clumsy, and that Dickens was irritated by her as early as 1842, but the letter as a whole is grateful, appreciative, and affectionate. Dickens clearly realizes that any woman, trained to physical timidity and immobility, would have a hard time keeping up with him, as would most men. Even in his eyes, measured by his demanding standard, she seems plucky.

The rigors of travel made them, quite literally, cling together. In Ohio, the coach they were travelling in had to pass for a long time over a corduroy road—a road made of logs laid over soggy ground to settle as they may and provide whatever support they can. Dickens compared riding over such a road to going up a steep flight of stairs in an omnibus. One moment they were flung up against the roof, the next they were thrown into a heap on the floor. As one side of the coach sank into the mire, they held on to each other for comfort. Dickens even tried tying Kate into place, in order to make her more comfortable. "Still, the day was beautiful, the air delicious, and we were *alone:* with no tobacco spittle, or eternal prosy conversations about dollars and politics . . . to bore us. We really enjoyed it; made a joke about being knocked about; and were quite merry. At two o'clock we stopped in the wood to open our hamper and dine; and we drank to our darlings and all friends at home."[16]

When the Dickenses returned in late July of 1842, their friends and children were overjoyed to see them. Indeed, Charley, the eldest child, was quite deranged with joy and suffered convulsions, which a doctor had to be summoned to treat. The children had been well in their parents' absence but not happy. The Macready household was run more severely than the Dickens house and the children had found it prim, gloomy, and unjoyful.[17] Their daily visits had not been pleasant. So one can imagine their happiness at their parents' return.

In *My Father As I Recall Him*, Mamie Dickens, who never married, would testify to what a delightful parent Charles Dickens had been. His nature, she said, was home-loving. No man ever existed so naturally inclined to derive his happiness from home affairs, and the more famous he got, the more pleasure he took in the circle close to him, particularly his children. He entered enthusiastically into all their interests. He helped them with the decorations of their rooms (which he daily inspected). He provided treats. He arranged for games and sporting events and birthday celebrations. But his genius for family entertainment expressed itself most strikingly at Christmas, the family festival *par excellence* and, indeed, the holiday which his own Christmas stories would help to secularize and turn into a celebration of the family.

Twelfth Night coincided with Charley's birthday, and in 1843, after his return from America, Dickens began a tradition of performing magic tricks at the Twelfth Night celebration. He and Forster had purchased the stock of a conjuror who was going out of business, and together, with Dickens as conjuror and Forster as his assistant, they astonished young and old alike on Twelfth Night and selected birthdays during the Christmas season. Dickens turned watches into tea-caddies, made pieces of money fly through the air, burned up pocket handkerchiefs without burning them. He caused a tiny doll to disappear and then to reappear with little messages and pieces of news for different children in the audience. But his greatest trick, the climax of all, was his manufacture in an ordinary gentleman's hat of a plum pudding.

On December 26, 1843, Jane Carlyle attended one of these Christmas extravaganzas, a birthday party for little Nina Macready. It was held at the Macready house but organized by Dickens, at least in part to cheer up Mrs. Macready and the children for the absence of the head of the household, on tour in America. Jane called it the most agreeable party she had ever attended in London. Dickens and Forster, she reported, exerted themselves so hard that perspiration streamed off them and they seemed drunk with their efforts. Dickens played conjuror for an entire hour and was the best Jane had ever witnessed, including ones she had paid money to see. He turned ladies' handkerchiefs into candies. He turned a box of bran into a guinea pig. And then he performed his *pièce de résistance*, emptying raw eggs, flour, and other appropriate ingredients into a hat and, in seconds, turning out a plum pudding, cooked and steaming hot, before the astonished eyes of children and grown-ups—even the skeptical former belle of Haddington.[18]

After the magic came the dancing. Gigantic Mr. Thackeray, old Jerdan of the *Literary Gazette*, and many other gentlemen of the arts were all "capering like Maenades." Jane would not dance, although Dickens begged her to waltz with him. She preferred to talk. She talked, therefore, the zaniest nonsense with Dickens, Thackeray, Forster, and Maclise. After supper, they went madder than ever, pulling crackers, drinking champagne, and making speeches. Jane thought that nowhere in London, not in the most aristocratic circles, was there more wit and brilliance and fun than in that room that night. A country dance was proposed. Forster seized Jane Carlyle by the waist and made her dance. Once on the floor, you had to keep moving or else be crushed, as on a treadmill. The room was that crowded. Jane cried out, "For the love of Heaven, let me go! you are going to dash my brains out against the folding doors!" And Forster replied, "Your *brains!!* who cares about their brains *here?* let them go!" The merriment surged, pooled, swelled, and was rising (in Jane's view) to something like the rape of the Sabines, when someone noticed it was midnight. Everyone made a rush for the coat room. Dickens, however, was determined not to stop, and left, with his wife, Thackeray, and Forster, vowing to continue the party at home.

But even while he was cavorting at Nina Macready's birthday party, dancing like a Maenad and pulling plum puddings out of hats, Dickens had worries on his mind. Or rather, he had worries he was trying to put out of his mind by his wild cavorting. He had just undergone the incredible strain of writing *A Christmas Carol* and his usual installments of *Martin Chuzzlewit* at the same time. He was almost thirty-two, seven years older than he had been when he produced *Pickwick* and *Oliver* and then *Oliver* and *Nicholas Nickleby* concurrently. It was getting harder to continue to pull *those* puddings out of hats. In all those seven years, with the exception of the trip to America, which had been a strain in a different way, he had been a work machine. And what did he have to show for it? The sales of *Martin Chuzzlewit* were consistently disappointing. And the *Carol*, which he had counted on to set him up financially, brought in much less money than he expected. He had switched publishers again (he had earlier moved from Bentley to Chapman and Hall, now from Chapman and Hall to Bradbury and Evans) in the hopes of increasing his profits, and it hadn't worked. He resented his publishers, each in turn, feeling he had made them rich without making himself the same. The specter of Sir Walter Scott, dying bankrupt, haunted him.[19]

His financial responsibilities were enormous—not just to Catherine and his children, but, more irritatingly, to his parents and brothers as well. His father, in particular, was a torment to him, for he never knew when he would be presented with another bad debt contracted by John Dickens. He set up his parents in a house in the country, but his father, far from being grateful, wanted to be in Paris or London instead. Eventually, without his son's consent, John Dickens rented out the house his son had taken for him and kept the money. He was always writing to Charles Dickens's publishers and bankers asking for loans. Nothing Dickens did for his father would satisfy him. "The thought of him besets me night and day; and I really do not know what is to be done with him. It is quite clear that the more we do the more outrageous and audacious he becomes."[20] He felt that all of them—father, mother, and brothers—looked upon him as something to be plucked and torn to pieces for their advantage. They did not care for him in any other way than as a provider. Their constant demands and the fear of ever more of them depressed him, weighed down his spirit, distracted him from work. The infuriating thing was that they were out of his control. He could not ever shut off that source of annoyance. "My soul sickens at the thought of them."[21]

He was beset, too, by his public, by constant requests for speeches, favors, endorsements, advice. He wrote a dozen letters a day and was always behind in his correspondence. In the latter part of 1843, he began to think longingly of leaving England altogether. He would take a long sabbatical on the Continent, in France or Italy, some place where he could live cheaply. Perhaps by renting out the Devonshire Terrace house again and by living cheaply abroad, he could cut down expenses and get ahead a bit. It seemed to him that, given his fame and success, he ought to be able to live like a rich man, and he kept finding to his bitterness that he could not. Distressingly, the old foe of Political Economy was discovering that for him, at least, a variation of the Malthusian principle seemed true. It was as though his dependents increased geometrically and his resources only arithmetically. Satisfied as he was with his family of four, overburdened financially as he already felt, he had to confront the fact that Catherine was pregnant again. She was, unusually for her, dull, depressed, and frightened about the birth. No wonder, when her husband's lack of enthusiasm for the new baby was so apparent. "We think of keeping the New Year, by having another child. I am constantly reversing the Kings in the fairy tales, and importuning the Gods not to trouble themselves: being quite satisfied with what I have. But they are *so* generous when they *do* take a fancy to one!"[22] Francis Jeffrey Dickens, their fifth child, was born early in 1844. Five more babies would follow him by 1852.

Dickens Dissatisfied

We do not know for certain what prompted Mrs. Henry Winter, after a silence of twenty-four years, to contact the man who had been dotingly in love with her and whom she had rejected when they were both young, but we do know the effect her letter had on him. Charles Dickens recognized the handwriting of the woman he had known as Maria Beadnell in the years before he had married, before he had become famous and successful as a novelist. "Three or four and twenty years vanished like a dream, and I opened it with the touch of my young friend David Copperfield when he was in love."[23] He wrote her a long letter in reply—and another, and another. He had told her the literal truth of his imagination: twenty-four years had vanished, and he was in love again, in love with Maria Beadnell, age eighteen.

Thinking back on the role she had played in his life, he became convinced she was its heroine. He had never been so in love as he had been with her. She had inspired in him whatever imagination, energy, passion, aspiration, and determination he had. She was the reason he had exerted himself to work his way up from poverty and obscurity. He would have done anything for her—even died for her. She was to have been his reward. But she rejected him. The disappointment was so great that, as he looked back on his life, Dickens thought it had stifled one side of his nature. Never since the rebuff from Maria had he been able to display affection completely—except to his children, and only when they were very young.

Mrs. Winter was not appalled at being turned, after the fact, into the heroine of the great novelist's life. His surge of emotion inspired confessions of similar feeling from her. She was also well into middle age and no doubt, like Dickens, was thinking about lives she might have lived, feeling the one she had chosen somewhat limited, investing the unchosen path with the glow of romance. Even respectable matrons, with prosperous businessmen husbands and two charming daughters may feel the impulse, in their thirties or forties, to re-establish contact with an earlier lover, to think that, if they had chosen this person instead of that, things might be more satisfactory, to wonder if it were possible to erase the past, to go back to the turning point and try again. Life must have seemed a very bitter joke to Mrs. Winter, who had chosen her husband on the grounds of prudence and who, out of prudence, had rejected one of the most successful men of her time just two years before his success became evident. How pleasant to think that he loved her still, that her image, his love for her, was behind everything he had accomplished, as he said it was.

Mrs. Winter was less deluded than Dickens. She warned him, as he pressed her to agree to a secret meeting without their respective spouses, that she was "toothless, fat, old and ugly,"[24] but he did not believe her. It was true that his wife, Catherine, who was forty while Maria was now forty-five, had grown old and fat—and boring, and silly, and lethargic. But she was an unusual case, a particularly vexing woman. If Catherine had aged badly it was her fault; something rotten in her character was expressing itself in her body. Maria Beadnell—charming, girlish, laughing Maria—she could not have aged.

They met, as arranged, on a Sunday at an hour when Catherine Dickens could be counted on to be out of the house. Mrs. Winter arrived at the Dickens residence between three and four, asked for Mrs. Dickens, was told she was out, and was offered the attention of Mr. Dickens instead, all as Dickens had foreseen. But his fantasy of a renewed attachment with the love of his youth was destroyed with one glance. Perhaps somewhere beneath the bulk of Mrs. Winter there was a youthful Maria struggling to escape, but Dickens could not perceive her. One wonders what sentimental platitudes he mobilized to get through the painful interview he had unquestionably imagined as the beginning of a seduction. The past—how long gone. One's children—how comforting, yet who could have imagined one would have them. Growing old—who could have foreseen that, either. Somehow he got through the time. Then he had to endure a dinner with Mr. and Mrs. Winter and Mrs. Dickens, which the secret lovers had arranged before they had seen each other again. But after that, Dickens went to any rhetorical length to avoid seeing the travesty of his romantic past. "Whoever is devoted to art," he told her, "must be content to deliver himself wholly up to it, and to find his recompense in it. I am grieved if you suspect me of not wanting to see you, but I can't help it; I must go my way whether or no."[25]

The woman who had inspired the representation of David Copperfield's love for Dora Spenlow now inspired Arthur Clennam's appalled response to Flora Finching: "Clennam's eyes no sooner fell upon the subject of his old passion, than it shivered and broke to pieces."

> Flora, always tall, had grown to be very broad too, and short of breath; but that was not much. Flora, whom he had left a lily, had become a peony; but that was not much. Flora, who had seemed enchanting in all she said and thought, was diffuse and silly. That was much. Flora, who had been spoiled and artless long ago, was determined to be spoiled and artless now. That was the fatal blow.[26]

With her disjointed volubility, her sentences connected by little sense and less punctuation, Flora stands out as one of the great successes of *Little Dorrit*. "I am so glad you like Flora," Dickens wrote to the duke of Devonshire. "It came into my head one day that we have all our Floras (mine is living and extremely fat), and that it was a half serious half ridiculous truth which had never been told."[27] The truth was the truth of time's power. Girlish charm, unmodulated after twenty-four years, is no longer girlish charm but eccentric affectation. Beautiful women age, thicken, and are no longer attractive. The dreams of one's youth become depressingly, ludicrously, the flabby realities of middle age. One can become famous and successful without becoming happy. One can have married at twenty-three a woman one loved dearly, then realize at forty-three that one has nothing in common with her but years spent in the same house and ten children one doesn't really want.

Researchers in developmental psychology tell us it is normal for a man between the ages of thirty-five and forty-five to undergo a period of acute change in which he re-examines his entire life and as a result of which he may desire to "modify" (in the words of the social scientist) "an oppressive life structure."[28] The oppressive life structure may be his occupation or it may be his marriage. The real prison, however, is probably harder to escape from than a job or a marriage. Jung, considering the monumental task of re-education confronting the psyche in the middle of life, laments that there are no colleges for forty-year-olds, to prepare them for the second half of existence. "Thoroughly unprepared we take the step into the afternoon of life; worse still, we take this step with the false assumption that our truths and ideals will serve us as hitherto. But we cannot live the afternoon of life according to the program of life's morning; for what was great in the morning will be little at evening, and what in the morning was true will at evening have become a lie."[29] In the past, said Jung, religions had served people as those colleges for forty-year-olds he whimsically imagined, but religions no longer have that hold on people's minds.

Unaided by the deeper side of religion (for Christianity had already become, for Dickens, little more than an organized form of sentiment, a species of practical benevolence), unaided even by the useful if unlovely formulations of the social scientists, Dickens faced the disintegration of his happiness alone, quite unaware that the radical dissatisfaction he was feeling was in some sense normal. Such an awareness could not have offered a solution, however, and it might not even have been consoling to a man of Dickens's nature. Perhaps it would have irritated him to think that what he felt could have been felt by others. Probably he would not have believed it. For it is partly the source of his greatness as a writer—though the source, too, of whatever smallness one may see in him as a moral being—that he could feel his own life so intensely and project his imagination so powerfully onto the rest of life that he seemed to be living in a world with only one real person in it, himself. He could be kind and genial to the rest, but they remained supporting players.

Dickens's writing changed noticeably after the publication of *David Copperfield* in 1850, when he was thirty-eight, and critics frequently compare the early works of Dickens with the later. The earlier works tend to be more humorous and optimistic than the later. The later works are more complicated, more symbolic. There are differences in both style and content. Even his manuscripts changed, showing a new mode of composition much less spontaneous in his later years, the passages worked over and over as they had not been in his youth. He was having a harder time writing, but his imagination was in many ways more powerful than ever, if less spontaneously inventive. Dickens's career provides an excellent example of Elliott Jaques's hypothesis that the mode and content of the work of artistic geniuses change radically at mid-life, that they must change if the artist is to continue to be fully creative. In his art, Dickens found ways to change and grow. He was by no means imprisoned within his occupation as a novelist. It was his domestic situation that seemed insupportable when, in the year 1855, at the age of forty-three, he was offered the false hope of remaking his life by the reappearance of Maria Beadnell.

What he craved was emotional intensity with another person, and he could not find it in his wife. Catherine Dickens was an amiable if limited person. To say that she was not Dickens's match in complexity, energy, and brilliance is to say nothing that would not have been true of virtually every other woman of her class and her time in England. "There was nothing wrong with my mother," her daughter Kate later said. "She had her faults, of course, as we all have—but she was a sweet, kind, peace-loving woman, a lady—a lady born."[30] Hans Christian Andersen praised her "womanly repose" and noted that a light came into her china-blue eyes when she spoke and that her voice was charming. She reminded him of Agnes Wickfield. That shows what an obtuse houseguest Andersen was, for it was precisely Catherine's lack of Agnes Wickfield's managerial talents that first made Dickens consciously dissatisfied with her.

With his love of orderliness and insistence on bourgeois comfort, Dickens demanded a well-run household. But Catherine no longer had the energy or the interest to manage the complex business of co-ordinating servants, dealing with tradesmen, disciplining children. She had given birth to ten children in sixteen years of marriage, and there were miscarriages in addition. Almost always pregnant or caring for an infant, she was exhausted. Living with one of the most energetic and high-spirited men in England, she was overwhelmed. Catherine seems to have given up—at least on running the household—and that job was taken over by her sister, Georgina Hogarth, who had been living with them from the time she was fifteen (as Mary Hogarth had lived with them in the early days of their marriage). By 1856 Georgina had effectively replaced Catherine both as head of the household and as Dickens's domestic partner. It was to their aunt Georgina that the children turned with their problems. Catherine, flattened by fatigue, lay on the sofa, increasingly irrelevant in her own house.

For her remained only the sexual role, a role in which she won little applause from her husband. Time made her no longer as exciting to him as she once had been. And she kept getting pregnant and producing all those babies! Dickens, who increasingly resented every new addition to the sum of his financial responsibilities, complained about his wife's fertility as though he himself had nothing to do with it. Moreover, all that childbearing told on her body, along with age and perhaps too much rich food. Little of the beauty of her youth—except her lovely blue eyes—remained distinct in the general plumpness of her face; her throat subsided fleshily, vaguely, into the amplitudes of the rest of her body. Eminently resistible as he now found her, Dickens must have despised himself a bit for not, after all, resisting her, but he transferred the blame for that, as he transferred the blame for all the irritations and inadequacies of their marriage, to her. *She* was the one who kept having babies.

Catherine's feelings in this situation have entirely to be imagined. Few of her letters are preserved (most of his are) to make her presumed despair known to later generations. She understood, from absences of enthusiasm, from trivial gestures, that he no longer found her appealing or even adequate to his needs. Somehow, what had seemed perfectly satisfactory to him once was satisfactory no longer. In her own mind, she was exactly the same person he had fallen in love with and married—good-natured, generous, not brilliant but solidly affectionate—and she did not know why that no longer satisfied him. Catherine could not understand what she had done wrong or in what way she had failed, but she knew she had failed, and was miserable. She could do nothing about it, say nothing, for her husband set the terms of their marriage and of their daily life. She had to accommodate herself to him. "My poor mother was afraid of my father," Kate Dickens said. "She was never allowed to express an opinion—never allowed to say what she felt."[31] And in her supine acquiescence, he undoubtedly found more material for dislike. If only his energy could be matched by some from another person! If only she would provoke him, excite him, resist him!

To his eyes, Catherine had become unresponsive, grudging, inert, close to inhuman. Had she really changed? Certainly she had aged. He had married a young woman, and she had turned into an older one. Perhaps the gap between them had widened in the years of her dedication to babies and of his to books. Perhaps there had always been an incompatibility between them, but he had been too busy to notice it—too busy establishing himself professionally, too busy assaulting the world to register insufficiencies closer to home. Nevertheless, he brought to bear on Catherine a rage which seems unjustified by anything she was, even granted that she had let herself become unattractive and lazy. Perhaps, as she left girlhood behind, Catherine became for him more and more the mother he hated and felt betrayed by, whom he blamed for keeping him at work when he was ten. It was Catherine keeping him at work now, always producing more children for him to support. And she refused to take responsibility for her own household, thrusting it onto other people, onto himself and Georgina. If Catherine lived now, she might well feel (as other women have felt) that her husband's anger at her had nothing to do with her and a lot to do with his mother. But Catherine, in 1855, could have had no such consoling thought.

When the fantasied reunion with Maria Beadnell and the hoped-for rebirth of his emotional life turned out to be a fiasco, Dickens was unable to laugh at himself or to accept his situation resignedly. It drove him, if anything, into a more acute state of despair. Would he never feel excitement with a woman again? Was he to be caged, confined, smothered within the limits of domesticity? Was it fair that one of the foremost novelists of his time should be denied the kind of emotional intensity in his life which he could project in his art? He envied French writers like Balzac and George Sand, who were not, in their writing, as constrained by their nation's morality as he felt himself to be. He envied the frankness possible in their fiction, and, no doubt, the fabled sexual expressiveness of their lives as well.

He was aware, above all, of a preternatural restlessness. He seemed unable to settle down to one task or one place, as though he could not find a comfortable point of repose in his life. He would sit down to work, get up, walk twelve miles, plan a trip to the Pyrenees, go back to his room, sit down, get up, pace the floor, make appointments and then not keep them. He went to Paris. He went to Boulogne. He was beginning to write *Little Dorrit*, and some of the restlessness was a writer's normal spillover of energy at the start of a project, before the form and discipline of the work have channeled it usefully. But Dickens himself connected the restlessness that tormented him with his unhappy home life, with the irritations of life with a woman he found incompatible, and with frustrated sexuality. He thought obsessively about his own restlessness, trying to convince himself it was somehow useful, that the wayward and unsettled feeling which so distressed him was part of the tenure on which he held his imaginative life—in short, that his misery was allied to his genius. But why had his genius been so untroubled in earlier life? Had he repressed his restlessness by riding over it like a dragoon? Why couldn't he go on keeping his discontent buried? "The old days—the old days! Shall I ever, I wonder, get the frame of mind back as it used to be then?"[82] What he called the skeleton in his domestic closet—his closet dissatisfaction—seemed to be growing larger and threatening to break down doors.

One outlet for Dickens's restless energy was provided by the amateur theatricals he organized for his household. In 1855 he had staged a melodrama by Wilkie Collins in the children's theater in Tavistock House, their London residence. It was called *The Lighthouse*. Dickens, an electrifying actor who entered wholeheartedly into his roles and used his voice magnificently, tearing every passion to tatters, played the central role of the lighthouse keeper haunted by the belief he had murdered someone. On January 6, 1857, in honor of the twentieth birthday of his eldest son, Dickens produced another Wilkie Collins melodrama, *The Frozen Deep*. He, Collins, Charley, Mamie, and Kate Dickens, and Georgina Hogarth, had rehearsed the play twice weekly for months. Dickens had supervised the construction of flats, which were painted by his friend Clarkson Stanfield of the Royal Academy. Admission was by invitation only, and Dickens had to insist that the invitations were not transferable as room was so extremely limited (partly due to the voluminousness of ladies' crinolines). He had to deal with the gas board to get special permission for the gas lights and yet to avoid an increase in his taxes. He managed every aspect of the production.

Dickens loved to act—there is a painting of him playing the role of Bobadil, the braggart, in Ben Jonson's *Every Man in His Humour*—and his amateur theatricals, like his later public readings, served his emotional needs in complicated ways. For one thing, acting was for him, as it had been for Shakespeare, an expression of human freedom and flexibility. For Shakespeare this image was counterbalanced by a sense of theater as shadow-activity, an emblem of the vanity of earthly life.[33] But for Dickens the theater seeemed increasingly truer than life. Aware in his youth (as in *Nicholas Nickleby*) of the comic limitations of actors and acting, Dickens, as he aged, grew oppressed by the not-so-comic limitations of life. Life did not measure up so satisfactorily as theater to his demands for intensity.

The theater answered, too, his need to control. For it was not just acting he enjoyed. He liked producing, co-ordinating the efforts of many people—the writer, the scene painter, the actors—liked seeing a work of art take shape through co-operative effort and not, as was more usual for him, in the loneliness of his study. Putting on a play was like writing a book in company, and performing it allowed him to "feel its effect coming freshly back upon me from the reader."[34] His performance was a text whose impact, unlike that of his novels, he could witness instantly. Watching his effect on an audience, establishing his power over an ever greater number of people visibly present before him, became increasingly important to Dickens.

Collins's melodramas, with their heightened emotionalism, were peculiarly suited to offer release from the monotonous and depressing irritation of his domestic life. In *The Frozen Deep*, which was to play, one way and another, such an important role in Dickens's life, he acted the part of a man who sacrifices himself to save the life of his rival in love. Richard Wardour discovers himself on an Arctic ice floe with Frank Aldersley, the man Clara Burnham has rejected him for and whom he has sworn to kill. But instead of killing Aldersley, Wardour carries him over snow drifts and ice floes, staggering on with the sick man and bringing him to safety, at the cost of his own life. Time after time, in rehearsal and in the four-performance run, Dickens sacrificed his life to save a man he hated. It was the role he felt he was enacting in his own life. He felt torn between the urge to sacrifice his own happiness for what he felt he owed to others and the urge to break loose and seek his own happiness at whatever cost. And this conflict registers in the way he keeps returning to the themes of self-sacrifice and self-indulgence in his novels of this period, in *Little Dorrit* and *A Tale of Two Cities*.

As Wardour, he triumphed. Most of the audience and many of the actors were in tears. "O reaction, reaction," he wrote to Collins when the public performances were over.[35] He would not let go of *The Frozen Deep*. When his friend Douglas Jerrold died in June, Dickens organized three more performances of the melodrama with a paying audience to benefit the widow and her family. He hired the Gallery of Illustration in Regent Street for the purpose. The play was becoming widely known. The queen herself requested and was given a special performance. Then Dickens, who had given public readings in the provinces to raise money for charity, got the idea of taking *The Frozen Deep* on the road. They would perform it in Manchester, in a theater that could seat three thousand! He would continue to play Richard Wardour, but it was out of the question for Georgina Hogarth and the Dickens girls to continue in the female parts. Their voices would never carry in such a large theater. They would have to be replaced by professional actresses.

That Dickens did not immediately think of Mrs. Ternan and her interesting daughters suggests that the story of his backstage meeting the previous spring with Ellen Ternan, crying at the scantiness of the costume she had to wear, may, after all, be apocryphal,[36] or that, if they did meet, the impression made upon the novelist by the crying ingenue was not so great. Or perhaps he was greatly attracted to her and precisely for that reason tried to find a different actress. He asked Mrs. Henry Compton to join the cast for the Manchester performances, but she was busy. Then, at the recommendation of the manager of the Olympic Theater, he asked Mrs. Ternan and her daughters, Maria and Ellen. Maria, the more talented actress, played the part of Clara Burnham, in whose arms Richard Wardour dies. Even though her back was to the audience and no one could appreciate it but Dickens, the distress and agitation on her face when she recognized Wardour were extraordinary. She had to kneel over him as he was dying and be said good-bye to. Dickens, playing the part of the dying man, testified that tears streamed out of her eyes into his mouth, down his beard, all over his rags, down his arms as he held her. "At the same time she sobbed as if she were breaking her heart, and was quite convulsed with grief. It was of no use for the compassionate Wardour to whisper, 'My dear child, it will be over in two minutes—there is nothing the matter—don't be so distressed!' She could only sob out 'O! It is so sad, O it's so sad!' and set Mr. Lemon . . . crying too. By the time the curtain fell, we were all crying together."[37] Ostensibly a tribute to Maria's wholehearted acting and her vibrantly compassionate nature, this account by Dickens of the Manchester performance also serves as a testimonial to his own power, his impact as an actor and the beauty of the self-sacrificing role he had chosen to play.

Dickens was moved by dependency and weakness in women—but it had to be an active, quivering, sensitive weakness, a weakness which could testify to his strength, not the bovine and lethargic weakness of his wife. Still, it is not wholly surprising that his fiercest response was evoked not by Maria Ternan but by her younger and less gifted sister, who was the same age as his favorite daughter, Kate, eighteen, the age that Maria Beadnell had remained in his mind, and who may or may not have cried months before at the thought of appearing on the stage in too little clothing. By the second of the two performances of *The Frozen Deep* in Manchester, after three days of rehearsal in London and a train ride up to the Midlands in the company of the Ternans, Dickens's life took a sharp new turn. He became obsessed with Ellen Ternan as an alternative to his domestic misery. He was in love.

A man who is dissatisfied with his marriage, if he has means and leisure, and if he is a person of honor who wants to avoid a conflicting entanglement, has many possible ways of distracting himself from his problem, quite apart from engaging in amateur theatricals. He can work very hard. He can take short trips. He can indulge in quick dissipations. He can vary his usual social milieu and seek out low-life dives. All this Dickens did, usually in the company of Wilkie Collins, his favored companion for adventure and self-indulgence, a man of considerable—and at this time to Dickens welcome—moral laxity (he kept a mistress). A man seeking to avoid confrontation with marital problems in a significant way can try to solve them, or bypass them, by buying a new house. This, too, Dickens had done, in the spring of 1857, acquiring Gad's Hill Place, near Rochester, which he had coveted from the time he was a child and his father had pointed out the house to him, saying that if he were successful, someday he could live there. But the most direct way for a man to signal (if only to himself) that a marriage is no longer serving his needs, and the classic way to do something about it, is to fall in love with another woman.

His despair now increased because there was an alternative to it. He imagined a specific happiness from which he was being kept by his wife and family responsibilities. Dickens did not embark immediately on a sexual relationship with Ellen Ternan, but that, if anything, increased his sentimental attachment to her. He began to polarize his life so that all the excitement of it lay in the secret part. His family routine seemed increasingly a hollow masquerade, no more than an oppressive wrapping over his true, passionate self. His inner torment reached a new stage, compared to which his previous despair seemed mild, and he was later to say that he had not known a moment's peace or contentment since the last night of *The Frozen Deep*. Having limited himself previously to vague hints about the source of his misery, Dickens began, soon after the close of the play, to speak (or rather to write, in carefully constructed letters) about his domestic discontent. From this time, the summer of 1857, we may date his years-long effort to shape his private life into a fiction, his most recalcitrant.

He chose as his confidant John Forster, one of his oldest and closest friends. Forster had always been his most trusted adviser on literary as well as on legal matters. (Forster had legal training, and although a writer himself, he acted as a kind of literary agent, in days before literary agents existed, for Dickens and other writers with whom he was friendly.) In the light of what he would write later, what Dickens wrote to Forster was a mild enough statement of the situation between himself and his wife:

Poor Catherine and I are not made for each other, and there is no help for it. It is not only that she makes me uneasy and un-happy, but that I make her so too—and much more so. She is exactly what you know, in the way of being amiable and comply-ing; but we are strangely ill-assorted for the bond there is between us. God knows she would have been a thousand times happier if she had married another kind of man. . . . I am often cut to the heart by thinking what a pity it is, for her sake, that I ever fell in her way; and if I were sick or disabled tomorrow, I know how sorry she would be, and how deeply grieved myself, to think how we had lost each other. But exactly the same incompatibility would arise, the moment I was well again; and nothing on earth could make her understand me, or suit us to each other. Her temperament will not go with mine. It mattered not so much when we had only ourselves to consider, but reasons have been growing since which make it all but hopeless that we should even try to struggle on. What is now befalling me I have seen steadily coming, ever since the days you remember when Mary was born; and I know too well that you cannot, and no one can, help me. Why I have even written I hardly know; but it is a miserable sort of comfort that you should be clearly aware how matters stand. The mere mention of the fact, without complaint or blame of any sort, is a relief to my present state of spirits—and I can get this only from you, because I can speak of it to no one else.[38]

It is a poignant document. Dickens's pity of Catherine's suffering seems genuine ("I am often cut to the heart by thinking what a pity it is, for her sake, that I ever fell in her way"), although the other side of it—his pity for himself—is so obvious as hardly to need statement. Despite their incompatibility, which time has exaggerated, as fame and success made him all the stronger and more expansive while she became more helpless and limited, the twenty years of their marriage has made some emotional bond between them. But he can only appreciate the force of the bond by imagining a disruption—sickness or disablement. And how interesting it is that he imagines himself getting ill and not Catherine, as though a solution to their problem might be found in some diminution of his strength, his health, his success, his fullness of being—or as though he should be punished for his wish to be rid of her.

Forster was not completely sympathetic. He replied that discontent is part of marriage; that it must be borne; that Dickens had a tendency to be too impatient; that he should look to his own flaws of character and try to mend them in hopes of bettering his relationship with Catherine. It was frustrating advice to receive when what he longed for was sympathy and an understanding of the unbearable claustrophobia he felt at home, but Dickens was so relieved to be talking about what was really on his mind that he took Forster's response with equanimity. "I agree with you as to the very possible incidents, even not less bearable than mine, that might and must often occur to the married condition when it is entered into very young. I am always deeply sensible of the wonderful exercise I have of life and its highest sensations, and have said to myself for years, and have honestly and truly felt, This is the drawback to such a career, and is not to be complained of. . . . But the years have not made it easier to bear for either of us; and, for her sake as well as mine, the wish will force itself upon me that something might be done. I know too well it is impossible."[39]

In this year, 1857, the Matrimonial Causes Act, which established secular divorce in England, was passing through its successive readings in Parliament. Dickens must have read reports of the debates in the newspapers and must have had tantalizingly before him the notion of being legally free of Catherine forever, free even to marry again. But it was impossible. Because even if the bill passed, as seemed increasingly likely, it was based on the fiction that one party in the marriage was guilty of its demise and the evidence of this guilt was adultery. If Catherine would commit adultery, he could be free of her. But that was preposterous. Immobile, conventional Catherine would never do anything so daring. And on the other hand, it was equally impossible that Dickens should present himself to the world as the aggressor, the guilty party, the adulterer. In this he was hardly unusual. Even after the Divorce Bill was passed, relatively few people in the period before World War I took advantage of it. And not until after World War I did the upper classes develop the sexual sophistication and contempt for the absurdities of the law necessary to produce the staged infidelities which became, for a while, a routine part of divorces by mutual consent.[40] So, for Dickens, as for many others, divorce could offer no solution to connubial misery. The best he could hope for was some separation from his wife, relieving him from the irritation of her daily presence, but not allowing him the comfort of re-marriage. It seemed that the vital part of himself would have to be sacrificed to that grotesque fiction of domestic harmony which he himself, in his novels, had helped to impose upon England.

In 1857-58, as Dickens moved towards and then effected a separation from his wife, he displayed a ferocious impulse to make life repeat the patterns of *The Frozen Deep*. In the summer of 1857, on a walking trip in Cumberland which was intended to work off some of his misery and restlessness, he strode up hills at such a rate that Collins, his companion, could not keep up with him, eventually tripped and sprained his ankle, and had to be carried by Dickens, as Dickens himself put it, "à la Richard Wardour."[41] Dickens seemed to do in whomever he was with and then look down upon his companions, however humorously, for their inability to keep up with him. With Collins as with Catherine, this was his way. Collins found it appalling: "A man who can do nothing by halves seems to me a fearful man."[42] And Forster, too, found all this charging up hills the expression of an impatience, impetuosity, and absence of inwardness in Dickens.

Melodrama has its power, but as a way of understanding marital discord it is not particularly useful. Trapped by the melodramatic patterns in his mind, Dickens projected all his difficulties onto outward circumstance, of which the grossest embodiment was Catherine, and he cast himself, improbably, in the role of victim. Perhaps because of his childhood trauma of abandonment,[43] for which he blamed his mother, Dickens continued to identify with the unprotected, fragile child and based some of his greatest work on the identification. But in his marriage, this fruitful fantasy made him fail to perceive his own power. He was male, with all the privileges of his sex; he was successful; he was rich, at any rate compared to his wife. Yet in his mind she appeared as the wounding and derelict parent. His own role was self-sacrifice. At the cost of his happiness, he had kept the family together. She had subsided and collapsed. If only (in the dualism of self-sacrifice and self-indulgence) he had thought of himself as frankly selfish and self-indulgent, he might have been kinder to Catherine in what followed.

The first gesture he devised to express outwardly the separation from Catherine that existed in his heart was interestingly equivocal. He asked the servant at Tavistock House to arrange for separate bedrooms for himself and his wife. His instructions were quite specific. Mrs. Dickens was to have the bedroom which they had formerly shared. His dressing room was to be turned into a bedroom for himself. The connection between the two rooms was to be walled up and covered over with bookshelves. He was to have a new iron bedstead. Who was being walled up? Who was being kept from whom? The gesture is a bit virginal, as though Catherine were a rapacious sexual pursuer who had to be held off. Yet the bookcase he would see, should he think of returning to Catherine, and the iron bedstead he would have to lie in, seem rebukes to himself, reminders to deny himself the easy consolations of sex, which, over many years of unhappiness, he had had a hard time resisting.

For Catherine, however, the gesture was not equivocal. It was a harsh and devastating rejection. That Christmas of 1857, which was celebrated in the nation at large with particular joy because of the news from India that Lucknow had been relieved, was hardly celebrated at all at Tavistock House. No theatricals in the children's theater. Mrs. Dickens was weeping, beginning to think she would be better off, subject to fewer indignities, if she were not living in the same house as her husband. Dickens could not throw her out of Tavistock House, but he arranged matters so that even that passive woman (prodded by her parents) came to think it better she should go.

In the spring of 1858, a bracelet which was intended for Ellen Ternan arrived at Tavistock House. It was a gift from Dickens which had been mistakenly delivered by the jeweler to Dickens's own house. Dickens claimed that Ellen Ternan was not his mistress, that he often sent gifts of jewelry to young ladies who acted in his theatricals. Although one can hardly accuse him of having arranged this incident, which upset his wife terribly, one might expect him to have exercised particular care as to the address of a present to a young lady, whether or not she was technically his mistress. But Dickens contrived to turn the episode against Catherine, as proof of a conception of her character which had been growing in his own mind and which he began trying out on other people: she was insanely jealous. Years before, when they had been living in Italy, he had undertaken the treatment by mesmerism of the wife of a friend, Madame de la Rue. They were as close as analyst and analysand, whose relationship theirs in many ways resembled, and Catherine had been disturbed by their intimacy and the sheer amount of time they spent together. Dickens said at the time that her suspicions had poisoned their relationship with the de la Rues, and eventually he made her apologize to Madame de la Rue for them. It was to the de la Rues, therefore, that Dickens wrote, developing his notion of Catherine as insanely jealous: "I don't get on much better in these later times with a certain poor lady you know of, than I did in the earlier [Villa] Peschiere days. Much worse. Much worse. Neither do the children, elder or younger. Neither can she get on with herself, or be anything but unhappy. (She has been excruciatingly jealous of, and has obtained positive proofs of my being on the most confidential terms with, at least Fifteen Thousand women of various conditions since we left Genoa. Please to respect me for this vast experience.)"[44]

When the jewelry incident occurred, Catherine accused her husband of having an affair with Ellen Ternan. He stood by his technical innocence and accused her of pathological jealousy. He reminded her of the de la Rue episode. She was displaying the same low mind now, repeating her vile suggestions. He had made her apologize to Madame de la Rue for her suspicions, as insulting to the lady involved as to him, and he would have her apologize to Miss Ternan now. Kate Dickens passed her mother's bedroom and found her crying as she put on her bonnet. "Your father has asked me to go and see Ellen Ternan," sobbed Mrs. Dickens, and her daughter claims to have stamped her foot and said, "You shall not go!" But Mrs. Dickens went. When she told her parents the story of Ellen Ternan's bracelet and the apology, the Hogarths said she should insist on a separation. Dickens at first resisted this suggestion but gradually acceded to it. Since he had managed things so that the suggestion of a separation did not come from him, he needed to feel no guilt about it.

Now his energies could be wholeheartedly directed towards convincing other people of his innocence. It was particularly important to convince Angela Burdett-Coutts, for not only did he respect her personally, she was also, in her wealth and power, an embodiment of the Establishment. In his account for Miss Coutts of his domestic misery, notice how what begins as a neutral tale of incompatibility becomes a story of oppression. "I believe my marriage has been for years and years as miserable a one as ever was made. I believe that no two people were ever created with such an impossibility of interest, sympathy, confidence, sentiment, tender union of any kind between them, as there is between my wife and me." Nature had placed an insurmountable barrier between them. Catherine was the only human being he had ever known with whom he could not get along, in communicating with whom he could find no common interest. Indeed, no one could get along with her. (At this point, one begins to suspect caricature.) Her own mother would be unable to live with her. Her own children couldn't stand her. "She has never attached herself to them, never played with them in their infancy, never attracted their confidence as they have grown older, never presented herself before them in the aspect of a mother. I have seen them fall off from her in a natural—not *un*natural process of estrangement, and at this moment I believe that Mary and Katey . . . harden into stone when they go near her."[45]

The truth of the matter seems to have been that Georgina, with more intelligence, inventiveness, and energy than her sister, presented a more attractive alternative to the children and so took over their care and their affection. Dickens thought that without Georgina his household could never have functioned, but perhaps without Georgina, Catherine would have risen to the occasion and been a more outgoing mother. (Her children seem not so much hostile and alienated as simply distant.) But Dickens, caught up in his compelling fairy tale, cannot resist elaborating on the image of Catherine as a monster who turns even her children to stone. "It is her misery to live in some fatal atmosphere which slays every one to whom she should be dearest." His own role, by implication, is entirely passive; he is innocence in monsterland, Una, or Sleeping Beauty, or Little Red Riding Hood—or Oliver Twist, passing unscathed through the den of thieves.

Miss Coutts took laconic note that the Dickenses were separating because of incompatibility. She was satisfied that there was no "criminal" connection at issue, and that was all she cared about. Her sympathies, however, tended to go to Mrs. Dickens. Dickens had shown a child hurt, a child dying in books such as *Dombey and Son*, *David Copperfield*, and *The Old Curiosity Shop* and the world had cried. He had shown children oppressed by fairy-tale monsters such as he imagined Catherine to be—unnatural, death-allied, slayers of life like Murdstone and Dombey. But he was not a helpless child. And his "oppressor," Catherine, was strikingly not a powerful, authoritarian figure. Miss Coutts would not cry for him on this one. The formula was inappropriate.

Dickens moved into the offices of his magazine, *Household Words*, while the separation was worked out. Forster represented Dickens, and Mark Lemon, the editor of *Punch*, whom Dickens had called the softest-hearted man in the world, represented Catherine. She was to have a settlement of £600 per year. She was to have her own house, and her eldest son, Charley, would live with her. But all the other children were to stay with Dickens. They could visit their mother if they chose to, but Dickens did not encourage them to—in fact, quite the opposite. Kate and Mamie took music lessons across the street from Mrs. Dickens's house at 70 Gloucester Crescent and never stopped to visit their mother. She was not invited to Kate's wedding. In later life, Kate felt guilty. "We were all very wicked not to take her part; Harry does not take this view, but he was only a boy at the time and does not realize the grief it was to our mother, after having all her children, to go away and leave us. My mother never rebuked me. I never saw her in a temper."[46] Dickens did not make his children choose between himself and their mother. He simply assumed that, as the law allowed, they would stay with him. And so they did. They were happy to. He was dynamic, funny, famous, charismatic, and powerful. Nevertheless, their staying with their father rather than their mother strikes *us* as so unusual that we wonder whether the mother may not have been the monster the father said she was. So we should remember that children were at this time the property of their fathers. Under law, a man's wife was his property, too. Married women had no legal status, no legal existence. They were entitled to nothing. When Caroline Norton, the writer, separated from her dissolute husband, she had to fight to be allowed even visits with her children. All the money Mrs. Norton earned from writing went to her scapegrace husband, whether she was living with him or not. In cases of divorce or separation, therefore, children more commonly went with the father than they do now. Then too, the Dickens children adored their father. Next to him their mother may have seemed irritatingly commonplace. Particularly for Mamie and Kate, the normal tendency of girls to overestimate their fathers and resent their mothers must have been exaggerated by the agreement of the outside world. They thought their mother was not worthy of their father. They blamed her for not keeping his love.

In retrospect, Kate believed that Ellen Ternan had been the cause of all the trouble. She, like much of London society, assumed there had to be Another Woman (it was not yet fashionable to conceive of the Other Woman as symptom rather than cause). But people who did not know the situation in the Dickens household as well as the Dickens daughters thought that the Other Woman was Georgina Hogarth, who had brought up the children and run the household for so many years. This was an unusually shocking suggestion, because in England at this time it was still illegal for a man to marry his deceased wife's sister; the relationship was considered incestuous. How much worse, then, to carry on illicitly with a living wife's sister! Thackeray thought he was standing up loyally for Dickens when someone at the Garrick Club said he was having an affair with his sister-in-law. "No such thing," said Thackeray. "It's with an actress." Hearing of this episode, Dickens was furious with Thackeray for spreading what he considered a great slander, although it was certainly the lesser of two slanders and closer to the truth. He could not accept any version of the story of his separation other than the one he himself chose to give out, the story of incompatibility bleeding into the tale of the monstrous Catherine. No blame. No blame. At least no blame on him. People whom he could not bring around to his way of seeing things, like Thackeray and Mark Lemon, he broke with.

Other people in those days separated. George Lewes left Agnes, continuing to support her and her children, even the illegitimate ones. Anna Jameson, the author, lived apart from her husband for most of their life, supporting herself by her pen. Mrs. Norton made her separation the basis of a campaign for women's rights. Other male novelists who lived separate from their wives were Frederick Marryat and Edward Bulwer-Lytton. The Bulwers' separation and that of Mrs. Norton were hardly discreet—Mrs. Norton sought publicity in order to dramatize the injustices which married women suffered under English law. In the Dickenses' separation, no issues were at stake, yet Dickens sought to tell his story as vigorously as Mrs. Norton. Behind his desperate attempts to justify himself must have lain the sense that he was doing something wrong. But towards whom did he feel guilty? Towards Catherine, for abandoning his role as husband, or towards his public for betraying his role as the bard of domesticity? Other people got separated, but few were in as peculiar a position as Dickens, who had so successfully appropriated for himself the role of exemplar and moral tutor. The London correspondent of *The New York Times* wrote that rumors of Dickens's having eloped to France with an actress were a lying scandal which ought to be scotched lest readers' faith in the wholesome lessons of *Pickwick, Master Humphrey's Clock*, and the Christmas stories be shaken by the author's failure to achieve in his own life the ideals of peace and harmony he wrote about.

Three days after the deed of separation was delivered to Catherine in June of 1858 after complicated and acrimonious negotiations, Dickens took a quite extraordinary step. It was a gigantic rebellion against the social structures in which his life was embedded, an absolute assertion of the uniqueness of his life and of the primacy of his imagination over all fact. He wrote a statement about his separation from his wife explaining himself and attempting to clear his name.

Then he had the statement published first in the *London Times* and later in his own *Household Words*. "Three-and-twenty years have passed since I entered on my present relations with the Public," his statement began, and he continued, in describing his ties to the Public, to use imagery bizarrely connubial. He has tried to be as "faithful to the Public as they have been to me." He has never trifled with the Public, or deceived it, or presumed upon its favors. He has always tried to do his duty by it. The document presents his relationship with the Public as the primary one in his life, and his marriage merely as an incident. His concern is all lest the Public think badly of him.

> Some domestic trouble of mine, of long-standing, on which I will make no further remark than that it claims to be respected, as being of a sacredly private nature, has lately been brought to an arrangement, which involves no anger or ill-will of any kind, and the whole origin, progress, and surrounding circumstances of which have been, throughout, within the knowledge of my children. It is amicably composed, and its details have now to be forgotten by those concerned in it.
>
> By some means, arising out of wickedness, or out of folly, or out of inconceivable wild chance, or out of all three, this trouble has been made the occasion of misrepresentations, most grossly false, most monstrous and cruel—involving, not only me, but innocent persons dear to my heart, and innocent persons of whom I have no knowledge at all, if, indeed, they have any existence—and so widely spread that I doubt if one reader in a thousand will peruse these lines, by whom some breath of these slanders will not have passed, like an unwholesome air.[47]

The monstrous and cruel misrepresentations he refers to were of course the suggestions that he was involved with another woman, whether Georgina Hogarth or Ellen Ternan, and the notion that not one reader in a thousand would not have heard these slanders suggests how badly Dickens was foundering in the fantasy that his private life was public, uniquely visible, centrally important to his readers. Of course, what the publication of his statement accomplished was precisely to spread the rumors about his private life far beyond the relatively small group of people in London who had heard them before. To spread them without convincing anyone that they were not true. How could the master manipulator of public response have conceived a step so misguided?

In a way, everything in his adult life can be seen as preparing for this debacle, for his misjudgment of people's response. He had had too much success in exerting his personal power. In his immediate lionization with the publication of *The Pickwick Papers* when he was twenty-four, in his experiments with mesmerism, which put another person's mind directly in his control, in his public readings and performances which established an almost hypnotic relationship with his audience, he was nurtured in a fantasy of omnipotence. He was convinced that there was a "particular relation (personally affectionate and like no other man's)"[48] subsisting between himself and the public, that vast feminine abstraction which wept and fainted and laughed on cue. He needed it to go on reacting as he wished. He needed its applause. He needed its love. He needed to retain his power over it. He had created another marriage, his successful marriage with the British public.

The statement in *Household Words* was followed, in mid-August, by an even more explicit account by Dickens of the separation. He had written it in late May and given it to Arthur Smith, the manager of his public readings, to use as he saw fit in putting rumors to rest. What Smith saw fit to do was give the letter to the *New York Tribune*, from which the copy was reprinted in many other American and English newspapers, spreading the news of Dickens's domestic misery even further throughout the world. Dickens claimed to be upset and referred to the document afterwards as "the violated letter," but he did not end his friendship with Smith as he had with so many others who contradicted his wishes about the public presentation of his private life.[49] So the violated letter constitutes another example of Dickens's contradictory wishes to assert and control and yet to appear as victim.

"Mrs. Dickens and I have lived unhappily together for many years," this amazing statement began, like a parody of a fairy tale. "Hardly anyone who has known us intimately can fail to have known that we are in all respects of character and temperament wonderfully unsuited to each other. I suppose that no two people, not vicious in themselves, ever were joined together who had a greater difficulty understanding one another, or who had less in common." It is a smoothly worked-up version of his statement to Miss Coutts, emphasizing Catherine's dereliction in the household and glorifying Georgina Hogarth as the family's savior, the person to whom all the children are devoted and who has a greater claim on Dickens's own affection, respect, and gratitude than anyone else in the world. With a passing reference to a "mental disorder under which [Mrs. Dickens] sometimes labours"—no doubt, her jealousy—he goes on explicitly, but without mentioning her name, to deny the guilt of Ellen Ternan. Two "wicked persons" (Catherine's mother and sister) had linked Ellen with the separation. But "upon my soul and honour," he wrote, "there is not on this earth a more virtuous and spotless creature than that young lady. I know her to be innocent and pure, and as good as my own dear daughters."[50] The "violated letter" expresses the myth of Dickens's marriage as he chose to present it, as he probably believed it, in its final form, and it is worth noting what role he casts himself in. He has done nothing. He is torn between two women, one good, one bad. The issue is household and family management. There is no question of erotic needs or sexual satisfaction. Dickens's marriage with the public was also, in its way, imprisoning; if Dickens was patriarchal in his relations with the public, the public was equally demanding, severely limiting him in the story he could tell. It would not permit the mention of anything which might bring a blush to the cheek of Miss Podsnap. In telling, even to himself, the story of his life, he had to make adjustments for the demands of family readers. In presenting the crises of adult life, he was forced back upon the structures and narratives of childhood crisis. He asked the public to respond to his domestic misery as they had to the trials of Oliver Twist, or Paul Dombey, or the young David Copperfield.

But the public was less a captive of its popular fictions than Dickens. It refused to believe that the most admired novelist of his country and age, the one with the fame, the money, the children, the magazine—and perhaps the mistress—was a victim. Jane Carlyle quipped that if one wanted a new way to describe a man who had ill-used his wife, one could say he had played the dickens with her.[51]

Many others saw the irony of the situation, as expressed in this contemporary comment, "Rumor says that this great novelist of the domestic hearth ran away with an actress; and his separation from his wife, although it does not prove this story, does show that he really was not happy at home, although he wrote so well about that kind of thing."[52] But the irony of his position was lost on Dickens. Other people had to tell him that it would not do to use the name *Household Harmony* for the re-constituted *Household Words*. (He used *All the Year Round*.) He believed too unshakeably in the fiction of his own innocence—that only the character of Catherine and not his own nature had kept him from the domestic ideal which he still endorsed—to see the joke.

Catherine moved to Gloucester Crescent, accompanied, at least for a time, by Charles, Jr., and Dickens's torment was over. The intolerable itch was scratched. Soon after the separation, he was heavily supporting the Ternan family and looking after Ellen and Maria. On occasion he had his proofs sent to him at Ellen's house. Kate Dickens believed that they had a child together, who died in infancy. He was, at any rate, deeply devoted to this woman who would always remain (she was twenty-seven years younger than he) the embodiment of eternal youth. The only unhappiness was leaving her as, for example, he was forced to do in 1867, when he went on a reading tour of America. He conceived the idea that she might join him there. He would look the place over and decide. If, shortly after his arrival in America, he telegraphed "All well," then Ellen was to join him. If he telegraphed "Safe and well," she was to stay put. The telegraph was to be sent to W. H. Wills, his assistant editor at *All the Year Round*, who would forward it both to Ellen in Italy and to Georgina at Gad's Hill, but of course only Ellen would know what it really meant.[53] The telegraph "Safe and Well" went out, and Ellen remained in Florence with her sister, receiving letters from Dickens forwarded through Wills so there would be no direct communication between the lovers. In this Dickens was a model of discretion. Indeed the affair with Ellen Ternan forced Dickens to lead a secret and subterranean existence. He could not allow her to be seen with him publicly (although he travelled with her, and she and Mrs. Ternan were with him when he was in a railway accident at Staplehurst), and she could not be received at Gad's Hill Place to mix with his daughters.

A powerful and new type of character appears in Dickens's later work, a man divided and tormented. Bradley Headstone, the schoolmaster in *Our Mutual Friend*, whose frustrated passion for Lizzie Hexam leads him to plan the murder of the man Lizzie loves, is one of these striking figures in later Dickens who seems to live two separate lives—an underground, volcanic emotional life and a placid, repressed life of service. In *Edwin Drood*'s John Jasper—a choirmaster in a quiet cathedral town who takes opium, has possibly murdered his own nephew, and is probably a devotee of the Indian goddess of destruction, Kali—the contrast between the underground life and the surface life of respectability verges on schizophrenia. In both cases, the man occupies a conspicuously respectable position in his community. His passionate emotional life is secret. He can find no way to integrate the two. The emotional impulses—the drive to emotional and sexual satisfaction—are imagined as destructive and murderous. In portraying these men who carry their respectability around with them like a burden, Dickens showed that he had come to understand imaginatively in his later years the truth that Freud was to articulate in *Civilization and Its Discontents*, that the achievements of civilization require a suppression of instinctual drives, that lust and aggression had to be ridden over and trodden down in order for books to be written, laws to be passed, families to survive. And he also understood that this got harder, rather than easier, to do as one aged.

I suspect that *The Frozen Deep* served as the template for the divided path of Dickens's later life, providing a structure for emotions and impulses obscurely felt. Two men, united by their love for one woman, deadly rivals, one of whom sacrifices himself for the other: Dickens would repeat the triangular pattern in *A Tale of Two Cities*. In *Our Mutual Friend*, the other possibility is played out when Bradley Headstone actually plans to kill his rival. But the triangularity becomes most interesting when the two rivals exist within the same man, as in John Jasper, whose waking rational side vows to destroy the other side, the drugged, murderous worshipper of Kali. By amalgamating the two instincts—towards self-sacrifice and towards self-indulgence—in one person, by merging into one figure the two men who are rivals in love, Dickens worked his way towards a psychological formulation way beyond in subtlety anything in his early fiction. It is a formulation of psychic economy especially congenial to the late nineteenth century and to our own post-Freudian age, and recent biographers of Dickens, picking up on it, invariably emphasize Dickens's enjoyment of his public readings of the murder of Nancy by Sikes—how his pulse would shoot up dangerously when he read that passage. They stress the writer's criminal sympathies and the way he sublimated his erotic and murderous energies into fiction and performance. I would add that the woman for whom the darker part of himself had to be sacrificed so that the other part of him could live was certainly not Catherine and not Ellen Ternan, either. It was the British public, his feminine abstraction, that ultimately demanding woman he had created for himself and could never ultimately satisfy.

Dickens may have felt he was bottling himself up, sacrificing his happiness for respectability, but in fact he neither stifled himself nor erupted self-destructively. He continued to write. For all the secrecy —perhaps because of it—he had a more satisfying life with Ellen Ternan than he had had with his wife. In however inept and muddled a fashion, he remade his life to suit himself for such "afternoon" as he had left to him. (He lived twelve years after his separation from Catherine, dying at fifty-eight.) In later life, he tended to have sympathy for any man he met who was unsuitably married. And he showed, in his writings, an understanding of repression in men and of complex erotic appeal in women. Moreover, there is something compelling in the gigantic, unself-conscious theatricality of Dickens's flailing against middle age and domesticity. There is something grand about living as though no one had ever lived before. He acted his plight out on the grand scale, in expectation of a matching grand-scale sympathy which never came.

But it must be said that Dickens seems to have learned little about himself from his sufferings—and less about the suffering of others. As he transferred all the blame to his wife in the matter of his marriage, he blamed most of his woes in later life on his male children, accusing them of shiftlessness and lack of energy, which they had inherited—as he thought—from their mother. Dickens's emotional development is not inspirational. It is a story of survival merely and proves only, as Jung said about his own reprehensible behavior to a young woman, that sometimes it is necessary to be unworthy in order to continue living.[54]

If, for Dickens, the upheaval in 1858 was to the good, allowing life to continue, the price for his wife was a kind of living death. His behavior towards her, accentuated by his self-righteous posturing, seems little short of murderous. Deprived of her children, deprived of any role, Catherine lived for twenty years after the separation. She lived quietly, like a lady, in the modest house in Gloucester Crescent. She remained very fat. When their son Walter died suddenly in 1864, Dickens did not even send her a note. When Dickens himself died, no one troubled to invite her to the funeral, although the scrupulous Miss Burdett-Coutts paid a formal condolence call on Catherine at Gloucester Crescent and not, as others did, on Georgina Hogarth at Gad's Hill. Catherine felt she had been wronged and hoped that posterity would vindicate her. Near the end of her life, she gave the letters which Charles Dickens had written to her in the course of their life together to her daughter Kate, with the request that they be published. She thought the letters, filled with expressions of devotion and affection, proved that at least there had been a time when Dickens loved her.

Kate did not agree. She found the expressions of love in the letters perfunctory. She thought they showed that even before his marriage Dickens had been resigned to doing without the kind of companionship he craved. She did not see his heart and soul in these letters, and she feared that others might eventually turn up (letters to Ellen Ternan) in which his heart and soul *did* appear, making the letters to Catherine look all the more hypocritical. In the late 1890s, she was thinking of destroying the correspondence her mother had entrusted to her.

It took George Bernard Shaw, whom she consulted on the matter, to convince Kate to save the letters and donate them to the British Museum. It took Shaw to get her to see that a case could be made for her mother. For Kate was an old-fashioned romantic, and she liked the story of a great man mismated and dragged down by an inferior woman. Shaw did not. He argued that "the sentimental sympathy of the nineteenth century with the man of genius tied to a commonplace wife had been rudely upset by a writer named Ibsen." He predicted that posterity would sympathize more with the woman sacrificed to her husband's uxoriousness to the extent of being made to bear ten children in sixteen years than with the man whose grievance only amounted to the fact "that she was not a female Charles Dickens."[55] Shaw seems to have convinced Kate thoroughly, for she later co-operated with Gladys Storey in the first attempt to tell the story of the Dickenses' separation from Mrs. Dickens's point of view. *Dickens and Daughter*, published in 1939, based on conversations between Gladys Storey and Kate Dickens Collins Perugini in 1923, is dedicated to the memory of Mrs. Perugini and of her mother, Mrs. Charles Dickens.

Although he thought he was unique, Charles Dickens, in his unrest and his impulse to blame it on the person with whom he had chosen to spend his life, was probably representative of many. Trying to be good, wanting to be loved, he made himself known in his own time as a model of (as they would have put it) ungentlemanly behavior. For us he provides a fine example of how not to end a marriage.

GEORGE
ELIOT
and
GEORGE
HENRY
LEWES

1854 – 1878

Prelude:
The Carlyles and the
Visiting Australian

One afternoon in their house on Cheyne Row, the Carlyles entertained a visitor from Australia. They had known Gavan Duffy for twenty years, from the days when he was a firebrand in Irish nationalist politics and an agitator for tenants' rights. They had known him when he was jailed by the English for treason. Ten years before, despairing of Ireland, he had gone to Australia, Britain's California, the land of opportunity, determined to prove that a man who had been called a traitor by the English in Ireland could rise to the top of the government of a free colony. By the time he came to visit London in 1865, he had already proved it. He was minister of lands for that vast continent. In the future he would rise even higher before retiring to devote himself to literary works, one of which, *Conversations with Carlyle*, would contain every word he could remember that the sage of Chelsea had uttered in their decades of friendship.

This day, as the three sat chatting in the second-floor drawing room, shielded from drafts by the folding screen which Jane Carlyle had covered in découpage with scenes of antique heroism and pathos, Duffy was paying close attention in order to be Boswell to Carlyle's Johnson. The latter-day Johnson was in a vile mood. He had been working on his biography of Frederick the Great for thirteen years, and now that he was nearing the end, far from feeling relieved, he feared that no one would read the book which, by taking so long to write, had blighted his life. When Duffy asked him if he would write another historical work after finishing *Frederick*, Carlyle answered grumpily. No one should be encouraged to write books at all these days, for nothing but junk was applauded—junk writers like Lamartine, with his windy platitudes, and George Sand, with her eroticism posing as morality.

From George Sand, it was but a short step to talking of sex and London's own female George.

Was it consistent, asked Mrs. Carlyle, to attack George Sand as a teacher of morals and to make so much of George Eliot in that respect? George Eliot, a moralist! Really, Mrs. Carlyle had to laugh. "When we first heard that the strong woman of the *Westminster Review* had gone off with a man we all know, it was as startling as if we had heard that a woman we knew went off with the strong man in the circus. But that the partners in this enterprise set themselves up as moralists was even more of a surprise. A marvelous teacher of morals, surely, and still more marvelous in that other character, for which nature has not provided her with the outfit supposed to be essential."

Duffy was flattered by this allusion to the personal appearance of literary London's most celebrated illicit couple. It included him among those who knew.

"And the gallant," he said (referring to Lewes), "the gallant is just as badly equipped as an Adonis and conqueror of hearts."

"The ugliest little fellow you could meet anywhere," said the sage of Chelsea. "But lively and pleasant."

For his guest's benefit, Carlyle explained that Lewes had been married to the pretty daughter of a disreputable member of Parliament from Wales. But she had openly produced all those dirty, sooty-skinned children whose father was Thornton Hunt. The household had broken bounds in all directions before he had met Miss Evans. So if he was now living sinfully with her, at least it could not be said he had broken up a healthy home in order to do so.

"His proceeding with Miss Evans is not to be applauded, but it can scarcely be said that he has gone from bad to worse."[1]

A Second Birth

It is so easy, looking backward, knowing the glorious fruits of a life, to assume that the glory was always evident, that the person destined for immortality looked confidently forward to his or her success, that people at the time acted deferentially and helpfully towards the one posterity would consider glorious. Nothing could be further from the truth of the life of George Eliot, who, at the time we begin her story was not George Eliot but Marian Evans, middle-aged, physically unattractive, lonely.

In 1851, after spending the first thirty years of her life in the Midlands, in and around Coventry, she began working in London for the *Westminster Review*, a liberal periodical of some stature which had been particularly distinguished when it was owned by John Stuart Mill and which now belonged to John Chapman, the publisher and bookseller.[2] Chapman and Marian Evans were the entire editorial staff of the *Westminster*, and since Chapman's time was heavily committed to his other businesses, Miss Evans virtually ran the magazine herself. She conceived and commissioned articles, did copy-editing, read proof, and wrote some of the copy—particularly the connective copy in the long surveys of new work abroad and in England. Although the work was unpaid and she had to live on the interest from a legacy of £2,000 left by her father, it provided her with an excellent education in contemporary thought and literature.

Superficially, her life was full. She boarded with the Chapmans, who had a large house in the Strand.[3] She participated in their complicated family life: Chapman's mistress was his children's governess and lived with the family; both wife and mistress recognized Miss Evans's presence as a further complication and watched constantly for signs of her attachment to Chapman evolving beyond the tolerable. The situation in the Chapman household must have been interesting but could hardly have been satisfying for the woman who was neither wife nor mistress. Still, there were pleasant social evenings. The Chapmans gave evening parties almost every week, and Miss Evans was always invited. Some of the people she met there—for example, Sir James Clark, the queen's physician—liked her so much that they invited her to dine at their homes. Most people were impressed by her intelligence, by her grey eyes, and by her voice, a deep, lovely instrument from which the provincial accent had been trained out when she was at boarding school in her teens. Ralph Waldo Emerson said of her, "That lady has a calm, serious soul."

Through her work for the *Westminster*, Miss Evans met Herbert Spencer, who was about her own age and held a position similar to hers on *The Economist*. His first book, *Social Statics*, had recently been published. It also happened that he lived just across the street from the Chapmans. With so much in common—scientific and philosophical interests, extraordinary intelligence, a taste for music—he and Miss Evans spent a lot of time together. He got reviewer's tickets to the opera, theater, and concerts, and Miss Evans was his favorite companion.

They enjoyed each other's company so much that it became a problem. Spencer, a man not conspicuous for social daring, was afraid that people might assume they were engaged because they appeared together in public so often. Even worse, Miss Evans herself might think that he was in love with her. He knew he was not in love with her and was never likely to be. He found her, with some reason, physically unappealing, and the lack of physical attraction was fatal. As strongly as his judgment prompted him to love her, his instincts would not respond.[4] He took the extraordinary step of warning her that he did not love her and had no intention of doing so. Then, embarrassed by his own lack of tact, he wrote another letter apologizing for having hurt her.

Miss Evans's response was characteristically self-deprecating. "I feel disappointed rather than 'hurt' that you should not have sufficiently divined my character to perceive how remote it is from my habitual state of mind to imagine that anyone is falling in love with me."[5] But despite the warning that her love would not be returned, she fell in love with him, or, more precisely, her passionate desire that there should be love in her life came to focus on Spencer. He was available. He was her equal. He was appropriate. He would do.

Aware of the unconventionality of her behavior, she made a declaration of her feelings, asking for his love. He said he could not give it. She asked, then, for merely his companionship and the promise that he would not attach himself to someone else, abandoning her. If that happened, she said, she must die, but short of that she could gather courage from his friendship to carry on with her work and to make her life useful. "I do not ask you to sacrifice anything—I would be very good and cheerful and never annoy you. But I find it impossible to contemplate life under any other conditions."

> Those who have known me best have always said that if I ever loved anyone thoroughly my whole life must turn upon that feeling, and I find they said truly. You curse the destiny which has made the feeling concentrate itself on you—but if you will only have patience with me you shall not curse it long. You will find that I can be satisfied with very little, if I am delivered from the dread of losing it.[6]

I do not want to weaken the impact of this letter, surely one of the saddest I have ever read, but lest Marian Evans sound entirely like a love-starved spinster, pathetically abasing herself for a crumb of affection, I must point out the letter's ending, which sounds another note. "I suppose no woman ever before wrote such a letter as this—but I am not ashamed of it, for I am conscious that in light of reason and true refinement I am worthy of your respect and tenderness, whatever gross men or vulgar-minded women might think of me." If the need for affection was characteristic of her, so too was pride in her radical rethinking of how to live, pride in the difference between her morality and that of most men and women. The strength of her desire to love and be loved was matched by the energy and daring she was willing to devote to satisfying that desire.

Still, she had been rejected, and it was a hard thing to take. Her self-esteem could hardly have been lower. When she told a friend in Coventry that she was being taken to the opera (for Spencer continued to perform that essential service), she said, "See what a fine thing it is to pick up people who are short-sighted enough to like one." It seemed that going to the opera would be the only sensual pleasure she would ever know. "What a wretched lot of old shrivelled creatures we shall be bye-and-bye."[7]

You would not say of all thirty-three-year-old women that they are middle-aged, but you would certainly have said it of Marian Evans in the summer of 1852. She felt the best was behind her; she looked into the future and saw no sources of renewal. She feared that old friends would die and that she wouldn't have the power to make new ones. She feared she had missed out on life. "You know how sad one feels when a great procession has swept by one, and the last notes of its music have died away, leaving one alone with the fields and sky. I feel so about life sometimes." A passage from Margaret Fuller's journal was achingly appropriate. "I shall always reign through the intellect, but the life! the life! Oh my God! shall that never be sweet?"[8]

At her advanced age, she could hardly hope for marriage. Even when she had been young, her father and brother had considered her a poor prospect. She was too ugly. Her only asset on the marriage market was her piety, and when she lost that her brother was furious, partly with the fury of the outraged religious conservative and partly with that of the property-owner whose tenant sublets to a welfare family. By the time of his death, her father must have given up hoping a husband would take over the care of Marian—hence the legacy, to enable her to be independent. Marian must have given up herself.

Yet she had a strongly affectionate nature, supported by a philosophical conviction that people should devote themselves to the happiness of others. In a phrase that she would use to describe some of her heroines, she was ardent, longing to attach herself to other people, other goals. How long can such a person survive as merely a welcome guest at other people's dinner parties? She longed for closer attachments, for an emotional connection which would be central to her life, from which new interests and activities would result as naturally as children result from lovemaking. Although she had accomplished a great deal (her translation of Strauss's *Life of Jesus* was an important contribution to progressive thought), although she had a position of some stature in literary London, although she enjoyed the respect and affection of everyone who met her, although—in sum—her lot was enviable compared to that of most unmarried women in Victorian England, she was lonely. Her powerful imagination could conceive of a life much richer than the one she led. As active as she was, she felt she could be doing more—and events would prove her right. She would look back on these years as a time of inertia and suffering. Her great energy, burning to be put to other uses—nurturing, intimacy, creativity—turned back upon herself for lack of an object. Idle, she brooded; brooding, she despaired.

To avoid feeling sorry for herself, she tried to suppress any awareness of her emotions at all. "If you insist on my writing about 'Emotions,'" she said to one friend, "why, I must get some up expressly for the purpose. But I must own I would rather not, for it is the grand wish and object of my life to get rid of them as far as possible, seeing that they have already had more than their share of my nervous energy."[9] In describing herself, she used the word *plucky* rather than *happy*. She would carry on, with resolute cheerfulness but not with joy, and it seems hardly likely that in this "carried-on" life the writing of fiction would have figured. Those parts of herself she would need in writing novels—passion, sympathy, dramatic power—were too close to the parts of herself she would have had to stifle in order to remain a plucky spinster.

Herbert Spencer was feeling so guilty that he even mentioned marriage to Miss Evans, as a kind of restitution for having engaged her emotions. But she was not interested in the mere form of intimacy. Still, he continued to see her, and one day George Henry Lewes[10] asked if he might join Spencer in his visit to Miss Evans. Another day, to Spencer's vast relief, Lewes decided to stay on alone with Miss Evans after Spencer left.

John Chapman had introduced them in 1851. He and his assistant happened to run into the literary journalist in a bookstore in the

Burlington Arcade. Lewes and Thornton Leigh Hunt had recently begun publishing *The Leader*, a radical weekly for which Hunt wrote the political sections and Lewes covered theater, music, and books. Despite his position in the literary world of the capital, Lewes did not make much of an impression on Miss Evans. Physically, he was unprepossessing—short and scruffy. And although he was the best writer you could get for a certain kind of scientific subject (exactly the right man, for example, for an essay on Lamarck), Miss Evans the editor valued him less as a writer and thinker than many other contributors to the *Westminster*. He had nowhere near the intellectual stature of John Stuart Mill, nor even of Froude, F. W. Newman, or James Martineau. He was a witty man who cultivated—in the Gallic fashion—a flippant manner, and this, too, did not impress the earnest Miss Evans. And he was, of course, married. Mrs. Lewes had recently given birth to her sixth child.

By the spring of 1853, Miss Evans's opinion of Lewes had changed. She now found him genial and amusing. "Like a few other people in the world, he is much better than he seems, a man of heart and conscience wearing a mask of flippancy."[11] Lewes, like Spencer, was supplied with free tickets to theater, opera, and concerts, and he took Miss Evans along with him. At some point, Lewes must have told her the truth about his marriage, and that more than anything—more than his kindness and attentiveness, more than the free tickets—must have changed her mind about him. Here was a man who needed her.

Lewes had married Agnes Jervis in 1841. She was then a beautiful nineteen-year-old with striking blonde hair, and the two seemed very much in love. Mrs. Carlyle, for one, got pleasure from seeing them together. But by 1849 she noticed a change. "I used to think these Leweses a perfect pair of lovebirds, . . . but the female lovebird appears to have hopped off to some distance and to be now taking a somewhat critical view of her little shaggy mate!" Jane Carlyle saw acutely. Mrs. Lewes had in fact hopped so far from her husband that she was having an affair with his close friend and partner, Thornton Leigh Hunt. (Hunt was married, too.) The child born to Agnes Lewes in the month that her husband was introduced to Miss Evans in the bookstore was fathered not by Lewes (the father of her first three children) but by Hunt. It was her third child by Hunt.

Agnes, her husband, and her lover all had views on sex and love that would have been called at the time "free-thinking" or "advanced" by some, "libertine" by others. They were inheritors of a heady eighteenth-century rationalist tradition: what was endorsed by religion and society was not always right. If anything, inherited institutions and traditional authorities were likely to be stupidly tyrannical. One had to be on the lookout. One had to rethink everything. One had to beware of authority. One had to rebel. Mr. and Mrs. Lewes believed that only love could bind people together and that neither law nor religion had it in its power to cement a union where feeling no longer existed. And although traditionally, by law, a woman's body belonged to her husband, they believed it was her own, to give to whomever she chose.

Taking the high rationalist line, Lewes refused to be outraged by his wife's infidelity. He registered no complaint when she gave birth to another man's child, and even allowed the baby to be given his name, in a spirit, one supposes, of communal responsibility—a spirited "no" to the pedantry of precise acknowledgment. He must have thought that Agnes's passion for Hunt would pass in time, or that a rational, sophisticated man who admired Gallic insouciance ought to be able to live with the fact of his wife's infidelity. In 1850 he believed in what was much later given the name of "open marriage." But in October 1851, when Agnes gave birth to another child he had not fathered, Lewes began to realize that what he had was not an open marriage, or a radical, free-thinkers' marriage, but no marriage at all. By the start of 1853, when Agnes was pregnant yet again by Hunt, Lewes had ceased to think of her as his wife, although he continued to support her and her children.

English law was not adapted to such subtleties of thought and behavior. It understood that a man had the right to exclusive enjoyment, sexually speaking, of his wife. It was horrified at the possibility that a man might have to pass his property on to children who were not really his. That, if nothing else, was sufficient reason for the strong stand the law took against adultery—that is to say, female adultery. Even before the Matrimonial Causes Act of 1857, English law allowed a man—albeit with great trouble and at vast expense—to divorce his wife for adultery.[12] But the law did not allow for quirky, eccentric attempts to live rationally, for private understandings of what did and did not constitute adultery. One illegitimate child was quite enough to convince the law that a man's wife had abandoned his protection, and if a man chose to wait for a second illegitimate child before he was convinced, then in the eyes of the law he had condoned his wife's adultery and forfeited his right to divorce her. That was George Lewes's situation when he began seeing Marian Evans daily and escorting her to the opera. In law, he had a wife, but in fact he did not. Legally tied to a woman from whom he could expect no love, no help, no comfort, he was in as much despair about his emotional life as was, for other reasons, Miss Evans.

In October 1853, the month that Agnes's third child by Hunt was born, Marian Evans moved out of the Chapmans' house, where she had come to feel claustrophobic, and into lodgings of her own in Cambridge Street. Now she had more freedom. She could receive whatever visitors she chose. When she turned thirty-four in the following month, she noted that she began her new year happier than usual. The signs of a closer professional tie with Lewes appear. When Chapman accepted a negative review by T. H. Huxley of Lewes's book on Comte, Marian intervened on her friend's behalf, begging Chapman not to run Huxley's piece. And when, in April, Lewes got sick and was unable to work, she wrote some of his copy for him. "No opera and no fun for me for the next month!"[13] Lewes's health did not improve swiftly or completely enough to suit either of them, and they began to talk about going to the Continent for his health. In July of 1854 they left England for Weimar, travelling together openly and sharing lodgings. From this moment on, until Lewes's death twenty-four years later, they would live together as though they were married.

From the beginning, they were delighted with each other and saw their union as a rebirth. "The day seems too short for our happiness, and we both of us feel that we have begun life afresh—with new ambitions and new powers."[14] They moved from Weimar, which they loved, to Berlin, and with the self-satisfaction of fresh love felt pity for anyone who had to come to such an ugly place alone or with a disagreeable companion. For them, even Berlin was charming. "I am happier every day," wrote Miss Evans to John Chapman, the one person to whom she felt free to describe her illicit happiness (presumably the lecherous publisher was proof against shock), "and find my domesticity more and more delightful and beneficial to me. Affection, respect, and intellectual sympathy deepen, and for the first time in my life I can say to the moments *'Verweilen sie, sie sind so schön.'* "[15]

"The literary couple," wrote Elizabeth Hardwick, "is a peculiar English domestic manufacture, useful no doubt in a country with difficult winters. Before the bright fire at tea-time, we can see these high-strung men and women clinging together, their inky fingers touching."[16] One has reason to envy the intellectual compatibility of Miss Evans and Mr. Lewes. They walked together, wrote together, read Homer, and learned languages together. Lewes's scientific interests were a source of new delight to Miss Evans; they even raised tadpoles together. Every night after dinner they read aloud to each other, for as much as three hours. On a typical evening she would begin with an enjoyable book (Boswell's *Life of Johnson*, for example), then subside to a dreary and dry one (Whewell's *History of the Inductive Sciences*), and then wind up with some German poetry, Heine perhaps. They read aloud the third volume of Ruskin's *Modern Painters*, and they read aloud Elizabethan plays.

Their new domestic life centered on work. Lewes was in the midst of writing his excellent *Life of Goethe* and Marian Evans was doing a translation of Spinoza which was destined never to be published. In addition, they wrote articles and reviews because they were constantly in need of money to support Agnes and her children as well as themselves. And what a lot of work they got done! Together they wrote almost half *The Leader*'s supplement for June 16, 1855, Miss Evans contributing a review essay, "Menander and Greek Comedy," and Lewes writing articles on Sydney Smith, Isaac Newton, and Owen Meredith, as well as a review of a French book on longevity.

Although posterity has reversed their positions, in 1855 when they returned from Germany and settled on the south side of the Thames in the London suburbs, Lewes was by far the more established professionally of the two, and with the self-assurance of the successful, he took more pleasure in Marian's success than in his own. His encouragement and his example of professionalism helped her to develop quickly from an editor into a freelance writer.[17] With money as motivation and with a little praise, he coaxed out her inclination to authorship.

She had long thought of writing fiction and had actually written the first chapter of a novel—a description of a Staffordshire village and the neighboring farmhouses. Gordon Haight estimates the date of composition as 1846. But she laid the fragment aside, never going further. "As the years passed on I lost hope that I should ever be able to write a novel, just as I desponded about everything else in my future life."[18] Some writers, as Freud believed, thrive artistically on misery. They write only when and because life seems to offer no other source of satisfaction. They write to create for themselves, in imagination, the satisfactions that reality seems to deny. But George Eliot was a writer of the other sort, for whom productivity depends upon contentment. In this way, too, she was a realist: she could not create her happiness through fictions, had to proceed to her work from a bedrock of fulfilled life.

When they went to Germany, Miss Evans took along with her the fragmentary chapter she had written years before, and one night in Berlin she read it aloud to Lewes. I want to underline that Lewes did not encourage her to bring the manuscript. She says it "happened to be among the papers" she brought with her. Nor did Lewes encourage her to read it aloud. "Something led me to read it to George."[19] Demurely, girlishly, she was blurring the traces of her own activity, and I emphasize the extent to which she took the initiative in this matter because history has so readily perpetuated the fiction that she was the passive party in the birth of George Eliot. But just as she was unafraid to ask for love from Herbert Spencer, she was aggressive enough to raise the possibility of writing novels to Lewes. All she needed in order to continue was the encouragement she had every human reason to expect he would offer in response.

Lewes's reaction to her reading of the fragmentary chapter could hardly be called overwhelming. On the basis of what he heard, he thought she might be able to write fiction, but he had his doubts. It was wholly descriptive, and everything else she had written was expository. In general, her mind seemed so powerfully analytic that one did not expect her to be creative. He wondered whether she would have the dramatic power necessary for fiction writing—the ability to imagine other people's thoughts and to invent dialogue for them. This was exactly her own doubt. Still she was sufficiently encouraged to continue to think about writing fiction, and as time went by, perhaps sensing her desire for such encouragement, Lewes urged her even more strongly: positively, she must try to write a story. He thought she might be able to pull it off by the sheer force of her intelligence.

One morning her desire to write finally coincided with sufficient self-confidence to form a resolution to do so. "As I was lying in bed, thinking what should be the subject of my first story, my thoughts merged themselves into a dreamy doze, and I imagined myself writing a story the title of which was—'The Sad Fortunes of the Reverend Amos Barton.' "[20] When she told Lewes about it, he said, "O what a capital title!" And so she set to work. To Lewes's amazement, the very first chapter of "Amos Barton" convinced him that her dialogue was excellent. The only other question was whether she could command pathos. Did it follow that a person who was strong in intelligence was correspondingly feeble in feeling, or that an analytical mind could not also imagine fiercely? One night in the fall of 1856 Lewes went to town on purpose to give her quiet to write, and she set out to prove she could evoke emotion, in treating the death of Milly, Amos Barton's wife. She was determined that the old dualistic chestnut about intelligence and emotion be laid to rest. She knew herself to be a deeply feeling woman as well as an intelligent one. When Lewes returned and read aloud what she had written, both of them were moved to tears. He went over to her, kissed her, and said, "I think your pathos is even better than your fun."[21]

Lewes sent "Amos Barton" to John Blackwood in Edinburgh, who, with his characteristic reticence, said the piece "would do." He ran it in *Blackwood's Magazine* and later published the completed series, *Scenes of Clerical Life*. Although Blackwood was aware that

"George Eliot" was a pseudonym, he believed his new author was a man, in all probability, a clergyman.[22]

To say that George Eliot was the child of the extraordinarily happy union of Marian Evans and George Henry Lewes is more than word-play.[23] Literary parthenogenesis being as impossible for Miss Evans as the biological sort is generally impossible, George Eliot would almost certainly not have entered the world without Lewes's participation. But what exactly was his role, the dynamics of his contribution? The usual explanation—that Marian was "not fitted to stand alone" and needed someone to lean on—is subtly misleading, making England's strongest woman novelist seem deficient and dependent.

The myth of George Eliot's dependency—a myth she may have chosen to perpetuate for her own purposes—originates with a phrenological reading of her character made in her Coventry days. Like many intellectuals of her time she looked to phrenology as a way of understanding herself, as contemporary intellectuals look to psychoanalysis. Charles Bray, her Coventry mentor, took her to London to have a cast made of her head for a phrenological reading. The reading confirmed that in her brain development Intellect vastly predominated. "Feelings" expressed themselves in another part of the topography of the skull, and from the bumps in that area, the skilled phrenologist could tell that Miss Evans's "Animal" and "Moral" instincts were about equal. The moral feelings were sufficient to keep the animal in order and in proper subservience but they were not "spontaneously active." In addition, her social feelings were very active, particularly "adhesiveness," a phrenological term for non-sexual love. "She was of a most affectionate disposition," Bray reported, paraphrasing the phrenologist, "always requiring someone to lean upon, preferring what has hitherto been considered the stronger sex, to the other and more impressible. She was not fitted to stand alone."[24]

Phrenologically speaking, Marian Evans had feared for a long time that her moral and animal regions were unfortunately balanced. That is to say, she felt herself to be a sensual person. When her father was alive, she had associated him with the restraining, moral part of herself, and when he died she suffered from a horrid image of herself "becoming earthly sensual and devilish for want of that purifying restraining influence."[25] The phrenological reading confirmed her fears about the sluggishness of her moral region: it was "not spontaneously active." But the part of her phrenological reading that posterity has chosen to emphasize is her dependence, the notion that she required someone to lean on, preferably a man, that she was not fitted to stand alone.[26]

In support of this characterization, we are told how Marian Evans threw herself at the feet of the aged Dr. Brabant, the Biblical scholar, offering to devote herself to his work. We are told how she repeatedly mistook intellectual friendships offered by men for offers of sexual love. We are told how, ignoring conventions, she paid men like Dr. Brabant the utmost attention, causing consternation in their families. We hear about the wife and mistress of John Chapman—how jealous they were of Miss Evans's intimacy with Chapman and how threatened they felt when she moved into their household. We are told about her attempt to throw herself on Herbert Spencer and the relief with which she sank onto the proffered arm of the already married George Henry Lewes. And in all this we are supposed to see a "need" —not a desire, mind you, but a neurotic "need"—for affection. In the face of all these terrified wives and families, of men who realize with dismay that this gentle woman who has captivated them wants even more than they thought—we are supposed to see a woman who cannot stand alone. What I see is a woman of passionate nature who struggles, amidst limited opportunity, to find someone to love and to love her; a woman who goes to quite unconventional lengths and is willing to be unusually aggressive—almost predatory—in her efforts to secure for herself what she wants. To want love and sex in one's life is hardly, after all, a sign of neurosis. And is it a sign of dependence for a woman to want love and sex from a man? It is a small matter of emphasis only, but it does seem to me to make some difference whether we think of one of the most powerful female writers ever as neurotically dependent on men or as brave enough to secure for herself what she wanted.

"Under the influence of the intense happiness I have enjoyed in my married life from thorough moral and intellectual sympathy, I have at last found out my true vocation after which my nature has always been feeling and striving without finding it."[27] I take seriously this account of how George Eliot seized her identity as a writer. I see the story of George Eliot's "birth" as a moving testimony to the connection there may be between creativity and sexuality. Lewes's editorial help and his encouragement at the start of her writing career were certainly important in George Eliot's birth, but they were responses to gestures Miss Evans made. They were not the motivating force. That came from inside her, welling up along with the joy, the self-esteem, and the sense of fulfillment which followed her belated acquisition of love. It was a second spring in her life, and its warmth released powers inside her which had been held back, powers which might earlier have drowned her meager, virginal equanimity.

Living in Sin

Although the union of Marian Evans and George Henry Lewes has been legitimized by time and by its progeny—the literary career of George Eliot—at the time it caused great scandal. We have heard the Carlyles' indignant reaction to the elopement a good ten years after it occurred, and we know the extent of Thomas Carlyle's sympathy— that it could not be said that Lewes had gone from bad to worse. It is, of course, one of life's persistent disappointments that a great moral crisis in my life is nothing but matter for gossip in yours. Still, it is somewhat of a shock to me that Carlyle's response to the moral complexities of the Lewes-Evans affair was so briskly superficial. The man who fervently believed that new times needed to generate new institutions did not, evidently, apply this belief to the institution of marriage. Nor did he see the relationship between a man and a woman as fit matter for anything but comedy.

For Marian Evans, on the other hand, falling in love with a man who could not marry her was a test case in personal ethics at the profoundest level. The relationship between a man and woman was to her as important as the relationship between human being and God had once been—the centrally serious business of life, an index of the degree of meaning you could infuse into the occupation of living. "Assuredly if there is any subject on which I feel no levity it is that of marriage and the relation of the sexes—if there is any one action or relation of my life which is and always has been profoundly serious, it is my relation with Mr. Lewes."[28] To a contemporary audience whose ethical arena has become almost exclusively the matter of what we call "relationships," George Eliot should seem a congenial figure.

By the time she went to Germany with Lewes in July 1854 (the same month that Effie Gray obtained the annulment of her marriage to Ruskin), Marian Evans had given a great deal of thought to the ethics and consequences of her actions. She did not live lightly in any case, and this seemed to her the major decision of her life. Piously evangelical in her youth, she had ceased, in her twenties, to believe in the literal truth of Christianity, whose myths, rituals, and worldly forms she rejected while clinging to its ethical spirit. She practiced— and many people in the twentieth century have followed where she and others like her in the nineteenth century led—a Christianity without faith, emphasizing *caritas*, good works and acts of loving-kindness, instead of belief. She believed in duty and self-sacrifice. But where did duty lie? In pleasing family and friends by conforming to conventional codes of behavior, or in staying with the man she had willed into central importance in her life? And what was to be sacrificed, "that which is the deepest and gravest joy in human experience,"[29] or the greatest good life offers after that, friendship and the esteem of others?

Long before meeting Lewes, she had formulated a response to the same kind of moral dilemma when she found it posed in *Jane Eyre*. We may read *Jane Eyre* as a female *Bildungsroman*, in which Mr. Rochester is a secondary—not to say a fantasy—figure. But when it appeared, many people assumed that the wild tale of a mad wife in the attic and attempted bigamy was no more than accurate reporting of a social problem. Mr. Rochester's marital plight seemed so plausible to a contemporary audience that many people assumed the author, "Currer Bell," was a governess in the home of William Thackeray, whose wife was mad and had been locked away, yet from whom he could not obtain a divorce. (That the novel was dedicated to Thackeray encouraged this illusion.) What *was* a man to do whose wife, like Thackeray's, was insane, or whose wife, like Lewes's, had left him, albeit with his consent? All self-sacrifice is good, Miss Evans had thought upon reading *Jane Eyre*, but one would like it to be in a nobler cause than that "of a diabolical law which chains a man body and soul to a putrefying carcase."[30] She thought Jane Eyre ought to have lived with Rochester as his wife. She was puzzled by the mistaken understanding of duty which impelled a woman to abandon the man who loved and needed her simply because of a legal fiction. If the law said Rochester was married to the madwoman in the attic, if the law said Lewes was married to Agnes after she had had three children by another man, then the law (in the words of Dickens's Mr. Bumble) is a ass!

So for her, the moral issue was clear, however painful the consequences of her choice. On the one hand was an arid legalism which would bind Lewes to Agnes and would refuse to authorize her life with Lewes; on the other hand, a radical redefinition of what constituted marriage. She would call herself Mrs. Lewes. She would be his wife. Whether or not they uttered the ritual oaths of fidelity, they would stay together always. They would help each other in distress, and the responsibilities of one would be the responsibilities of the other. It was to be a regular marriage in every way but one: it was validated only by personal commitment. John Mill and Harriet Taylor had long before decided that in a matter so entirely personal no authority beyond themselves was relevant, but unlike them, Lewes and Miss Evans were prepared to act on their beliefs.

They believed that other rational people, not blinded by orthodox morality, could be brought to see things as they did. Of course most people were not rational—they knew that. Most people were immovably attached to a particular, restrictive narrow morality which they associated with the Church. Miss Evans would not even broach the subject to her brother, for example, for three years. She knew he was provincial and conservative. She knew she could not keep him and Lewes, both. She was prepared to give up her brother, to give up everyone, all her friends, her entire social life. That she would give them up if necessary was the bargain she made with her fate.

But everyone wants to be understood by at least *one* disinterested person. While they were still in Germany, Lewes and Miss Evans tried to explain their side of the matter to a few selected friends. Above all, they wanted to contradict the rumor that Miss Evans had seduced Mr. Lewes away from his wife and children. The Brays, Miss Evans's old friends in Coventry—intellectuals, writers, progressives—were her test case. She explained that Mr. Lewes had been in constant correspondence with his wife since they left England; that his wife had had all money due him in London; that he intended to separate from her but never intended to renounce his financial responsibility for her. She asked them to believe nothing they heard of her beyond the fact that she was attached to Lewes and living with him, which was scandalous enough. She pronounced herself quite willing to endure the consequences of the step she had deliberately taken.

How eagerly she must have waited for this letter to make its way to England and for the reply to reach Germany. She could imagine their refusing to have anything to do with her again. She could imagine their graciously congratulating her on her happiness and wishing her well. Either response would have been fine. But I doubt that she took into account the human desire to avoid important issues—or imagined that the Brays, however magnanimous, might find matter for offense in her letter quite apart from the issue so singularly present in Miss Evans's mind. In fact, the ladies were irritated because Marian, out of an exaggerated delicacy, had addressed the letter to Mr. Bray, and not, as was her custom, to Mrs. Bray and Miss Hennell as well. Were women, then, of no account? They were irritated, too, that she seemed so ready to give them up, seemed almost to be boasting of it.

Lewes turned for support to Carlyle, among other people, and here too there were comical cross-purposes. Lewes's explanation of his separation from Agnes was received by Carlyle with sympathy; he wrote back approving the dissolution of such a marriage. He filed Lewes's letter away in an envelope marked "G. H. Lewes and

'Strongminded Woman.' " But he wanted to be reassured that Lewes had not eloped with the strong-minded woman, and instead Lewes wrote back that the strong-minded woman had not caused the separation. "As well assure me her stockings are both of one colour; that is a very insignificant point! No answer to this second letter," Carlyle wrote to himself.

The people who passed the test were as distressing as those who failed it, for they were as likely to be libertines as not. John Chapman, for one, that practiced philanderer, had no trouble accepting the Lewes-Evans union—and using it for his own purposes. When he fell in love with the estimable Barbara Leigh Smith and tried to convince her to live with him openly, he held before her the example of Marian Evans and G. H. Lewes. "Rely upon it we shall be happy yet. Lewes and M.E. seemed to be perfectly so." This is exactly what most people predicted would be the result of such behavior as Miss Evans's —a bad example, an invitation to anarchy, a wedge in the stones of the temple walls. Marian herself, if she knew of it, would have been furious and chagrined. That was not what she had in mind.[31] But where *was* the line between free-thinking and libertinism to be drawn? When was unconventional behavior justified by one's deepest feelings, and when was one merely self-indulgent?

Few people in 1854 were willing to concede the morality of Mr. Lewes's and Miss Evans's position, and few bothered to distinguish between Lewes's high-minded behavior and the profligacy of Thornton Leigh Hunt, who continued to sleep with and father children upon his own wife while he was sleeping with and fathering children upon Agnes Lewes. (Twice the women gave birth to his children within two weeks of each other.) The venom which the sexual behavior of Lewes and of Hunt could arouse may be seen in a letter from Thomas Woolner, the sculptor and member of the Pre-Raphaelite Brotherhood, to William Bell Scott.

By the way—have you heard of two blackguard literary fellows, Lewes and Thornton Hunt? They seem to have used wives on the ancient Briton practice of having them in common: now blackguard Lewes bolted with a ——— and is living in Germany with her. I believe it is dangerous to write facts of anyone nowadays so I will not any further lift the mantel and display the filthy contaminations of these hideous satyrs and smirking moralists—these workers in the Agepomone—these Mormonites in another name—stink pots of humanity.[32]

George Combe, the great phrenologist and Charles Bray's mentor in that science, was mortified by the news of Miss Evans's elopement. Believing as he did in the physiological basis of all behavior, he wondered if there was a history of insanity in her family. "An educated woman who, in the face of the world, volunteers to live as a wife, with a man who already has a living wife and children, appears to me to pursue a course and to set an example calculated only to degrade herself and her sex, if she be sane."[33] He thought that Hunt, Lewes, and Miss Evans (he did not distinguish among them) had greatly hurt the cause of religious freedom, and he, for one, intended to cancel his subscription to *The Leader*.

His irritation forced his disciple, Bray, into an interesting defense of Miss Evans. Combe thought that believers in the "greatest happiness for the greatest number" principle had all the more to fulfill the obligations of married life. Bray, in Miss Evans's defense, replied that she and Lewes intended to fulfill the obligations of married life: the nature of those obligations was the issue. Showing he had understood Miss Evans's argument even if he didn't approve, he invoked the concept of natural law to distinguish between Lewes's state in regard to Agnes—legally married but unmarried in natural law—and his relationship to Miss Evans—legally unmarried but married in natural law.

But Combe remained unconvinced. Would it be doing justice to his own female domestic circle, he asked Mr. Bray, to re-admit this tainted woman to it? How would the other ladies feel about entering a circle which makes no distinction between women who act disreputably and those who keep their honor unspotted? The vulgar implication here, to be sure, is that if no social distinction were made between the spotted and the unspotted, a lady would hardly go to the trouble of keeping herself pure. There must have been, then as now, many people for whom the fear of social ostracism acted as the only check on behavior, as well as many more who simply took care that their indiscretions not be known. Marian Evans was particularly concerned to distinguish between her behavior and unprincipled hedonism. "Light and easily broken ties are what I neither desire theoretically nor could live for practically. Women who are satisfied with such ties do *not* act as I have done—they obtain what they desire and are still invited to dinner."[34]

But easy stories drive out complicated ones, and the most familiar and vulgar version of the matter will gain the widest currency. It was almost impossible for Miss Evans and Mr. Lewes to substitute for the popular tale of a *femme fatale* stealing another woman's husband the much subtler story of a husband, abandoned by his wife, refusing to abandon his own responsibilities to her, unable to divorce her yet unwilling to live with her, unable to re-marry yet constructing a relationship which was equivalent to marriage. Almost no one could accept the crucial point that Lewes was not *really* married at all.

"I do not well understand how a good and conscientious woman can run away with another woman's husband," said kindly Mrs. Jameson, who had, by her own choice, been separated from her own husband for twenty years. To her correspondent in Germany, Ottilie von Goethe, Goethe's daughter-in-law, Mrs. Jameson described Lewes's companion as first-rate in intellect and science and attainments of every kind, but "very *free* in all her opinions as to morals and religion."[35] One of the noteworthy things about the gossip occasioned by the Lewes elopement was how rarely the gossipers drew any connection between the scandalous story and the facts of their own lives. The closer people's plight to Miss Evans's or Lewes's, the more they seemed to cling to the differences. No wonder George Eliot would make a point in her fiction of the moral necessity of comparing experience. No wonder she understood so thoroughly the failure of most people to see their lives as analogous to anyone else's, and that this was the greatest failure of the imagination. Perhaps it was her experience of being the center of scandal that made her elevate tolerance and sympathy to the highest of virtues.

Over and over she asserted how serious, how moral (if rightly understood) her union was. She insisted she had nothing to hide. "I have done nothing with which any person has the right to interfere. I have surely full liberty to travel in Germany and to travel with Mr.

Lewes. No one here seems to find it at all scandalous that we should be together."[36] That, to Chapman. To Bray she insisted she was her own master. She was too old, she told him, for people to suppose he was answerable for her. "So far as my friends and acquaintances are inclined to occupy themselves with my affairs, I am grateful to them and sorry they should have pain on my account, but I cannot think their digestion will be much hindered by anything that befalls a person about whom they troubled themselves very little while she lived in privacy and loneliness."[37] Although she realized how unconventional her behavior was, she had taken the measure of her infraction and was prepared to pay, without irritation or bitterness, the price of renunciation by all her friends, certain in the knowledge that the person she devoted herself to was worth any sacrifice. (Certain, too, that what she gave up was inessential to her, "a person about whom her friends troubled themselves very little while she lived in privacy and loneliness.") Friends to whom she wrote explaining her behavior were sometimes offended by the self-congratulation they detected in her words.

That any unworldly, unsuperstitious person who is sufficiently acquainted with the realities of life can pronounce my relation to Mr. Lewes immoral I can only understand by remembering how subtle and complex are the influences that mould opinion. But I *do* remember that, and I indulge in no arrogant or uncharitable thoughts about those who condemn us, even though we might have expected a somewhat different verdict. From the majority of persons, of course, we never looked for anything but condemnation. We are leading no life of self-indulgence, except indeed, that being happy in each other, we find everything easy. We are working hard to provide for others better than ourselves, and to fulfill every responsibility that lies upon us. Levity and pride would not be a sufficient basis for that.[38]

Levity? Perhaps not. But pride? Certainly.

She was proud of herself. She had acted according to her principles. She had had the courage to scorn conventional behavior, conventional rewards, conventional approval. Her union with Lewes was a triumph of natural morality in the face of absurd and tyrannical laws. Those of her friends who could understand this redefinition of moral behavior were worthy of being kept; the others were a loss she could accept. Had she pretended to shame and remorse, conforming herself to the popular plot that she had sinned and needed to be forgiven, I think her union with Lewes would have been found more acceptable. It was "the pretence of a sanctioned union," in the jealous words of the novelist Eliza Lynn Linton, which was most offensive, and which, morally speaking, was the most serious and challenging aspect of the affair. What makes a marriage valid? its endorsement by church or state? or the commitment of the people involved? That was the question her behavior posed, and her radical stance was calculated to undermine morality as it had been known and to re-establish it on a more serious, a more existential, basis.

Allies

George Eliot's fame had little effect upon the way she and Lewes lived together. They had always kept to themselves and lived quietly. Because of the irregularity of their marriage, George Eliot could not be received in society, although Lewes, according to the strange moral logic of the time, was acceptable and frequently invited to dine out. In the early years they did not entertain at all and received even the closest friends rarely. They refused in general to put people up at their house. Sara Hennell, virtually a member of the family, was offered a bed for one night only. George Eliot realized they were "brutally inhospitable," but claimed it was in the interest of their work. Solitude, at first the product of ostracism, turned out to have advantages, and it is a question whether in fact the world banished her or she the world. At one point, there seemed to be a chance of Lewes's obtaining a divorce abroad, but the chance fell through and his companion was not sorry. "I prefer excommunication. I have no earthly thing that I care for, to gain by being brought within the pale of people's personal attention, and I have many things to care for that I would lose—my freedom from petty worldly torments, commonly called pleasures, and that isolation which really keeps my charity warm instead of chilling it, as much contact with frivolous women would do."[39]

Like Traddles and Sophie, like David Copperfield and Agnes, like Walter Gay and Florence Dombey, like the happy couple at the end of almost any Dickens novel, these two display towards each other nothing but goodwill, affection, an urge to self-sacrifice, and gratitude. No rosy children surround them, as the happy couple should be surrounded in a Dickens novel. Instead, books are their children. They embody all the ideals and principles of that most assertive of Victorian tracts on marriage, *David Copperfield*, which repeatedly told its readers that "there can be no disparity in marriage like unsuitability of mind and purpose."[40] If ever a couple was united in purpose it was Marian Evans and George Henry Lewes, dedicated to Duty, to Work, to Love, spreading warmth and light from their domestic hearth in the most approved style of Victorian domestic fiction. They were the perfect married couple. Only—they weren't married. One cannot help but wonder how different things might have been had they been married in accordance with, and not in opposition to, the customs of their culture. How much did their happiness depend upon the irregularity of their union?

Because they were not respectable, they were spared the burdens of respectability. They did not have to be nice to each other's friends. They did not have to give dinner parties. They did not have to put up with guests for the weekend. They did not have to appear together in public. Treated as sinful lovers, they remained lovers. Since their union was disapproved by society, their energies went into justifying it, enjoying it, making other people believe in it—not wishing there were less of it, wishing themselves more free. For some people stability flourishes where the apparatus of stability is absent. Simone de Beauvoir, whose lifelong relationship with Sartre was in many ways similar to that of George Eliot and George Henry Lewes, says that she and Sartre thought of themselves "as" married, gave their relationship a name (morganatic marriage) even before they had worked out its details, and played at being a particular *petit bourgeois* couple, Monsieur and Madame M. Organatique, but "by wriggling into their skins for a joke we emphasized the difference." Once, when it seemed they could be saved from a painful separation by dual appointments that legal marriage could make possible, Sartre urged de Beauvoir to marry him. She said no immediately. "Any modification of the relationship we maintained with the outside world would have fatally affected that existing between the two of us."[41]

George Eliot knew her priorities. Her work and her intimacy with Lewes were most important; both were served by being cut off from the world. All she gave up was a superficial social intercourse which she did not much enjoy, preferring a walk with Lewes in the Zoological Gardens to pallid conversations over clear consommé. Ill health also kept her close to home. She had no carriage and was too frail to go walking far in London. Gradually they developed the rule of never paying visits; anyone who wanted to see them had to come to their house, which, from 1863 on, was The Priory, a two-story structure in the St. John's Wood district near Regent's Park, sufficiently remote to ensure quiet, surrounded by a brick wall. She was at home every Sunday, and brilliant people came to call, but the women were either so emancipated as not to mind what was said about them or they had no social position to maintain.

One of the guests who made his way to the Leweses' door in 1869 was Charles Eliot Norton, an American gentleman, later a Harvard professor, accompanied by his wife, Susan. They were received by Lewes at the door of The Priory with characteristic animation. By this time the woman living in sin had become Britain's voice of morality. George Eliot had written *Adam Bede, The Mill on the Floss, Silas Marner*, and *Felix Holt*, and her fame had quite eclipsed her husband's.

There was nothing formidable about George Henry Lewes. He was not dignified or stately. What you noticed about him was rapid motion. To a fastidious man like Professor Norton, he seemed slightly vulgar, like an old-fashioned French barber or a dancing master. He was ugly, vivacious, and entertaining; you expected him to take up a fiddle and start to play. His talk, in its liveliness and the gestures which accompanied it, seemed more French than English, and both mind and mouth seemed always to be running over. He was amazingly versatile, able to talk equally well about philosophy, science, and literature, but perhaps for that very reason you tended to suspect his depth. Professor Norton had to remind himself that both Darwin and Lyell had spoken highly of Lewes's accomplishments. "Not a man who wins more than a moderate liking from you," he concluded.[42] He did not say that such a frivolous-seeming man was hardly a fit mate for George Eliot, but others thought it. George Eliot herself seemed aware of an incongruity, and in describing Lewes to her friends invariably pointed out that his impact was not weighty. It was, in fact, the lightness and buoyancy of his spirits that made him attractive to her, so dreadfully given herself to despondency. Sometimes she had to summon her deepest resources to make the coming day seem worthy of its inevitable weariness, whereas Lewes was cheerful even in ill health, was never a prey to moods, and was healthy in his relationship to his work, which he enjoyed in the doing and whose presentation to the public he faced without anxiety.

Although the Leweses had much in common, although they shared all their intellectual pursuits—reading books together, learning languages together, following each other's work—their attraction for each other was, like many erotic ties, based upon the differences between them, differences of bearing and of temperament. What made Lewes suspect in the eyes of the visiting American scholar—his light-heartedness, his good cheer, his Gallic pose of frivolity—had initially made him unimpressive to Marian Evans, too. Yet it was what she came to find most appealing in him.

Before Lewes, she had been attracted to men who demanded looking up to, men who would require sacrifices and were prepared to give little in return: Dr. Brabant, Chapman, Herbert Spencer. Towards these men she experienced the impulse towards self-surrender which she portrayed so brilliantly in Dorothea Brooke's response to Mr. Casaubon, the feminine impulse to over-value a man's work and to derive one's identity from it. But Lewes never inspired such feelings. "Do not for a moment imagine that Dorothea's marriage experience is drawn from my own," George Eliot wrote Harriet

Beecher Stowe after the publication of *Middlemarch*. "Impossible to conceive any creature less like Mr Casaubon than my warm, enthusiastic husband, who cares more for my doing than for his own."[43]

He was prepared to devote himself to her, and she accepted an immense amount of devotion. It became understood between them that without his help she could not write. Her fear of failure almost stifled her; she needed him to deflect the world's dislike. Her first book, *Scenes of Clerical Life*, which consists of three sketches, was originally supposed to be longer, but Blackwood, her publisher, unwisely admitted that he didn't like the third story so much as the first two, and his sensitive author insisted on stopping right there. Early in their relationship, Lewes warned Blackwood in a letter to refrain from saying anything unpleasant to George Eliot.

> Like "Oliver Twist" he is for ever "asking for more." He seems to me a sort of obverse of that Roman Emperor who had a slave at his elbow to whisper constantly to him "Remember you are mortal." *He* wants a friend at his elbow to whisper "You see, George, you really are not a confounded Noodle."[44]

Lewes was the consoling slave at her elbow.

To her friends, even her closest friends, and for the entire length of her career, he had to repeat warnings such as the one he gave Blackwood about suppressing any negative response to her work. Only the most effusive praise was acceptable. Lewes went to extraordinary lengths to keep hostility from her. Once he went so far as to misread a letter which contained some criticism, omitting an entire section and then conveniently "losing" it. He also intercepted newspaper reviews, allowing her to see only the laudatory ones. You can easily imagine the risks of practicing this sort of vigilance on behalf of someone beloved: benevolence can lead to contempt; the protector can grow to resent the inequality of the burden, his or her unvarying strength, the other's weakness. If this does not happen you can be sure that the pattern of dependence has not been adopted unilaterally, and it becomes ambiguous who is dependent on whom for what. One can need to be needed. George Henry Lewes seems to have been this sort of person, and George Eliot was wise enough not to be too strong. Her need meshed with his, making him an equal partner in her acts of creation. For twenty-four years he went on cheerfully deflecting criticism, helping her with business matters, answering mail, being indispensable.

Writing is usually a lonely profession, but George Eliot had the knack of turning men into collaborators. In addition to Lewes, there was John Blackwood, her excellent Scottish editor and publisher. Without the intermediary of an agent, except Lewes, she corresponded with Blackwood in Edinburgh on matters of content, printing, sales, distribution. She entered enthusiastically into all these business affairs, when she allowed herself to enter at all. She was a difficult author, rejecting any interference with her text and subject to unaccountable resentments in business matters, but Blackwood handled her with tact and patience. The relationship between them was stormy and in some ways more overtly flirtatious than her relationship with Lewes. After the great success of *Adam Bede*, her second book, she began to think of changing publishers. She felt he was beginning to take her for granted. She thought someone else would appreciate her more. Although Blackwood had generously and spontaneously doubled her royalty for *Adam Bede*, she was angry at him; he had insufficiently exercised himself on her behalf when rumors spread that a Mr. Liggins was the author of *Adam Bede* and when a sequel to the book was announced by an unscrupulous publisher.

Lewes joined her in letting Blackwood know that other publishers wanted her. His phrasing was unfortunate: "My precious time is occupied with declining offers on all sides—every one imagining that he can seduce George Eliot."[45] This remark passed between the Blackwood's offices in Edinburgh and London, creating outrage everywhere. If many people were trying to seduce George Eliot, well, no wonder, since Mr. Lewes himself had shown the way, said an employee less gentlemanly than Mr. Blackwood. The favored metaphor in the Blackwood offices for what was happening was that George Eliot was selling herself to the highest bidder.

George Eliot stayed with Blackwood for *The Mill on the Floss* and *Silas Marner*, but she gave *Romola* to Smith and Elder for the immense sum of £7,000. The transaction was not a pleasure. She felt guilty towards Blackwood, who had always treated her well, and she felt guilty towards Smith who, she thought, had given her too much money. In a sense she was right, for *Romola* was not a popular success. Smith lost money on it. After that unsatisfactory fling, and for the rest of her career, she stayed happily with Blackwood, for, as she had written him when she first thought of leaving him for another publisher, "I prefer, in every sense, permanent relations to shifting ones."[46]

If their dual solitude was anchored on one side by their mutual devotion to her work, it was also anchored by their devotion to Lewes's three sons, who called Marian *"Mutter"* and seem to have been closer to her than they were to their natural mother. After being educated in Switzerland, two of the boys wound up in Natal, but Charles Lewes came to London to take up a junior position in the post office, which Anthony Trollope, the novelist and a friend of the family, had been able to secure for him. At a time in their lives when both would have preferred to live in the country, convinced that Marian suffered in health and spirits in the city, the Leweses nevertheless resolved to make a home there for young Charles. "I languish sadly for the fields and the broad sky; but duties must be done, and Charles's moral education required that he should have at once a home near his business."[47] George Eliot was the kind of person to welcome duties and obligations of that sort. Not only were they a spiritual discipline, they also gave shape to a life which might otherwise be paralysingly subject to whim. Fortunate are those, she said, who have a peremptory reason for living in one place rather than another.

By turning their backs on the search for happiness in their daily lives, by committing themselves to each other, to their work, and to Duty, the Leweses managed to be as happy together for the twenty-four years they lived together as any two people I have heard of outside fantasy literature. Of course, theirs was not the happiness of fantasy literature at all: not passionate, not romantic, not played out upon the peaks of life but on its plains. It was founded on a stoical, a tragic sense of life. "There comes a season when we cease to look round and say 'how shall I enjoy?' but as in a country that has been visited by the sword, pestilence, and famine, think only how we shall help the wounded and how find time for the next harvest—how till the earth and make a little time of gladness for those being born without their own asking."[48] There was something mournful in George Eliot's contentment. She never knew the exhilaration, let us say, of an opera singer who has given a splendid performance and been applauded by thousands. Although she became the most lauded and respected female novelist in England, she found that "the merely egotistical satisfactions of fame are easily nullified by a toothache."[49] Her pleasure came from daily life and from the abiding sense of the worth of her writing. What better sources?

She asked for little partly because she knew she was not beautiful; she did not consider herself, in worldly terms, a prize. She asked for little, too, because the experience of loss and death had tempered her expectations. Her mother died when she was seventeen, and her father, to whom she was even more strongly attached, renounced her when she was twenty-one over her loss of faith, reconciled with her uneasily, then died when she was thirty. The only way she could reconstruct the network of love she had known as a child in her family was through marriage. So she came to that relationship with the utmost seriousness and the intention that she and the man she chose would be twin pillars supporting all meaning in life—he the center of her life as she was of his. She didn't look for excitement. She didn't look for happiness, although she found it. She looked to be of use to someone who in turn would find her existence indispensable. Lewes, for different reasons, approached his second marriage with a chastened set of expectations. Asking for little, they secured for themselves a joint life of exceptional richness.

Ill health was the tax they believed they paid for their contentment. "We have so much happiness in our love and uninterrupted companionship, that we must accept our miserable bodies as our share of mortal ill." And, "We are always the same—happy in everything except our livers and stomachs."[50] Lewes, like Carlyle, was cursed with chronic dyspepsia and rarely got through a day without discomfort. "O dear O dear when *will* people leave off their foolish talk about all human lots being equal? as if anybody with a sound stomach ever knew misery comparable to the misery of a dyspeptic."[51]

She suffered periodically from incapacitating illnesses which aspirin and antibiotics might have cured. Lacking routinely useful medications, they sought health in Continental spas. They travelled whenever George Eliot finished a book, having then the time and additional motive—to avoid reviews.

Their health seems consistently to have improved in warm climates, and one wonders why they did not, like the Brownings, simply leave England. Harriet Beecher Stowe assumed it was only a question of money, and she rejoiced at the success of *Middlemarch*, among other reasons, because it would allow her friend to buy a place in the sun. But that was not it. Their moral roots were English. They refused to cut themselves off. George Eliot feared becoming selfish if she lived in too pleasant a climate. In her bargain with life, the body's humiliation was the soul's enrichment; one prospered at the other's expense. As her lack of beauty was connected with her spiritual radiance, her domestic happiness seemed connected with the bodily misery she shared with her husband. By 1873 she was comparing the two of them to two medieval saints painted by a very naïve master. "Our bodies seem to shrink, like the *Peau de Chagrin*, with every year of happiness."[52]

Even before Thornton Lewes returned from Natal in 1869, sick with the spinal disease of which he would shortly and excruciatingly die, death was in her thoughts. The queen, who had been widowed in 1861, was mourning on the grand scale by withdrawing from most of her public duties. When her journal was published, George Eliot read it with particular sympathy, because, as she said, "I am a woman of about the same age, and also have my personal happiness bound up in a dear husband whose loss would render my life simply a series of social duties and private memories."[53] Thornton's death, devastating in itself, seemed to her also the beginning of their own. Her ponderous but deeply feeling mind began to make its way towards another truth about the nature of emotional life, and, as so often with George Eliot, the metaphor was commercial: loving someone is like an increase of property—at the same time that it brings joy, it brings fears about loss. Sometimes, in the midst of her happiness, she would cry suddenly at the thought of the necessary parting from Lewes that lay in the future. Like everyone else in the world who has lived in harmony with someone for a very long time, she wondered—even while he was alive and well—how she would live without him. She wondered which of them ought to die first. On the whole she thought she would prefer the pain of being left behind for the sake of being able to nurse him. "Death seems to me now a close, real experience, like the approach of autumn or winter, and I am glad to find that advancing life brings the power of imagining the nearness of death I never had of late years." She thought continually of death, almost to the eclipse of life, "as if life were so narrow a strip as hardly to be taken much reckoning of." For the blessedness of loving, she said, we pay a heavy price in anxiety.[54]

In 1877, when Lewes was sixty and she was almost as old, she was suffering horrible pain from kidney stones and he was barely able to walk. She recovered, but Lewes seemed to get worse. One person who saw him at this time said he looked like he'd been gnawed by rats. George Eliot watched his health with a grieving heart. The man whose lightness of step had so delighted her in their prime could hardly get around. In late November 1878, after a short bout of enteritis, Lewes died. He also had cancer and would soon have died of that, if not the other.

John Blackwood, though sickly himself, thought about descending from Scotland to take care of the author he had worked with for so many years. He did not know how she could manage herself and her grief. She never left the house. The servants heard her crying and sometimes screaming. She saw no one except Charles Lewes, who handled her daily affairs as his father had done. At first, she could not bear even to read the letters of condolence; Charles merely informed her who had written them. She was a "bruised creature," shrinking from even the tenderest touch. She wanted to live only to do certain things for Lewes's sake: she wanted to ready for publication the manuscript he had been working on, and she wanted to establish a fellowship in physiology in his name. So she watched her diet and she did enough work to keep her mind from imbecility. But her attachment to life was fragile. By the following July, she had diminished to 103 pounds.

Except for the three men she consulted about setting up the Lewes Studentship, one of whom was John Walter Cross, who handled her investments, she saw no friends until March—four months after Lewes's death. She could not pretend to be interested in anything but thinking of Lewes, of her own past happiness, of her grief. She feared that even her closest friends would find her sorrow wearisome. She did not want to pain them, but she could not relinquish her grief, so she stayed alone. The more she realized how thoroughly her happiness for twenty-four years had been founded on securing Lewes's happiness rather than her own, the more her desolation increased. She did not know how to seek happiness directly.

Oblivion through work was impossible. She could barely summon up strength and concentration to do the editing of Lewes's manuscript. Work of her own was out of the question. She had finished *Impressions of Theophrastus Such* before Lewes's death; in fact, sending the manuscript to Blackwood was practically Lewes's last action. But afterwards, George Eliot refused to let Blackwood bring the book out: it would seem disrespectful to Lewes. The type had been set, but no books could be printed. Eventually, feeling guilty about keeping all that type tied up, she allowed Blackwood to print the books but not to distribute them. When the book finally appeared in May, it bore a note from the publisher explaining that the manuscript had been in his hands since the previous year but its publication had been delayed because of the "domestic affliction" of the author. The unsentimental Scotsman did this entirely to soothe the feelings of the widow, whose prolonged mourning he had by March begun to consider morbid, and encouraged by "pretended sympathizers."[55]

In the eyes of the world, there seems to be no right way of handling bereavement. If you are rendered incapable of living by grief—like Victoria and George Eliot—you are thought morbid. If you smile to hide tears and go on as best you can, you are likely to be thought unfeeling. If you re-marry quickly you are suspected of having been insufficiently attached to your first spouse, and if you don't, you are insufficiently committed to the business of living. Wisely, George Eliot followed the path of her own grief to its natural conclusion. Although that winter seemed the end of her life, spring followed.

She was rebellious. That was a good sign. Although everything seemed difficult which before had seemed easy, although she now had to find reasons for continuing in life when before Lewes had supplied the reason, she could not bring herself to feel that her life was no use. She could not resign herself to continuing her death-in-life. She found herself repeatedly turning for help with financial matters to John Walter Cross, a forty-year-old banker whose mother the Leweses had befriended ten years before. Cross, whom George Eliot called variously "Johnny" and "nephew," handled her investments, helped with the drafting of the Lewes memorial fellowship, and advised her about the many requests for loans she got from friends and relatives. She was by now quite wealthy, and since she was resolved to continue Lewes's support of his wife, children, and grandchildren, her financial arrangements were complicated and extensive.[56]

Cross was young. He was useful. He worshipped her. And his mother, to whom he had been devoted, had died a week after Lewes. Each of them felt maimed. Each lacked a crucial emotional support. Grief, unless for the loss of the same person, is not a particularly binding emotion, but the determination to recover from it is. Johnny, perhaps because he was younger, was the more determined to discipline himself and to find new interests for his life. He thought it might be good to read Dante. Marian agreed. She would even do it with him. For the next twelve months, they read together through the *Inferno* and the *Purgatorio*, construing and discussing every line. She was the teacher, and the man of business became her pupil. She had the pleasure of watching her own experience kindle enthusiasm and understanding in him. He had the pleasure of feeling himself in the control of a woman in some ways more powerful than himself, who, nonetheless, depended on him in other ways. Somewhere in this strangely shifting duet of dominance, the erotic spark was struck. Like Paolo and Francesca (though not, like them, mournfully) they credited the book. "The divine poet took us into another world," wrote Cross. "It was a renovation of life." By May, he had induced her to play the piano again. "I am much stronger than I was," she said, "and am again finding interest in this wonderful life of ours."[57]

A year and a half after Lewes's death, in April 1880, she agreed to marry Cross, and the wedding took place shortly thereafter, on May 6, in St. George's, Hanover Square. Marian was given away by her stepson, Charles Lewes, and the other people present were all members of John Cross's family. They left almost immediately for the Continent. She had tried, obliquely, to prepare her closest friends for this shocking development. Two weeks before the wedding, for example, she went to say good-bye to Georgiana Burne-Jones, who knew only that Marian was going abroad. Mrs. Burne-Jones felt (but who knows with what retrospective insight) that her friend had something on her mind she wasn't saying. "I have always remembered though the weariness she expressed of the way in which wisdom was attributed to her. 'I am so tired of being set on a pedestal and expected to vent wisdom—I am only a poor woman' was the meaning of what she said if not the exact phrase, as I think it was."[58] But she told no one explicitly of her wedding plans. Instead she left notes for five close friends to be delivered on the day of the wedding. Clearly she felt she was doing something of which her friends would not approve. But the furtiveness in her wedding plans and departure for the Continent may have been part of the pleasure, if it really is true, as one expert has said, that guilt is the cutting edge of sex. She had lived guiltily for twenty-four years with Lewes in one way. Now she had another. For although Cross was an old friend, wealthy, eligible —in all those ways a suitable person for Marian Evans to marry—he was twenty years younger than she. Again she had managed to find an object for her love which defied easy social acceptance.

Anne Thackeray, the novelist's daughter, had done something similar three years before. At the age of forty, she married Richmond Ritchie, twenty-four, just barely out of university.[59] George Eliot had reacted with tolerance. She knew Miss Thackeray and Ritchie, and thought the nearly twenty years' difference between them might be bridged by his solidity and gravity. "This is one of several instances that I have known of lately," she wrote at the time, "showing that young men of even brilliant advantages will often choose as their life's companion a woman whose attractions are wholly of the spiritual order."[60]

Now, with the newly married couple on their honeymoon, Charles Lewes went about London explaining his stepmother's action, generously, sympathetically, for he felt he owed her everything good in his life. One of the people he called upon was Anne Thackeray Ritchie and she related the "thrrrrrrilling" conversation to her absent husband. Lewes had said he regarded Mr. Cross as an elder brother. He said that his father had not a grain of jealousy in him and would only have wanted her to be happy. He said his stepmother was of such a delicate and fastidious nature that only the most ideal tête-à-tête would satisfy her.

> I asked him if she had consulted him and he said no, not con-sulted, but that she had told him a few weeks ago. She confided in Paget (her doctor) who approved and told her that it wouldn't make any difference in her influence. Here I couldn't stand it, and said of course it would, but it was better to be genuine than to have influence, and that I didn't suppose she imagined herself inspired, though her clique did. It rather shocked him, and he mumbled a good deal. . . . George Eliot said to him if she hadn't been a human with feelings and failings like other people, how could she have written her books.[61]

Lewes could not have felt he needed to justify to Anne Ritchie his stepmother's marrying a man so much younger than herself. There was something else, another "failing": that she had re-married at all. Some people still thought that fidelity should extend beyond the grave. Hamlet, perhaps, was extreme in thinking that none doth wed the second but who killed the first; still, if love is unique, as the romantic tradition supposes it is, how could you love a second time? It seemed retroactively to dilute the importance of the first attach-ment.[62]

The situation was paradoxical. A quarter of a century earlier she had bypassed marriage to live with Lewes, and people were upset. Some were offended by her re-marrying, yet she hadn't ever really been married. Some, radical friends who approved the unconven-tionality of her relationship with Lewes, now felt vexed at her lapse into conventionality. St. George's in Hanover Square, indeed! One consistent reaction was that of her brother Isaac, who in his unimagi-native rectitude had refused to have anything to do with her while she was living in an unsanctioned union. Now that she was a respectably married woman, he broke his silence of twenty-five years to offer his congratulations and assure her of his love. "The only point to be regretted in our marriage," she wrote back, not allowing it to escape his attention that there was something to be regretted, "is that I am so much older than he, but his affection has made him choose this lot of caring for me rather than any other of the various lots open to him."[63]

The appeal of a handsome, vigorous man of forty, wholly devoted to her, to a woman of sixty who has achieved everything professionally she could hope to achieve, who, moreover, has always doubted her own attractiveness, is so obvious to me that it would seem to need no comment. But even contemporary commentators find Cross hard to accept. "Cross was probably a mistake," writes one. "In all his public appearances he is firmly on the dull side."[64] But if anything his businessman's ignorance of the higher culture was piquant and attractive to her. "Thou dost not know anything of verbs in Hiphil or Hophal or the history of metaphysics or the position of Kepler in science, but thou knowest best things of another sort, such as belong to the manly heart—secrets of lovingness and rectitude."[65] If the devoted companion of George Henry Lewes could not hide the pleasure of having to do, for a change, with a man who did not know the place of Kepler in science, are we to understand that as a betrayal of her attachment to Lewes? It would be more generous—and more revealing—to take it as testimony to the multiplicity of human instincts, which can be satisfied by one person only at the cost of partial shutdown.

Her response to Cross was more fulsomely sentimental than her response to Lewes had been. "Best loved and loving one—the sun it shines so cold, so cold, when there are no eyes to look love on me. I cannot bear to sadden one moment when we are together, but *wenn Du bist nicht da* I have often a bad time." At about the time she wrote that, during their courtship, she wrote her friend Mrs. Burne-Jones about a woman who had made an inappropriate match, "Remarkable men so often choose a succession of stupid women (if not evil ones) that there should be some tolerance for a woman who does the corresponding thing."[66]

Never without noble reasons for doing what her strong-willed nature impelled her to do, George Eliot presented her decision to re-marry as a spiritual discipline, an attempt to avoid selfishness. "Marriage has seemed to restore my old self. I was getting hard, and if I had decided differently I think I should have become very selfish." Her self-sacrifice was matched by that of Cross, who declared, "The great object of my life now will be to justify her trust and to fulfill worthily the high calling which I have undertaken." I do not mean to discount their rhetoric, for it seems to me that the formulas with which we choose to present our actions are by no means a negligible part of them. Yet the response to this unlikely marriage that pleases me best is that of excellent Barbara Bodichon (née Smith), who said that she would have done exactly the same as John Cross if she had been a man and Marian had let her. "You see I know all love is so different that I do not see it unnatural to love in new ways."[67]

They spent a good part of their honeymoon in Venice, which seemed to them a town of toys erected by petulant children with vast resources. They loved its beauty, quiet, and dustlessness. The season of heat and mosquitoes had not yet arrived. They read Ruskin on Venetian architecture, making grateful use of his knowledge but trying to shut out his wrathful innuendoes against the whole contemporary world. In the mornings they examined works of art or buildings of interest, not hurrying, and then were taken about in a gondola to see the most changeable of cities in all lights and from as many points of view as possible. It was idyllic. And then, after two weeks, something terrible happened. John Cross became ill. It may have been one of those Venetian fevers, generated by the filth in the canals, which travellers at that time were prey to. Under the influence of fever, Cross jumped from the balcony of their room at the Hotel de l'Europe into the Grand Canal, to be rescued by gondoliers, examined by the chief medical officer of Venice, given chloral.

It is difficult, now, not to think of Venice as a place where age pursues youth in sinister ways, yet George Eliot does not seem to have thought that her husband jumped out of the window to escape her. She feared insanity, revealed to Dr. Ricchetti that there was madness in the Cross family. Gordon Haight, her biographer, believes that what happened to Cross in Venice was acute mental depression, although Cross himself, in his documentary life of George Eliot, describes his illness as physical, attributing it to bad air and lack of exercise.[68]

In response to a frantic telegraph from George Eliot, Cross's brother, Willie, joined them in Venice, and the weakened man was moved by easy stages to Innsbruck, Munich, Wildbad, and, by July, back to England. She responded to his illness with strength. It seemed more natural to her to have anxiety than to be free from it and only hoped she would not run down "like a jelly fish" when the anxiety was over.[69]

That summer and fall, while Cross continued to improve, they stayed in the country, at the house George Eliot and Lewes had purchased in Surrey, near Godalming. Now they made the formal calls which they had not had time to do before the wedding, visiting Cross's married sisters in Lincolnshire and Cambridgeshire. A female guest at one of these dinners observed the incongruous pair in their new felicity. "George Eliot, old as she is, and ugly, really looked sweet and winning in spite of both," wrote Mrs. Jebb. The famous author was cleverly dressed in a dark satin dress to show off her slenderness but to hide the angularity of age. Nevertheless, Mrs. Jebb felt sorry for her. There was not a person in the room—including her husband—whose mother she could not have been. That she adored her husband was clear, and Mr. Cross seemed devoted to her in return. But Mrs. Jebb suspected her of being inwardly tormented by jealousy, for such a marriage was against nature. Cross might forget the twenty years' difference in their ages, but his wife never could.[70]

At last, by December, their beautiful townhouse on Cheyne Walk, overlooking the river, was ready. Moving the books from The Priory had been a huge job which Cross had supervised, and their move to London had also been held up by intermittent illnesses of Marian's. But nothing serious. Two weeks after they moved in, she developed another minor illness. A sore throat. The doctor was called in but was not concerned. Sleep, he said, was the best medicine. She took some cold beef tea jelly and an egg beaten with brandy, then dozed. Her husband listened to her breathing. He hoped it was curative sleep, but what he heard was death coming on. When another doctor arrived, four hours later, she complained of a pain in her side, then lost consciousness forever, and the next day Cross wrote, "I am left alone in this new House we meant to be so happy in."[71]

There was some talk of burying George Eliot in Westminster Abbey, as she wished, but even the agnostic T. H. Huxley did not think it was appropriate, pointing out that the Abbey was a Christian church, not a Pantheon. "George Eliot is known not only as a great writer, but as a person whose life and opinions were in notorious antagonism to Christian practice in regard to marriage," he wrote. "One cannot have one's cake and eat it too. Those who elect to be free in thought and deed must not hanker after the rewards, if they are to be so called, which the world offers to those who put up with its fetters."[72] She was therefore buried near Lewes in Highgate Cemetery, where her grave and Karl Marx's remain almost uniquely accessible in the treacherous bramble thicket which has covered most of the Victorian graves, protecting all but the giants from prying modern worshippers.

A hundred years after her death, a memorial stone was installed in the Poet's Corner of Westminster Abbey. It bears the name she was born with, Mary Ann Evans, and the name she lives by in memory, George Eliot, but refers to neither of her husbands—except perhaps, obliquely, in the quotation from "Janet's Repentance" inscribed around the four sides, "The first condition of human goodness is something to love: the second something to reverence."

JANE

WELSH

and

THOMAS

CARLYLE

1821–1866

Mr. and Mrs. Carlyle

They had been living in London since 1834. Their house on Cheyne Row in Chelsea, near the river, was a center of intellectual life. Although the Carlyles, like many city-dwellers, liked to complain about the noise, the dirt, and the empty excitements of urban life, their move to London from Scotland was a complete success. Their marriage was a success as well—not without its strains and absences of satisfaction, of course, but stable, and in unique ways satisfying to both of them. Each had fulfilled the compact made at the time of their engagement. Thomas had done his allotted days' writing to such good effect that *Sartor Resartus*, *The French Revolution*, and *Cromwell* had been born (for the Carlyles, too, talked of books as their children); as a thinker and man of letters he was respected beyond what Jane could have imagined possible back in Haddington. She had proved a superlative housewife, so clever at managing on a limited budget that no one could tell exactly how much money the Carlyles had: they seemed to live like people of good taste who had more money than they needed.

Some people said Jane was the cleverest woman in London, and, quite apart from her husband, she had her own following. George Lewes visited her with his wife Agnes, and Dickens came with John Forster. Erasmus Darwin (Charles Darwin's brother), Thackeray's daughters, the political exiles Giuseppe Mazzini and Godefroy Cavaignac, were all members of her circle. Her friends had the highest estimate of her talents on the basis of her conversation and her brilliant letters. Dickens thought she would have been a great novelist, and Forster agreed. She was a personage in her own right. George Eliot sent her and not Mr. Carlyle copies of her first two novels. Mazzini and Cavaignac, a French Republican in exile for conspiracy against Louis-Philippe and the younger brother of a future president of France, came principally to visit her, not Mr. Carlyle. Indeed the dashing Cavaignac was a little bit in love with her, and she with him. In her own salon, anchored by a successful husband, she could resume the flirtations which had made her young womanhood such fun. People were charmed. With men, she tended to be more French in her style, more disparaging for example of the institution of marriage, more epigrammatic (she practiced writing epigrams in her diary), but her great subject—especially with women—was herself as heroic housewife in the service of exasperating genius, a comic topos treated nowhere better than in the letters of Jane Welsh Carlyle.

There were those, even her friends, who thought she tried too hard to be clever. One evening, talking, as she thought rather wittily, to Cavaignac, she was interrupted by a brusque rebuke. "Spare me your cleverness, Madame. *Je ne le veux pas—moi!* it is not my pleasure to rank among those for whom you have to make minced meat of yourself!" Cavaignac found something tortuous and self-destructive in Jane's display of wit; it required too great a suppression of her sentimental side, her sweetness, and the warmth which endeared her to many people. Other people, less friendly to Jane, saw her as a self-important bluestocking who had never quite managed to rid herself of provinciality. Her conversation consisted largely of monologues, set pieces, narratives, and the stories were often too long. Her Scotch accent was too pronounced. She called too much attention to herself and demanded too much deference. There were other women in London equally clever—Mrs. Brookfield, Mrs. Procter, Lady Harriet Ashburton—who made less of a fuss about it and didn't seem to have to try so hard.

If her great subject was daily life—its problems and absurdities—her best audience was the person who followed the continuing drama on a daily basis, her husband. For his sake she squeezed each day like a citrus fruit, making it yield up its last drop of narrative interest. All through the day, she generated character sketches, ludicrous incidents, mock heroic accounts of running the household, until, sitting in front of the drawing-room fire in the evening, she could lay them before him, a Scottish Scheherazade. She gloried in her role. To feel herself interesting and amusing to one of the greatest men of his age as he sat quietly smoking his pipe after his labors was her reward for a lot.

Yet there is some evidence he wasn't really listening. In that dreadful thirteen-year period, from 1852 to 1865 when he was working on his life of Frederick the Great, spending the day, as he put it, immersed in Prussian Blockheadism, it is true that he looked forward to the horseback ride he allowed himself when his lonely, silent struggle was done for the day and to the hour he spent with Jane in the drawing room, smoking his pipe, perhaps sipping brandy, listening to her amusing stories. This was the bright spot of his day. But he loved her stories for their "spontaneous tinkling melody," in other words as background music, while, it is to be feared, the narrative of Prussian Blockheadism continued in the forefront of his mind. He would tell her, day after day, about (let us say) the Battle of Mollwitz, while Jane, sitting silent, half listening, thought about her own illnesses and imagined herself to be dying.

In the years of his unnervingly endless work on Frederick the Great, and reaching a nadir perhaps in 1856, Carlyle felt wholly alone, with no supporter in the world except his wife. He had lost a lot of his following with the publication in 1849 of the extremely reactionary *Latter-Day Pamphlets*, and any hopes he may have had of a public career, a political position (such as John Stuart Mill was to have), he realized would never be fulfilled. But if many people thought him a crackpot curmudgeon, his wife never wavered in her belief in his greatness. Later he would thank her for her "valiant strangling of serpents day after day done gaily . . . as I had to do it angrily and gloomily," but at the time Jane's vivacity and love made little dent in his loneliness and despair. He wanted a man with a mind like his to commune with. Jane, for all her humor and wit, could not discuss Prussian Blockheadism as it ought to be discussed. He wanted to talk with someone just like himself. Failing that, he wanted the attention of a woman whose attention would be flattering to him in the way a wife's could never be, since it was owed him.

Before we focus on the inner life of the Carlyles in this difficult

period of the mid-1850s, with its inevitable dissatisfactions and failures of communion, it would be well to emphasize the outward poise
of their marriage. Against the world's hostility, whatever form it
took—tiresome visitors, hapless servants, a recalcitrant, hard-to-run
house, bedbugs, ugly interiors, maddening noises—they stood united,
with Mrs. Carlyle firmly and joyously playing the role of her husband's protector, slaying the serpents without so that he could
concentrate on slaying the serpents within. That gaunt, convenience-
less house ran on Jane's spirit the way houses today run on electric-
ity. Rather, the house ran on servants, and the servants ran on Jane.
She hired and fired them. She encouraged them to draw water, light
fires, air bedrooms—to do whatever needed to be done. She also
supervised repairs on the house, encouraging the workmen, while
Carlyle escaped the uproar and retired somewhere else to write. She
kept foolish people away from him, either putting them off with
charmingly written excuses or, if that failed, by entertaining them
herself. When they were called to account by the tax assessor, it was
of course Jane who went. At the last minute Carlyle had said that
"the voice of honour" seemed to call on him to go himself. "But
either it did not call loud enough," Jane commented, "or he would
not listen to that charmer."[1] For both the Carlyles, the quintessential
expression of Jane's role within the marriage was her continuing
battle to protect her husband from the crowing of cocks.

Although it is a strange accident of language that the fight Carlyle
most thanked Jane for fighting on his behalf was this war against
cocks, no one who has been awakened in darkness by cock crows will
be tempted to put down his resentment of cocks as wholly symbolic.
He was extremely sensitive to noise. A dog barking kept him from
work; a cock crowing kept him from sleep. Beyond that, the noises
aroused in him a fury which in itself upset his work. Noise was an
insult to his creativity and genius. "A man has work . . . which the
Powers would not quite wish to have suppressed by two-and-sixpence
worth of bantams," he said, and she agreed. "We must extinguish
those demon fowls or they will extinguish us."[2] And "the world,
which can do me no good, shall at least not torment me with its street
and backyard noises."[3] Jane understood the way in which the cocks
were an obsession with her husband, involving a question of his ego

and status—"a question, Shall I, a man of genius, or you, 'a sooty washerwoman,' be master here?"[4] She was willing to do battle to establish that he and not the sooty washerwoman (or whoever owned the cocks) was master.

There was never any question but that establishing his mastery was her job, not his. Once, when Jane left a house party at Addiscombe to return to London on some cock business, the other guests asked Carlyle why he hadn't gone himself. He replied that she could manage it better. And she did. Usually a letter or a conversation with the owner of the cocks, alluding to her husband's genius and sensitivity to noise, was enough, but Jane was prepared to go to even greater lengths: she once considered buying the house next door to theirs to silence the cocks. Even in her dreams, she fended off cocks.

> I was dreaming last night about going to some strange house, among strange people, to make representations about cocks! I went on my knees at last, weeping, to an old man with a cast-metal face and grey hair; and while I was explaining all about how you were an author, and couldn't get sleep for these new cocks, my auditor flounced off, and I became aware he was the man who had three serpent-daughters, and kept people in glass bottles in Hoffman's Tale![5]

Constructing a soundproof room on the top floor of the house in Cheyne Row was the Carlyles' last desperate defense against the cocks, but even there the cocks triumphed over the great author. In addition to being hot and airless, the soundproof room was not entirely soundproof. Carlyle hated the room. It was an example of shoddy British craftsmanship, a falling away from past standards of which somehow, surely, the cocks were another example.

Most of the Carlyles' great cockfights were in the early 1850s, but in 1865, not long before Jane died, the whole business started up again, like a reprise of the main theme before the end of the symphony. Thanks to her heroic efforts at exterminating nuisances she had won her victory over noise many years since when, one night, lying in bed, she heard with horror the old summons to battle, the crowing of a cock. She had been ill. She no longer had the strength, the hope, the energy required for such skirmishing. She lay anxiously in bed listening to the cock crow and waiting to hear Mr. C.'s foot stamping frantically on the floor above as it had of old. But Mr. C. did not hear it. He was, at the moment, morbidly tuned in to the sound of railway whistles. After a night of anxiety, Jane, despite a headache, went briskly to work the next morning. She discovered that a hen-hutch had been erected more or less overnight in the garden next door with nine large hens and one very large cock sauntering under their windows. She arranged, with her usual efficiency, that the cock be shut in a cellar all night until after the Carlyles' breakfast. In exchange she bound herself (one wonders if the *quid pro quo* was really necessary) to tutor a little boy in reading three days a week. When Carlyle heard the story, he clasped his wife in his arms and called her his guardian angel. "No sinecure," she commented at the end of her mock-heroic account of this affair to her friend Mrs. Russell. It was one of her last great pieces of mock-heroic writing, but Carlyle, editing Jane's letters after her death, screened out the comedy and regarded this episode as particularly moving. "The noble soul heroically started up . . . and with all her old skill and energy gained victory, complete once more. For me—for me! And it was her last!"[6]

So long as Carlyle clasped her in his arms and called her his guardian angel, Jane was content to do battle on his behalf. She took care of him; he was grateful. She sacrificed; he thanked her. That was the equilibrium of their marriage, but in the mid-1850s it broke down, in a manner characteristic of marriages in which the wife feels she has given up a lot for her husband's sake. All of a sudden, he is not grateful enough. She feels herself taken for granted. She feels herself slighted and somebody else favored. Jane kept telling herself that she had been an only child, an heiress, sought by many. Had she given up wealth, ease, and position, had she sacrificed her talents and turned herself into a household drudge so that her husband should spend his evenings at the feet of another woman, listening to her stories and not to Jane's?

Lady Harriet Ashburton, with her inherited privilege, her looks, her clothes, her townhouse in London, country house, shooting lodge in Scotland, with the scale of hospitality she was able to deploy, commanded considerable glamour. She was one of the greatest hostesses of her time, and to Thomas Carlyle, she was Gloriana, a mythical, romantic figure whose attention carried with it the flattery of all aristocracies past and present. She was the perfect antidote to his daily immersion in Prussian Blockheadism, and, although the Carlyles had known the Ashburtons since 1845, he began to spend more and more time at Lady Harriet's houses—Bath House in London, the Grange at Addiscombe—as his work on Frederick the Great dragged on.

Jane, of course, was welcome to accompany him, but she chose to do so less and less. Travelling in those circles, she felt like an animate suitcase with Mr. Carlyle's name on it. It was too clear she was invited only as his wife. Her stories did not go over as well in this sophisticiated company as they did in her own home. She felt badly dressed and frequently patronized by Lady Harriet, who did not take Jane's illnesses as seriously as she thought they ought to be taken. The house parties at Addiscombe were particularly trying for Jane. She had nothing whatever to do. Carlyle could continue reading and writing even in luxurious circumstances, but luxurious circumstances cut the ground out from Jane's being. She needed bugs to rout, servants to chide, cocks to fend off. Without the daily struggle of her household she had no role; she had no identity, no material for molding into letters and anecdotes. She was reduced to playing shuttlecock and changing her clothes several times a day, as she had in her youth. But there were no suitors at Addiscombe to make it tolerable—and amusing to talk of. The youthful fiction that she was being kept by this vain show from serious intellectual work was no longer credible. She kept on complaining about fashionable life, but the comic tension was gone and only a self-righteous, somewhat spoilsport tone remained.

I was thinking the other night, at "the most magnificent ball of the season," how much better I should like to see people making hay, than all these ladies in laces and diamonds, waltzing! One grows so sick of diamonds, and bare shoulders, and all that sort of thing, after a while. It is the old story of the Irishman put into

a Sedan chair without a bottom: "If it weren't for the honour of
the thing, I might as well have walked!"[7]

That was for public consumption. The real and sadder story—Jane's
fear of not measuring up in glamourous company—comes out in her
diary, where she dreads, even before it takes place, a trip to the
Grange. "To have to care for my dress at this time of day more than I
ever did when young and pretty and happy (God bless me, to think
that I was once all that!) on penalty of being regarded as a blot on
the Grange gold and azure, is really too bad. *Ach Gott!* if we had
been left in the sphere of life we belong to, how much better it
would have been for us in many ways!"[8]

Jane's diary, begun in 1855, was a significant event in the joint life
of the Carlyles. By no means a neutral recording of daily occurrences,
it is a crafted work with a theme—the misery that Carlyle's relationship with Lady Harriet caused Jane, the unfairness that all her sacrifices for him should be repaid with such neglect. It constituted, I
would suggest, Jane's revenge on her husband—a spectacularly successful one—for the wounds he had caused her in marriage. If Carlyle, at this low point in his life, thought about his wife's inner life,
it was to regret that she had so few resources for keeping herself
amused at Addiscombe. He understood that taking care of him was
her full-time occupation, but he did not realize how devastating an
absence was created when that occupation, even for a weekend, was
removed from her. After years of gratitude to her for having given up
her self in his favor, he now wished she had more self—so she could
leave him alone with his fantasies. If he saw that his friendship with
Lady Harriet gave her any pain, he merely thought the pain was
unreasonable. Their relationship was sexually innocent. Moreover
such intimacy with the great should be flattering. What could Jane
object to? Jane, perhaps, tried to give some signs of her misery, but
she would joke to friends that as long as she was standing on two
feet, Mr. Carlyle never even noticed that she was ill. And it went
against every instinct of self-presentation to underscore misery. Gai-
ety was her mode. To make the essential points about their married
life—as they had done in their courtship—they had to turn to the
written word.

Imagine then Carlyle's feelings when, after Jane's death, he picked up her journal and read this entry:

> That eternal Bath House. I wonder how many thousand miles Mr. C. has walked between there and here, putting it all together; setting up always another milestone and another betwixt himself and me. Oh, good gracious! When I first noticed that heavy yellow house without knowing, or caring to know, who it belonged to, how far I was from dreaming that through years and years I should carry every stone's weight of it on my heart.[9]

She writes of walking and walking with no goal but to tire herself. Life is a kaleidoscope with a few things of different colors—mostly black—which fate shakes into new combinations; but the few things, pre-eminently her inner torment, remain always the same. She writes with irritation of having to turn down an invitation she would have accepted if she had only herself to consider, and with irritation at having to spend the evening mending Mr. C.'s trousers. She, an only child! She is constantly galled by what she has given up.

> Alone this evening. Lady A. in town again; Mr. C. of course at Bath House.
>
> > When I think of what I is
> > And what I used to was,
> > I gin to think I've sold myself
> > For very little cas.[10]

Folk ditties haunt her imagination, giving her sorrow a lineage.

> > Oh little did my mother think,
> > The day she cradled me,
> > The lands I was to travel in,
> > The death I was to dee.

Rarely romantic, Jane in this mood had no patience whatever with great passions and offered a gloss on another Scottish song:

> Oh waly, waly, love is bonnie
> A little while when it is new;
>   But when it's auld
>   It waxeth cauld,
> And melts away like morning dew.

"Beautiful verse, sweet and sad," she said, "like barley sugar dissolved in tears. About the morning dew, however! I should rather say, 'Goes out like candle snuff' would be a truer simile."[11] Carlyle, reading all this after Jane's death, was appalled.

The journal, which she kept from October 1855 to July 1856, is not unrelievedly a record of complaint, but even incidents which do not directly touch upon Lady Ashburton and Mr. Carlyle tend to sound the theme of sacrifice, inviting a comparison between what life might have been and what it has become. One day, for example, Carlyle, walking in Piccadilly, was stopped by a man who got out of a carriage to talk to him, "an iron-grey man with a bitter smile." It was George Rennie, the one of Jane's Haddington beaux who had gone on to become governor of the Falkland Islands. The day after his chance meeting with Carlyle, Rennie came to call on Jane, who sprang into his arms and kissed him a great many times. "Oh, it has done me so much good this meeting! My bright, whole hearted, impulsive youth seemed conjured back by his hearty embrace. For certain, my late deadly weakness was conjured away! A spell on my nerves it had been, which dissolved in the unwonted feeling of gladness. I am a different woman this evening. I am well!"[12] She was so excited she was afraid she wouldn't sleep (sleeping was always a problem for Jane), but the unwonted joy made her sleep better than ever.

It must be noted, however, if only for its incidental human interest, that this reunion with a former lover turned out little better for Jane than Dickens's reunion with *his* sweetheart from the past. The Rennies invited the Carlyles to dinner before a soirée at Bath House. Jane had been fretting over the need to buy a new dress for the Bath House affair, but now she bought it happily. George Rennie would see that the smart girl of his province had not become a "*dowdy* among London women of 'a certain age.'" But "like everything looked forward to with pleasure," their dinner with the Rennies was a complete failure. They had all become established adults, behaving properly at a dinner party. "The Past stood aloof, looking mournfully down on me. . . . It was a London dinner Party, *voilà tout!*" For a change, it was a relief to go to Bath House. She felt more at home there than she did with this rigidified relic of a past passion, who had the nerve to discuss such unromantic subjects as the possibilities of war with America.[18]

The diary generally recorded things at once too trivial and too significant to write in letters to friends, returning over and over to Lady Harriet.

> April 11. I called on "my lady" come to town for the season. She was perfectly civil, for a wonder.[14]

> 18 June. On the 7th we went to Addiscombe and staid till the 11th. The place in full bloom and her ladyship affable. Why? What is in the wind now? As usual in that beautiful place, I couldn't sleep.[15]

She writes—but in French—about the unfairness of marriage laws: how women may lose their families for committing misconduct but men may drive them to the misconduct through hardness and disdain and not be punished for it in any way. Sometimes harsh treatment and difficulties of character in her husband drive a woman not precisely to misconduct but "to something, and something not to his advantage, any more than to hers," Jane said darkly.[16] She and her friend Mr. Barlow followed with great fascination the trial of a man named Palmer accused and convicted of poisoning his wife for her life insurance. "Mr. Barlow says 'nine-tenths of the misery of human life proceeds, according to *his* observation, from the Institution of Marriage!' He should say from the demoralization, the desecration, of the Institution of Marriage, and then I should cordially agree with him."[17]

Jane's problem was largely solved in May 1857 by the sudden death of Lady Harriet Ashburton. By July 1857, Jane's mood had changed completely. The gloom lifted. She resolved to stop giving voice to despondent thoughts. "It is not a natural voice of mine, that sort of egotistical babblement, but has been fostered in me by the patience and sympathy shown me in my late long illness. I can very easily leave it off, as I did smoking, when I see it to be getting a bad habit."[18] She did leave it off. She began to encourage Mr. Carlyle again about the writing of *Frederick the Great*, although she seems never to have read beyond the second volume. She could lift herself out of her own misery enough to be horrified by the massacre of Englishwomen at Cawnpore, to think that all other problems shrink to nothing beside their dreadful fate, and to wonder what sort of God rules a world in which it could happen. "It isn't much like a world ruled by Love, this."[19]

The question is, for whom was the diary written? Was it an outlet for her sorrow, written for herself only? Or was it in some way intended to be read? Parts of it seem to have no rhetorical purpose: the practicing of witticisms, for example. But the way that most of the journal is shaped to emphasize a theme—Carlyle's neglect of her, his galling attentions to Lady Harriet—suggest that Jane was trying to tell her side of the story to the world, and particularly to one person in it, Mr. C. himself. He had hurt her; she wanted to hurt him back. Only her method (the diary) and not her strategy (revenge through guilt) was peculiar to Jane. Usually women make their wounds known to their husbands in other ways: minor sickness, complaint, anger, coldness, and sexual unavailability. Thomas Carlyle was impervious to any of these tactics and it required a written statement of Jane's wrongs, read after her death, to put him into the appropriate state of guilt. But guilt is woman's revenge on man for the liabilities of marriage.

Few women in history—or even literature—were more successful at making their husbands feel guilty than Jane Carlyle. Paulina and Hermione together hardly did better with Leontes. Carlyle saw the story of her life as she had laid it out for him in her letters and journals to be found after her death, a story of great promise, great gifts, great advantages sacrificed for a man who ultimately neglected her, and he swallowed the story hook, line, and sinker. It transformed his life. No more obsessions with train whistles. Now he was morbidly obsessed with regret, tuned in to the high-pitched wail of past disharmony.

Jane Carlyle died in London suddenly, of a stroke or heart attack, on April 21, 1866, while Carlyle was in Scotland being lionized. "How pungent is remorse," he wrote, "when it turns upon the loved dead, who cannot pardon us, cannot hear us now! Two plain precepts there are. Dost thou intend a kindness to thy beloved one? Do it straightway, while the fateful Future is not yet here. Has thy heart's friend carelessly or cruelly stabbed in thy heart? Oh, forgive him! Think how, when thou art dead, he will punish himself."[20] Froude reports that Carlyle spoke about Jane constantly after her death, and always in the same remorseful tone, always with bitter self-reproach. "He had never properly understood till her death how much she had suffered, and how much he had himself to answer for."[21]

As expiation, he conceived the idea of making her genius and his own unworthiness known to the world. Shortly after her death he wrote his reminiscence of her and after that he began the long and extremely painful task of preparing her letters and "memorials"— including even the *de profundis* diary—for publication: arranging, annotating, and commenting. *Reminiscences*, for one, records Carlyle's guilt as much as it records Jane's life.

I doubt, candidly, if I ever saw a nobler human soul than this which (alas, alas, never rightly valued till now!) accompanied all my steps for forty years. Blind and deaf that we are: oh, think, if thou yet love anybody living, wait not till death sweep down the paltry little dust-clouds and idle dissonances of the moment, and all be at last so mournfully clear and beautiful when it is too late!

She had from an early period formed her own little opinion about me (what an Eldorado to me, ungrateful being, blind, ungrateful, condemnable, and heavy laden, and crushed down into blindness by great misery as I oftenest was!), and she never flinched from it an instant, I think, or cared, or counted, what the world said to the contrary.

Ah me! she never knew fully, nor could I show her in my heavy-laden miserable life, how much I had at all times regarded, loved, and admired her. No telling of her now. "Five minutes more of your dear company in this world. Oh that I had you yet for but five minutes, to tell you all!" This is often my thought since April 21.[22]

Ending the reminiscence, Carlyle called it his "sacred shrine and religious city of refuge from the bitterness of these sorrows," a kind of "devotional thing."[23] But in re-reading her letters, he got the idea of creating more than a personal monument to her. He would let the world know the quality of her gifts, let them appreciate how much she had sacrificed to him. "As to 'talent', epistolary and other, these letters, I perceive, equal and surpass whatever of best I know to exist in that kind. . . . Not all the Sands and Eliots and babbling *cohue* of 'celebrated scribbling women' that have strutted over the world in my time could, it seems to me, if all boiled down and distilled to essence, make one such woman."[24]

The preparation of Jane's letters for publication took Carlyle some eleven months' work in 1868–69, "sad and strange as a pilgrimage through Hades."[25] "Perhaps," he wrote in his journal, "this mournful, but pious, and ever interesting task, escorted by such miseries, night after night, and month after month—perhaps all this may be wholesome punishment, purification, and monition."[26] Jane's letters did not make Carlyle look good, especially when encased in his remorseful annotations, which emphasized her misery and his own guilt and ignored her joyous, playful deployment of her great comic complaint. At the cost of his own reputation, he would build a monument to the literary talent she had sacrificed for him, emphasizing the faults in himself which had made her life, as he thought, wretched. Froude calls it a "beautiful" gesture, "unexampled in the history of literature," the most heroic act of a heroic life, typical of Carlyle in its humility and truthfulness,[27] and I agree that Carlyle's determination to publish Jane's writings should be seen for the courageous and imaginative act it was. But it is also true that Carlyle, by means of this gesture, may have triumphed in the end, had the last nip in their private cockfight. As it stands, her genius, her sacrifice, and her suffering are *his* creation, a literary artifice based on her raw materials, surely, and sculpted according to her directions, but willed into permanent existence by him.

After Carlyle's death, with the publication of Froude's biography and the *Reminiscences* and Jane's letters, the domestic life of the Carlyles entered the public domain, as Carlyle intended it should. Like Hamlet asking Horatio to absent himself from felicity awhile to tell his tale, Carlyle had entrusted Froude with the telling of his story—and Jane's. Froude understood that the *Letters and Memorials* were to be published separately, as a monument to Jane's literary talent, but he was also given permission to use the Carlyles' intimate papers in whatever way he saw fit in the writing of his biography.

It is a magnificent, compassionate work, portraying a genius whose very strength and breadth of thought unfit him for the small negotiations of daily life. Because his vision is essentially tragic, Froude does not *blame* Carlyle for making his wife wretched any more than one would blame Othello for mistreating Desdemona. Nevertheless, his work is structured on an ironic (and implicitly critical) principle: Carlyle sees to the heart of society but not into the mind of his partner for life. He is a great man, a great thinker, but a pathetic human being. He hurts Jane without knowing it, and he is lonely and wretched at the same time. Froude basically adopts Jane's view of the marriage as suggested by the 1855-56 diary—an heiress debased to a servant and neglected in her middle age for a more glamourous woman, her serious illnesses not understood or sufficiently sympathized with. And I have no doubt that that is how Carlyle, seeking punishment and expiation, would have wanted the story told.

When Froude's biography appeared in 1882, it created a sensation. Froude's complex portrait, with its large and tolerant understanding of human nature, was debased to a simple one—the great Carlyle, the sage and prophet, had been a terrible, a cruel, husband. The idol had feet of clay. Some people were appalled not only by Carlyle's behavior to Jane but by what they recognized to be possibilities within themselves. Was this marriage so different from their own? Others, reading Froude's biography more stupidly, saw it as an attack on the great man's character, which they hastened to defend. The "anti-Froudians" tried in every possible way to place Carlyle back on his pedestal, and most of these attempts involved personal attacks on Froude, or Geraldine Jewsbury (Jane's close friend, upon whom Froude had relied for intimate details), or Jane herself. In their view, the great man was guilty of nothing. If he spent a lot of time with Lady Harriet Ashburton, it was out of a perfectly understandable fondness for an unusual lady. Jane was jealous because she realized that Lady Harriet did better than she did the sort of thing she aspired to. She projected her own self-hatred onto her husband. In other words, if this was a bad marriage, it was Jane's fault. She was the guilty party, a "highly neurotic woman" and no wonder—since she'd grown up knowing Latin like a boy, reading Virgil at nine, doing math at ten, and writing a tragedy when she was fourteen.[28]

A hundred years have gone by since the controversy over Froude's portrait of the Carlyles' domestic life. Is it possible to view the matter any differently now? Is it possible to discard the fiction of "fault"? to bypass blame? even tragic limitation, the ironies of greatness? If so, we might well begin by denying that this was an exceptionally wretched marriage. There is a joke which congratulates the world that the Carlyles married each other: that way only two people were miserable, not four. But what strikes me is the singular economy of their union. Any alliance which lasts as long as theirs is bound to have moments—even months or years—of divergence of paths, failures of attention or sympathy on one side or the other, boredom, resentment, as it is equally bound to have moments of joy and intimacy resulting from nothing other than the occasional awareness of a shared past, a shared future—moments of gratuitous sweetness as well as moments inevitably sour. In the long view, the Carlyles seem uniquely compatible. She gave him the stability and affection he needed to work; he gave her the frustration and annoyance she required to thrive. The strains in the Carlyles' marriage which began to appear in the late 1840s and brought it close to the breaking point in the mid-1850s—strains associated with Lady Harriet Ashburton's role in Carlyle's life—seem to me generated by the structure of traditional marriage, of which theirs, for all its peculiarities, is a classic example. The strains do not seem to result from the individual characters of these two people, nor are they usefully seen as "his fault" or "hers." Carlyle had set a machine in motion, she on her side of the room and he on his, he writing and she running the household—a seemingly symmetrical and balanced structure. In time, however, flaws emerged. The woman felt she had paid too high a price. Thomas Carlyle required a written statement, chronicling his offenses. But he got the point—that he had wounded his wife. And he felt guilty, as she had intended he would. That was her revenge, as inflicting guilt will always be a revenge of the less powerful, whether male or female.

The Carlyles' was a particularly deep conflict.[29] To say that they clashed in many ways and in many ways disappointed each other is to say no more than that they were married, and for a long time. They acted out the possibilities of the form. Together, they created their individual uniqueness. He created himself with her help and support, and she created herself, in service, in mockery, in resistance. Perhaps they lived sexless and childless, perhaps they were not happy, but they were certainly a couple, and by writing about it, they made of their marriage a spectacle we in later days can witness, with tensions and resolutions we can participate in vicariously.

Postlude I:
Carlyle and the
Punch-and-Judy Show

Charles Eliot Norton, that peripatetic American man of letters, found himself in London in the winter of 1872, at loose ends. His beloved wife, Susan, had died in Dresden the previous February, after childbirth. His house in Cambridge was still rented out. So, despite his grief and desperate sense of rootlessness, he tried to make the most of his time in Europe, visiting with great writers and thinkers, as had always been his habit.

The two men in England Norton respected most were Carlyle and Ruskin, and on December 13, 1872, he had them both to lunch. Carlyle was a distinguished seventy-seven, a renowned conversationalist, the sage of his era. The reputation which he had lost with the publication of the notorious, reactionary *Latter-Day Pamphlets* in 1850 had come back to him with age. That he had been fully rehabilitated was signalled by his installation as rector (an honorary post) at Edinburgh University in 1866, the year—the very week—that Jane died, at the pinnacle of her husband's success.

On the day of Norton's lunch, Carlyle brought his host and fellow widower a little bread-and-butter gift, a copy of *Sartor Resartus*. He and Ruskin, fifty-three, were in their sweetest moods, and they were perfectly at ease with each other. The talk, full of humor, devoid of arrogance, was the best that Norton, a connoisseur of talk, had ever heard. It touched on Frederick the Great, Barbarossa, Walt Whitman, the penalties of life in London, the horrors of shopping, Rousseau, magazines, old Scottish women, and *Don Quixote*, which Carlyle said was among the best books ever written.

After lunch, a Punch-and-Judy was performed in the street in front of Norton's study windows. Norton had arranged it especially for Ruskin, because he knew Ruskin enjoyed the play and also liked seeing the amusement of the audience of children. So Ruskin watched Punch beat Judy and Judy beat Punch and Punch beat Judy again, and he also watched the children laughing. Carlyle withdrew to the fireside and smoked a pipe. When Punch was over, Carlyle talked kindly to the children in the street, kissing a little girl who stood by the door. "Poor little woman! dear little woman!" he said. Then the men talked together some more, and at sunset Ruskin took Carlyle home in his carriage.

Postlude II:
Carlyle and the
Jamaica Rebellion

In October 1865 in Jamaica, one of the less-far-flung outposts of the Empire, trouble occurred. One hundred and fifty black men armed with sticks marched on the fort at Morant Bay in order to rescue a man imprisoned there. Scuffling led to serious fighting with policemen, and before long people on both sides were getting killed. When the news reached the governor, Mr. Edward John Eyre, in Spanish Town, he immediately called the riot a rebellion, declared a state of martial law, and sent a detachment of troops to Morant Bay. These troops suppressed the "rebels" with a vigor amounting to ferocity.

For many days, quick trials produced verdicts of death, and the sentences—execution by hanging or firing squad—were carried out immediately. Prisoners who were not killed were flogged. If the natives ran away at the soldiers' approach, they were shot for running away. One Lieutenant Adcock returned from a foray, having burned seven houses, to find that sixty-five prisoners had been collected in his absence. "I disposed of as many as possible," he commented, "but was too tired to continue after dark. On the morning of the 24th I started for Morant Bay, having first flogged four and hung six rebels."[1]

Governor Eyre became convinced that George William Gordon, a black member of the Jamaica House of Assembly, was responsible for all the unrest. After running him down and allowing him the merest form of a trial, the governor had Gordon hanged. In his own eyes, he was acting quickly to suppress a dangerous insurrection. He remembered—as what Briton in the colonies did not?—the massacre of British men, women, and even children at Cawnpore in 1857, and the memory encouraged and justified every ferocity. He was suppressing a mutiny not as small as Jamaica but as large as the Empire, as vicious as the dreams of revenge he imagined were harbored by subject barbarians.

Still, some people thought he had acted too quickly and severely in ordering Gordon's execution, that the execution, indeed, was no better than murder. Concern spread back to England, where the Jamaica incident aroused extraordinary interest among Victorian intellectuals. Jane Carlyle, at an evening gathering at the home of Lady William Russell, without her husband, engaged in conversation on the subject with one irate gentleman. According to Jane,

Hayward was raging against the Jamaica business—would have had Eyre cut into small pieces and eaten raw. He told me *women* might patronize Eyre—that women were naturally cruel, and rather liked to look on while horrors were perpetrated. But no *man* living could stand up for Eyre now! "I hope Mr. Carlyle does," I said. "I haven't had an opportunity of asking him; but I should be surprised and grieved if I found him sentimentalising over a pack of black brutes!" After staring at me a moment: "Mr. Carlyle!" said Hayward. "Oh yes! Mr. *Carlyle!* one cannot indeed swear what he will *not* say! His great aim and philosophy of life being 'The smallest happiness of the fewest number!' "[2]

Jane Carlyle did not have to know her husband particularly well to predict what line he would take on this issue. Although he had, in his earlier days, celebrated revolutionary energies, he increasingly respected the men who could channel and contain those energies, revering the leaders, scorning the masses of people who were led, until it was difficult to tell the difference between Carlyle's position and that of a simple worshipper of the authoritarian exercise of power. On the subject of blacks, he had expressed himself in 1849, in an essay he called "The Nigger Question," to the effect that blacks were intended for work and to be mastered. His essay had been scathingly rebuked by John Stuart Mill in an answering one: "The Negro Question."

The great adversaries who had once mistakenly thought they

shared intellectual bonds now squared off. Mill, outraged by Governor Eyre's disregard of law and human rights, organized a committee which sought to have him removed from office and prosecuted for murder, while Carlyle accepted the chair of the Eyre Defence Fund, saying that the nation owed Eyre honor and thanks for his defense of civilization and "wise imitation" should similar emergencies arise. "The English nation have never loved anarchy, nor was wont to spend its sympathy on miserable mad seditions, especially of this inhuman and half-brutish type, but always loved order and the prompt suppression of seditions." Both sides claimed to be fighting for law; but whose law? and laws protecting what—order or freedom? the strong or the weak? heroic Englishmen or their "half-brutish" subjects?

A kind of litmus paper for political assumptions, the Eyre controversy clarified orientations towards power. The great writers and thinkers of mid-Victorian England aligned themselves with or against Governor Eyre like two hockey teams ranged for the face-off. Behind Mill, opposing Eyre, were the liberals and scientific progressives, including Darwin, Huxley, Spencer, and George Henry Lewes. Behind Carlyle, defending Eyre, were the romantic authoritarians, including Dickens, Ruskin, Tennyson, Tyndall, and Kingsley.

Huxley put it this way: "If English law will not declare that heroes have no more right to kill people in this fashion than other folk, I shall take an early opportunity of migrating to Texas or some other quiet place where there is less respect for hero-worship and more respect for justice. . . . The hero-worshippers who believe that the world is to be governed by its great men, who are to lead the little ones, justly if they can, but if not unjustly drive or kick them the right way, will sympathize with Mr. Eyre. The other sect (to which I belong) who look upon hero-worship as no better than any other idolatry, and upon the attitude of mind of the hero-worshipper as essentially immoral . . . will believe that Mr. Eyre has committed one of the greatest crimes.[3]

The Eyre affair resurrected some of the issues of the Emancipation controversy thirty years before as well as Mill and Carlyle's "Negro Question" fight of 1849. Carlyle had argued that the domination of one group by another, of black by white, of slave by master, was "natural," whereas Mill had pointed out that the people had a way of calling "natural" whatever arrangement happened to work to their advantages. And even if such domination were "natural," did not human law exist to counteract the brutality of nature? Similar arguments were made about women's rights, too, one side holding it was "natural" for women to be subject to men, the other denying it. This was unsurprising, since the great democratic movements of the nineteenth century—emancipation, nationalism, universal suffrage, women's rights, even trade unionism—were connected, among other ways, in that they all attempted to redistribute power in the face of claims that the status quo was divinely ordained. However sympathetic they were to the plight of the disadvantaged, the supporters of Eyre tended to support, as a solution to the problem, a paternalistic exercise of power rather than a redistribution of advantage.

Eyre stood trial eventually, but the result was inconclusive. He was neither punished strongly enough to suit Mill nor vindicated strongly enough to suit Carlyle. What the Eyre affair suggests to me is a connection between the way you look at things like the exercise of authority in matters of government and the way you look at things like the exercise of authority within a family; it suggests a connection between politics and sex. Although the alignment is not absolute— Leslie Stephen, who opposed Eyre, was something of a domestic tyrant—the men who backed Eyre mostly tended to uphold strong male authority within the family and to expect submissiveness from wives. If, as with Ruskin, a strong-willed wife showed signs of what we might call self-assertion, those signs were read as rebelliousness, defiance, and hostility, and they led to a state of war between them as inevitably as between a ruler and any subject who resists his rule. Dickens married a cipher, made her even more of a cipher during many years of married life, and by middle age resented her for being the nonentity he had made her, thus reproducing in his private life the imperialist Englishman's mixture of benevolent condescension and contempt for his colonies. Mill, on the other hand, tried so hard to avoid the traditional male-dominated balance of power within marriage, that he enacted a parody of the patriarchal situation and in the name of sexual equality was, if anything, dottily deferential. Both outlooks shared the image of the family as a state, with the man as ruler, the wife as executive class, the children (if any) as the dependent masses to be cared for. They disagreed only about the degree to which the "governed" should participate in power. Was this little state an absolute monarchy or a democracy?

The underlying metaphor for marriage has changed, and much contemporary discussion is based on the image of marriage as a business partnership. In *The Subjection of Women*, Mill offered the example of commercial partnership to show that there need be no absolute master in voluntary associations, still less that the law need determine which of two people it should be. In *Man and Superman*, in one of his many puckish jibes at the bourgeois practice of marriage, George Bernard Shaw noted that while a proposal to abolish marriage would be tolerated in neither England nor America, "nothing is more certain than that in both countries the progressive modification of the marriage contract will be continued until it is no more onerous nor irrevocable than any ordinary commercial deed of partnership." Marriage counselling nowadays emphasizes "the marriage contract," an unwritten agreement at various levels of consciousness between a man and woman about their obligations and expectations.[4] The contractual model, which assumes two people of more or less equivalent status in law, seems a decided advance for women. But whether one thinks of a married couple's relation as that of ruler and ruled or that of business partners, the issue of equality—of the ideal balance of power between two parties—is a crucial one, and not significantly easier to define in terms of the one metaphor than the other.

Equality is to sexual politics what the classless society is to Marxist theory: the hypothesis that solves the problem. Anyone who thinks about human relationships as negotiations of power will quickly and inevitably come to consider the ideal of equality. But despite the number of people who pay lip service to this ideal, few have been able to pin down exactly what it means or to describe how this desirable state may be achieved. One of the most persistent in the attempt was D. H. Lawrence. His ideal of sexual equality involved the yoking of two strong selves and required the maintenance of self, not its surrender. But every time Lawrence tried to describe his ideal (largely through Rupert Birkin, in *Women in Love*), he got tongue-tied. "It is a difficult, complex maintenance of individual integrity throughout the incalculable processes of interhuman polarity." Or, "It is a maintenance of self in mystic balance and integrity—like a star balanced with another star." Lawrence's image of the "star-balanced equilibrium" for the ideal relationship between a man and a woman has struck a responsive chord in the twentieth century, but Birkin's fiancée, Ursula Brangwen, was probably not the last woman to suspect that behind the lure of the star-balanced equilibrium lay just another sun wanting another planet to circle it. Before going into cosmic orbit, how does one find these things out?

Another persuasive attempt to define equality—one which abjures measurement and metaphor both—is Erik Erikson's.[5] Calling the ideal "mutuality," Erikson elucidates the psychological truth of the prayer of Saint Francis, "Grant that I may not so much seek to be consoled as to console; to be understood as to understand; to be loved as to love, for it is in giving that we receive." Erikson warns that to approach any human encounter in a demanding spirit is to solicit disappointment. We can never be given enough. But if we ask only to give, to nurture and strengthen someone else, we will find ourselves strengthened in the process. In a marriage that works well, one person's needs strengthen—do not deplete—the vitality of the partner who responds to them, in the same way that a child's demands strengthen the parent who ministers to them by reinforcing his or her sense of competence, vitality, identity. In Erikson's view, all intimate human relationships repeat the relationship between parent and child in that help given helps the helper as much as the ostensible object of help. Both partners in a marriage are equal in that each depends on the other for the development of the strengths appropriate to his or her time of life. This is attractive, yet I can't help but wonder if Erikson's ideal of mutuality isn't the old ideal of self-sacrifice presented now in the inspirational language of psychological health.

Personally, I prefer images to definitions. The scene in *Women in Love* which shows Ursula replying skeptically to Birkin's notion of the "star-balanced equilibrium" ("I don't trust you when you drag in the stars. If you were quite true, it wouldn't be necessary to be so far-fetched") is, taken as a whole, a more convincing version of equality between a man and a woman than Birkin's murky definition, taken by itself. I like the images of sexual equality offered by some American films of the thirties and forties, notably those which continue the tradition of the sparring lovers of Shakespearean and Restoration comedy.[6] Some time in the future, the dynamics of equality may be understood, perfected, and described. In the meantime, sparring remains one of the most convincing images we have of it. *Adam's Rib,* with Spencer Tracy and Katharine Hepburn as attorneys for the prosecution and defense in the same court case, presents one appealing version of a marriage of equals. *Pat and Mike* offers another. In this one Hepburn plays Pat Pemberton, a superb athlete who fails consistently when her fiancé, a handsome, socially impeccable college administrator, is in the audience. The looks he throws her as she plays tennis or golf are supposed to be reassuring, but they assume her failure, seek to console her for it, and so end up by guaranteeing it. This is the film's cautionary version of sexual partnership. His strength depends on her weakness. And Pat can be obligingly weak. Tracy as Mike Conovan, Pat's Runyonesque manager, proves to be the better husband for her, partly because he has a vested interest in her success (talk about marriage as business partnership!) and partly *because* he is her social inferior. The film suggests that a woman has to transgress some barrier—class in the case of Pat and Mike, but age might be another—to secure an equal partner and to redress the power advantage which belongs to the man on grounds of gender.

Traditional marriage shores up the power of men in subtle ways which I believe few men—even sensitive men of the greatest goodwill towards women—appreciate. When you are playing tennis and the wind is blowing from your back, you may not be aware of the wind at all and think only that you are playing very well. All your shots go in swift and hard. It isn't until you change courts and the wind is blowing against you that you appreciate the force of the wind. Power is like that. You feel it most when it is working against you. Women sometimes marry to find that the wind is suddenly blowing against them. I am speaking now of spirited women, strong women, who are the most likely to resent the sudden change. They feel overwhelmed in marriage by husbands who have been raised to act, if not to be, strong in their dealings with the outside world and to expect devoted care from a woman in the family. Both their outward strength and inner dependency are reinforced by the usual order of things in marriage. So that women who are sensitive to power negotiations in their relationships—and women seem to be particularly sensitive to power —may prefer men with some handicap. (By handicap, I simply mean the absence of one of those surpluses, or advantages over women, with which men are traditionally expected to enter marriage—height, money, age, social status, achievement.) Or they may avoid marriage altogether. For "50-50," the rule of fair partnership, is a deceptively lucid ideal. How do people achieve it? How do they keep from slipping into 49-51? Splitting the household chores is a beginning, but only a crude one, on the path to achieving the psychopolitical equality many of us aspire to.

Judy Benjamin's lawyer husband, in the film *Private Benjamin*, advises a client on how to protect himself in marriage: "Pre-nups, baby! Pre-nups is the only way to go." (He is also speaking to the dark side of our contemporary sense of marriage as business partnership.) But Judy's husband dies on their wedding night, leaving her as dependent as ever. She cannot understand the behavior of another film heroine, in *An Unmarried Woman*, who refuses to marry the attractive artist played by Alan Bates. But by the end of *Private Benjamin*, Judy, too, will reject marriage. Pre-nups can't help her. Only the army—which, as we all know, makes a man of you—can help. *Private Benjamin* and *An Unmarried Woman* are among some films of the late seventies and early eighties which focus on what marriage can—and mainly cannot—do for women. The suspicion grows that it cannot do very much.[7]

My aim throughout this book has not been to show that Dickens or Ruskin or Carlyle were "bad" husbands, but to present them as examples of behavior generated inevitably by the peculiar privileges and stresses of traditional marriage. It is probably clear that George Eliot and George Henry Lewes are, in one sense, the heroine and hero of the book. In their case, devotion, stability, and equality grew outside the bounds of legal marriage—whether in accord with some psychological quirk of human nature which resists fulfilling promises, or because sanctioned marriage bears some ineradicable taint which converts the personal relationship between a man and a woman into a political one, I cannot finally say, although both may be true. I hope it is also clear that some of the other women I have written about are heroines, too: Harriet Mill for her thinking about marriage and her desire to reform it, as well as for making the most of a very weak hand, and Effie Gray for realizing she was in a mess (not crazy, as her husband said) and getting out of it. To think of Catherine Dickens as a heroine is impossible, but, in the annals of marriage, perhaps she has earned a place as a martyr. Above all, my heroine is Jane Carlyle. Feisty Jane went down fighting, demanding equal time, and writing about it all in marvelous prose which just might outlast her husband's. Because of her, the Carlyles' marriage seems, in the strange afterlife which literature grants, to be also a marriage of equals, where equality consists—as perhaps it must, in an imperfect time such as hers, or ours—in perpetual resistance, perpetual rebellion.

A Chronology

1821   Jane Baillie Welsh meets Thomas Carlyle.

1823   Francis Place tries to distribute information on birth control, assisted by seventeen-year-old John Stuart Mill; Mill is arrested on obscenity charges but the case is dismissed.

1826   Jane Welsh marries Thomas Carlyle.
        Harriet Hardy marries John Taylor.

1828   The Carlyles move to Craigenputtock.

1830   Harriet Taylor consults her minister about marital dissatisfaction; he arranges an introduction to John Stuart Mill.

1831   John Stuart Mill meets Thomas Carlyle.

        Maria Beadnell refuses to marry Charles Dickens because of his lack of prospects.

1833   Arthur Hallam, friend of Tennyson, fiancé of Tennyson's sister Emily, dies suddenly, aged twenty-two.

1834   The Carlyles move to 5 Cheyne Row, Chelsea.

1835   The manuscript of the first volume of *The French Revolution* is burned while in Mill's possession; the Carlyles are momentarily relieved that the bad news Mill has come to tell them is not that he has decided to elope with Mrs. Taylor.

1836   Darwin returns from the *Beagle* voyage of five years.

Ruskin falls in love with Adèle Domecq, daughter of his father's partner in the sherry trade.

Dickens marries Catherine Hogarth.

1837   Anne Thackeray, first child of W. M. Thackeray, the novelist, and his wife, is born. Another daughter, Minny, will be born the next year. Then Mrs. Thackeray will be committed to an institution, on grounds of mental instability, for the rest of her life. Thackeray, unable to re-marry, will devotedly raise his daughters.

Charles Dickens, Jr., the first child of Charles Dickens the novelist and his wife, Catherine, is born. Dickens is already famous for *Pickwick Papers*, which he concludes in this year; he has begun *Oliver Twist*.

Victoria, aged seventeen, ascends the throne of England.

1838   Mamie Dickens born.

1839   Charles Darwin marries his cousin Emma Wedgwood, daughter of the great chinaware manufacturer, Josiah Wedgwood; they take up residence in Upper Gower Street, London; in December, William Darwin is born. Darwin reads Malthus's *Essay on Population*, a key factor in generating his theory of natural selection.

Kate Dickens born.

1840   Queen Victoria, dreading only the prospect of having many children, marries her cousin, Albert of Saxe-Coburg.

1841   Anne Elizabeth Darwin born.

Walter Landor Dickens born.

Emily Tennyson announces her engagement to a lieutenant in the navy; it is eight years after Hallam's death, but many people are horrified by her betrayal of him.

1842   The Carlyles meet Mr. and Mrs. Baring (later Lord and Lady Ashburton).

The Darwins settle at Down, Kent; Mary Eleanor Darwin born, dies.

1843   Henrietta Darwin born.

1844   Thackeray and Jane Brookfield, each unhappy in marriage, vow to be close friends for life.

Francis Jeffrey Dickens born.

1845   Alfred d'Orsay Tennyson Dickens born.

George Howard Darwin born.

1847   James Simpson, the Edinburgh physician, publishes his discovery of chloroform as an anaesthetic, revolutionizing the procedure of childbirth.

Jane Eyre published with a dedication to Thackeray, leading many people to suppose (mistakenly) that its author was a governess in Thackeray's household and that the novel's portrait of Mr. Rochester and his mad wife was based on Thackeray and his.

Sydney Smith Dickens born.

Elizabeth Darwin born.

1848   Ruskin marries Euphemia Gray in Scotland, on the day of the Chartist demonstration in London.

Pre-Raphaelite Brotherhood founded, with the goal of truth to nature; it includes John Everett Millais, the painter.

Emma Darwin gives birth to Francis Darwin, her seventh child; four days later, Charles Darwin makes inquiries about chloroform.

1849   Mary Ellen Peacock marries George Meredith.

John Taylor, husband of Harriet Taylor, dies of cancer.

Henry Fielding Dickens born.

1850 Leonard Darwin born; Charles Darwin administers chloroform to his wife.

Dora Annie Dickens born. Dickens insists on use of chloroform for the delivery.

Tennyson marries Emily Sellwood, to whom he has been engaged since 1838; *In Memoriam*, his extended elegy for Arthur Hallam, is published.

1851 John Stuart Mill marries Harriet Taylor.

Marian Evans (the future George Eliot) meets George Henry Lewes.

William Brookfield, the popular minister, after a quarrel with wife, forces her to end her friendship with Thackeray.

Horace Darwin born; Annie Darwin dies, aged 10.

Dora Annie Dickens dies, aged 1.

Thomas Love Peacock's wife (Mary Ellen's mother), who has been mad and locked away for twenty-five years, finally dies.

1852 Ruskin, as J. M. W. Turner's executor, discovers and burns his pornographic sketches.

Effie Ruskin, as a charitable act, arranges to have chloroform sent from Scotland to the Fate Bene Fratelli, nursing friars with a hospital on one of the islands of the Venetian lagoon.

Edward Bulwer Lytton Dickens born.

1853 The Ruskins spend part of the summer at Glenfinlas, taking along John Everett Millais for the sake of his education; Ruskin works on the index to *The Stones of Venice;* Effie and Millais fall in love.

Queen Victoria is given chloroform for the birth of her fourth son, eighth child, Prince Leopold.

1854 The Ruskins' marriage annulled by the ecclesiastical court; the judgment cites Ruskin's "incurable impotency," which allegation he resents.

Marian Evans and George Henry Lewes "elope" to Germany, beginning their lifelong union.

1855 Effie Gray marries John Everett Millais.

Maria Beadnell re-enters Dickens life but proves to be a disappointment.

1856 Jane Carlyle records in her diary increasing misery about her husband's attentions to Lady Harriet Ashburton; she follows with interest the trial of Palmer, the man accused of poisoning his wife for her insurance policy; George Rennie, one of her Haddington beaux, re-enters her life but is disappointingly adult.

Charles Waring Darwin born, the Darwins' tenth and last child.

1857 The Matrimonial Causes Act establishes secular divorce in England.

Dickens meets Ellen Ternan.

Lady Harriet Ashburton dies; Jane Carlyle's depression lifts.

Millais's reputation as an artist begins to decline.

Women and children are massacred at Cawnpore, during the Indian Mutiny.

Madeleine Smith of Glasgow accused of poisoning her lover, a poor shipping clerk, who has been threatening to prevent her marriage to a man of higher social standing by making public her love letters; Miss Smith acquitted after a sensational trial which Jane Carlyle follows in the newspapers; public sentiment strongly in favor of Miss Smith.

1858 Ruskin meets Rose La Touche, with whom he will fall in love; he is thirty-nine and she is nine.

Dickens separates from his wife and explains himself to the public by statements in many newspapers.

Harriet Taylor Mill dies in France, where she and husband had gone in search of health.

The birth of "George Eliot," the novelist, with the publication of *Scenes of Clerical Life;* Mrs. Carlyle, sent a copy by the author, decides he is "a man of middle age, with a wife from whom he has got those beautiful *feminine* touches in his book, a good many children, and a dog."

Mary Ellen Peacock Meredith elopes to Capri with Henry Wallis, a painter who has used George Meredith as the model for Chatterton in his painting, *The Death of Chatterton.*

Queen Victoria's daughter, the Princess Royal (known as Vicky), is married to Prince Frederick William of Prussia and almost immediately becomes pregnant, which her mother considers "horrid news."

1859 Publication of *The Origin of Species;* Mill's *On Liberty; Adam Bede;* and *A Tale of Two Cities.*

William Morris marries Jane Burden.

In America, a member of Congress shoots a Washington lawyer for "a systematic career of guilty intercourse with his wife" and is acquitted, to general delight.

1860 Kate Dickens (Dickens's daughter) and Charles Collins (Wilkie Collins's brother), modelling for Millais's *The Black Brunswicker,* get increasingly attached to each other and eventually marry; Kate's mother is not invited to the wedding; it is thought that Miss Dickens has agreed to marry the sickly Collins in order to escape the unpleasantness of her father's household.

1861 Queen Victoria is widowed.

Marian Evans and George Henry Lewes, on their way to Florence, stop at the Avignon cemetery to visit Harriet Mill's tomb and find the inscription sweetly excessive.

Mill is writing *The Subjection of Women*.

Madeleine Smith marries George Wardle, an associate of William Morris; they will have two children and become members of the Socialist League; after his death she will move to America, re-marry, and die in Brooklyn at the age of ninety-two.

1863   Fairy-tale wedding of Albert, Prince of Wales, to Alexandra, who caught the popular imagination because she had grown up poor, but Jane Carlyle is sniffy: "Such a noise about that 'Royal marriage!' I wish it were over."

1865   The publication of the popular volume *Sesame and Lilies*, including the essay "Of Queen's Gardens," establishes Ruskin as a major authority on the nature of women.

Governor Eyre puts down with brutal efficiency an uprising among black subjects in Jamaica, causing controversy in England over the proper exercise of authority.

1866   Thomas Carlyle installed as rector at Edinburgh University; Jane Welsh Carlyle dies.

1867   John Stuart Mill, as a member of Parliament, initiates the first parliamentary debate on women's suffrage by proposing that the word *man* be replaced by the word *person* in the Reform Bill under discussion.

1868   Mr. and Mrs. Charles Eliot Norton of Cambridge, Massachusetts, stay with Dickens and his family at Gad's Hill, then take up residence near the Darwins, with whom they become good friends. Visiting Oxford, Norton meets George Henry Lewes, who tells him, with tears in his eyes, how his wife came to write fiction.

1869   Carlyle reads through all Jane's letters, preparing them for publication, "task of about eleven months, and sad and strange as a pilgrimage through Hades."

Mill publishes *The Subjection of Women*.

Charles Eliot Norton dines with Mill at Blackheath and with

Ruskin at Denmark Hill; for the first time he meets Carlyle, who tells him America would be the mightiest nation in the world if it had a king and if it put its "nagurs" back into slavery or killed them off by massacre or starvation.

1870 Dickens dies, leaving *The Mystery of Edwin Drood* unfinished; his will gives £8,000 to Georgina Hogarth and to each of his sons, Charles and Henry; £1,000 plus an annuity until she marries is left to his daughter, Mamie; and £1,000 goes to Ellen Ternan.

Married Woman's Property Act guarantees a wife's right to her own earnings, savings, and so on.

1872 Charles Eliot Norton, recently widowed, has Ruskin and Carlyle to lunch, arranging a Punch-and-Judy show for Ruskin's amusement.

1873 John Stuart Mill dies. Norton breaks the news to Carlyle, who says, "What! John Mill dead! Dear me, Dear me! John Mill! how did he die and where? And it's so long since I've seen him, and he was the friendliest of men to me when I was in need of friends. Dear me! it's all over now," and tells Norton the story of Mill's debilitating intimacy with Harriet Taylor.

1877 Anne Thackeray, forty, marries her cousin Richmond Ritchie, twenty-three.

Darwin's eldest son marries Sara Sedgwick, the younger sister of Charles Eliot Norton's dead wife, Susan.

Leslie Stephen, after the death of his wife Minny, Thackeray's younger daughter, courts the beautiful widow Julia Duckworth. They will marry and have four children; the third will become known as Virginia Woolf.

1878 Marian Evans's companion of twenty-four years, George Henry Lewes, dies.

1880 In May, Marian Evans, sixty, marries John Walter Cross, forty; she dies in December.

1881 Carlyle dies. Publication of his *Reminiscences*, including the memoir of his wife which unveils his remorse. From this time, people will debate the Carlyles' marriage. Controversy will increase with the publication of Froude's biography of Carlyle in 1882 and 1884. The self-styled defenders of Carlyle and "anti-Froudians" will blame Jane Carlyle, calling her an over-educated, neurotic woman.

1903 George Bernard Shaw proclaims (in *Man and Superman*), "The confusion of marriage with morality has done more to destroy the conscience of the human race than any other single error."

Notes

Selected Bibliography

Index

Notes

1. Sir Leslie Stephen, *The Mausoleum Book*, introduction by Alan Bell (Oxford: Clarendon Press, 1977).
2. It is possible to read *Jane Eyre* as a critique of the family along the same lines. Jane charges John Reed, the spoiled son of her foster family, with being a despot like Caligula and castigates herself for allowing him to treat her as a slave. Her adult encounters with Rochester are conscious attempts to re-adjust the usual balance of power between men and women. She is successful, at least in part, because of Rochester's blinding and maiming in the fire which destroys his house.

   Henry Kissinger has said that power in a man is aphrodisiac to women, but the absence of power may be equally alluring. Witness the perennial popularity of narratives about love between a woman and an attractive man who is suddenly maimed and made dependent, from *Jane Eyre* to the film *Coming Home*, in which the heroine prefers the paraplegic Vietnam veteran to her macho officer-husband. Buñuel's film *Belle de Jour*, about an upper-middle-class Parisian who works in a brothel for kicks until her surgeon-husband is blinded and crippled by one of her clients, is virtually a case study of the connection between power, sex, and marriage.

   On women's alliances with socially or economically disadvantaged men as conscious or semi-conscious attempts to redress the usual power arrangement in marriage, see also Jane Marcus on Virginia Woolf's choice of Leonard and Beatrice Webb's choice of Sidney: "The only solution for the woman who wanted independence, an intellectual and social partnership, instead of the slaveries and servilities of middle-class marriage, was to choose a mate who was an outsider, below her class, infatuated with her beauty and distinction, and indebted to her for her small income, which allowed him to pursue his own intellectual work." (Review of *A Victorian Court-ship: The Story of Beatrice Potter and Sidney Webb*, in *Victorian Studies* [Spring 1981], 579.)

3. Despite our willingness to assert love's importance in marriage, we seem to have some trouble in knowing exactly what it is. In my own effort to answer this question, I turned to a relatively sophisticated textbook on court-ship, marriage, and the family, which offers a chapter titled "What is Love?" It tells me first that love is a relationship which progresses through various stages: rapport, self-revelation, mutual dependency, and personality need fulfillment. It then instructs me on the difference between *eros* and *agape*, sexual and selfless love, with a considerable charge in favor of the latter. It then cites Fromm to the effect that love is an art, something to be practiced and worked upon. It distinguishes at length between immature and mature love. (Immature love is born at first sight and is the sort you think will conquer all, demands exclusive attention, is characterized by ex-ploitation, is built upon physical attraction and sexual gratification, demands changes in the partner to satisfy its own needs and desires but is itself static and egocentric, romanticizes itself and refuses to face reality, and is irresponsible, failing to consider the consequences of actions, *whereas* mature love is a developing relationship which deepens with realistically shared experiences, is built upon self-acceptance, seeks to aid the loved one without constantly striving for recompense, includes sexual satisfaction but not to the exclusion of other kinds of sharing, can accommodate the growth and creativity of the loved one, enhances reality, making the partners more com-plete and adequate, and is responsible, gladly accepting the consequences of mutual involvement.) Finally, the textbook provides me with a "Caring Relationship Index." All this the textbook does so that I, and other anxious students like me, may know if we love, and if we do love, whether we love in the right (mature) way. I am put in mind of the perplexity of some of John Wesley's followers, who, believing that love of God was the way to Heaven, as Wesley told them, wanted him to explain to them how they would know if they loved God or not.

On the repression of the subject of power as it affects human relationships, see Robert Seidenberg, *Marriage Between Equals* (Garden City, New York: Doubleday, Anchor Press, 1973. Orig. titled *Marriage in Life and Literature* [New York: Philosophical Library, 1970]). This intelligent and unpre-tentious book by a psychiatrist deserves to be more widely known.

4. See especially David Kantor and William Lehr, *Inside the Family: Toward a Theory of Family Process* (San Francisco: Jossey-Bass, 1976), which identi-fies three basic family structures, each with characteristic aspirations and mechanisms. The "closed" family, the most traditional, values discipline, strong central authority, unity, clear roles, and loyalty. The "open" family seeks to gain the consensus of all members of the family for action and em-phasizes tolerance and cooperation. The "random" family is a collection of

individuals who acknowledge a minimal connection, making collective action difficult but offering considerable freedom and encouraging inventiveness. Families rarely exist in one form at all times but adopt one form or another for various aspects of life. I am simplifying Kantor and Lehr's complicated and subtle model of family interactions, in which power is only one of a few valences. Nevertheless, their models of family systems are like political structures.

5. See, for a classic feminist exposition of *Jane Eyre*, Sandra M. Gilbert and Susan Gubar, *The Madwoman in the Attic: A Study of Women and the Literary Imagination in the Nineteenth Century* (New Haven and London: Yale University Press, 1979), 336–71.

6. Robert Hurley, trans., *The History of Sexuality, Volume I: An Introduction* (New York: Pantheon Books, 1978).

7. Lillian Faderman, *Surpassing the Love of Men: Romantic Friendship and Love Between Women from the Renaissance to the Present* (New York: William Morrow, 1981), esp. 190–203.

8. See Sigmund Freud, "The Most Prevalent Form of Degradation in the Erotic Life" ("Three Contributions to the Psychology of Love"), in *Creativity and the Unconscious: Papers on the Psychology of Art, Literature, Love, and Religion*, ed. Benjamin Nelson (New York: Harper & Row Torchbooks, 1958), 173–86. On Victorian sexuality, see also J. A. and Olive Banks, *Feminism and Family Planning in Victorian England* (New York: Schocken Books, 1964); Fraser Harrison, *The Dark Angel: Aspects of Victorian Sexuality* (New York: Universe Books, 1977); Keith Thomas, "The Double Standard," *Journal of the History of Ideas* 20 (1959): 195–216; Jeffrey Weeks, *Sex, Politics, and Society: The Regulation of Sexuality Since 1800* (London and New York: Longman, 1981).

9. See Christopher Lasch, *The Culture of Narcissism: American Life in an Age of Diminishing Expectations* (New York: W. W. Norton, 1979). See also Lasch's *Haven in a Heartless World: The Family Besieged* (New York: Basic Books, 1977), especially for its critique of the sociology of the family and its rediscovery of the anti-romantic studies of American courtship and marriage by Willard Waller, as in *The Family: A Dynamic Interpretation* (New York: The Dryden Press, 1938).

10. See Karl Scheibe, "In Defense of Lying: On the Moral Neutrality of Misrepresentation," *Berkshire Review* 15 (1980): 15–24.

JANE WELSH AND THOMAS CARLYLE
(THE COURTSHIP)

1. *The Collected Letters of Thomas and Jane Welsh Carlyle*, ed. Charles Richard Sanders, Kenneth Fielding et al., Duke-Edinburgh Edition, 9 vols. to date (Durham, N.C.: Duke University Press, 1970–), 2:196. Henceforth

referred to in the notes as Duke-Edinburgh. The most recently published volume of this magnificent edition covers material to 1837 only, and Carlyle lived to 1881. I calculate that more than two dozen volumes will be needed to complete this epic task.

2. Thomas Carlyle, *Reminiscences*, ed. James Anthony Froude (New York: Charles Scribner's Sons, 1881), 327–28. This story was originally told by Geraldine Jewsbury in the brief biography which formed the basis of Carlyle's reminiscence about Jane.

3. Ibid., 346.

4. Ibid., 363–64.

5. Duke-Edinburgh 1:363.

6. Ibid., 366.

7. Ibid., 420.

8. Roughly, "All for glory and her!" Carlyle is intending to quote from Schiller's *Thirty Years' War* in which Duke Christian of Braunschweig goes into battle with a motto on his standard alluding to his passion for the countess of the Palatinate, a great king's daughter from whom he wished to win a tribute to his courage. But Christian's motto was "Alles für Gott und Sie"; he fought for her and God, not for glory. Moreover, the great translator of German thought is guilty here of a grammatical error. The German preposition *für* takes the accusative, *sie*, and not the dative, *ihr*. Duke-Edinburgh 2:15; see also 2:26 and note.

9. Duke-Edinburgh 2:20.

10. Ibid., 26.

11. Ibid., 38.

12. Ibid., 17.

13. Ibid., 18.

14. Ibid., 38.

15. Ibid., 108.

16. Ibid., 114.

17. Ibid., 251–52.

18. Ibid., 197, 286, 321.

19. Ibid., 317, 416, 420.

20. Ibid., 427–28.

21. Duke-Edinburgh 3:250.

22. Ibid.

23. Ibid., 264.

24. Duke-Edinburgh 2:313–14.

25. Duke-Edinburgh 3:266.

26. Ibid., 281.

27. Ibid., 394.

28. Duke-Edinburgh 4:102–3.

29. Duke-Edinburgh 2:132.

30. Duke-Edinburgh 4:141.

Notes

1. I'm told that English radicals are so accustomed to this happening that whenever it rains on a demonstration they point to Heaven and say, "See. He knows which side His bread is buttered on."

2. Mary Lutyens, *The Ruskins and the Grays* (London: John Murray, 1972), 106. My chapters about the Ruskins could not have been written without Mary Lutyens's three brilliantly edited collections of their letters, of which this was the last to be published.

3. Quoted in Peter Quennell, *John Ruskin: The Portrait of a Prophet* (London: Collins, 1949), 56–57.

4. From Ruskin's statement to his proctor in the nullity suit, published in J. Howard Whitehouse, *Vindication of Ruskin* (London: George Allen and Unwin, 1950), 15. Effie revealed the facts of her marriage to her parents in a letter of March 7, 1854, including the information that after six years, Ruskin had told her his "true reason" for not making love to her, "that he had imagined women were quite different to what he saw I was, and that the reason he did not make me his Wife was because he was disgusted with my person the first evening 10th April." See Mary Lutyens, *Millais and the Ruskins* (London: John Murray, 1967), 156.

5. See Mary Lutyens, *Young Mrs. Ruskin in Venice* (New York: The Vanguard Press, 1966), 21. (Published in England as *Effie in Venice*.)

6. See Michael Brooks, "Love and Possession in a Victorian Household: The Example of the Ruskins," in *The Victorian Family: Structure and Stresses*, ed. Anthony S. Wohl (New York: St. Martin's Press, 1978), 82–100, for a discussion of how the elder Ruskins' smothering affection worked against independence in their son.

   Freud's brief essay "Medusa's Head" suggests a psychoanalytic approach to Ruskin's alleged fixation on pubic hair. To Freud, the bizarre imagery of the mythic Medusa's head, surmounted by snakes instead of hair, expresses a man's horror at seeing a woman naked and perceiving that she has no penis. His castration anxieties aroused, he fastens attention on her pubic hair and transforms it (symbolically) into an over-abundance of the thing whose absence so terrifies him. Hence the imagery of hair as snakes, to express the terrifying aspects of female sexuality. It might be noted that in his later years Ruskin frequently mentioned the Medusa and was obsessed by visions of snakes. See *Standard Edition of the Complete Psychological Works of Sigmund Freud*, ed. James Strachey (London: Hogarth Press) 18: 273–74.

7. R. W. B. Lewis, *Edith Wharton: A Biography* (New York: Harper & Row, 1975), 53.

8. Quoted in Susan Chitty, *The Beast and the Monk: A Life of Charles Kingsley* (New York: Mason/Charter, 1975), 86.

9. See A. Dwight Culler, "Introduction," in *Apologia Pro Vita Sua*, John Henry Cardinal Newman (Boston: Houghton Mifflin, Riverside Edition, 1956).

10. Chitty, *The Beast and the Monk*, 87–88.

11. James Atlas gives a recent example in his biography of Delmore Schwartz. Schwartz and his wife, an uneasy couple, were visited one night by Norman Jacobs, who had just read Léon Blum's *Du mariage* and described to them Blum's theory of why couples suffered on their wedding night from what he called "physical disharmony." "It was because men tended to confine their sexual experience to prostitutes before marriage, Jacobs explained, while their wives lacked any sexual experience at all. Delmore and Gertrude became increasingly tense as Jacobs talked on, and when his enthusiastic peroration ended, a terrible silence ensued. Not until that moment did it occur to their well-meaning visitor that he may have been describing a situation all too familiar to his auditors." James Atlas, *Delmore Schwartz: The Life of an American Poet* (New York: Avon Books, 1978), 117.

   Even in this decade, when pre-marital sex is the rule rather than the exception, there may be wedding night trauma, though of a different kind. Can society's sudden approval quench one's private pleasures as society's disapproval did before?

12. James Anthony Froude, *My Relations with Carlyle* (New York: Charles Scribner's Sons, 1903), 23; also 4–7, 17, 21, 22. On her deathbed, so that Froude would not doubt her sincerity, Geraldine Jewsbury repeated the accusation with details: "The morning after his wedding-day he tore to pieces the flower garden at Comely Bank in a fit of ungovernable fury." Froude was convinced by the solemnity of the deathbed scene and by the singularity of the details that, despite Geraldine's reputation as something of a flibberti-gibbet, she was relating absolutely what Mrs. Carlyle told her. And to doubt Mrs. Carlyle was impossible. A more vivid but less reliable source of information about the Carlyles' intimate life is Frank Harris, who, in his autobiography, cites as his source Sir Richard Quain, a physician who attended the Carlyles in their later years. Sir Richard (according to Harris) had examined Mrs. Carlyle when she was in her late forties and found her to be a virgin. Mrs. Carlyle was also alleged to have described to the doctor how Carlyle on their wedding night "lay there, jiggling like" until she started laughing and he ran out of the room with one contemptuous word: "Women!" Frank Harris, *My Life and Loves* (New York: Grove Press, 1963), 209–11.

13. See, for example, Salvador Minuchin, *Families and Family Therapy* (Cambridge: Harvard University Press, 1974).

14. J. Howard Whitehouse, *Vindication of Ruskin* (London: George Allen and Unwin, 1950), 14–15.

15. George Eliot, *Middlemarch*, Book 4.

16. Lutyens, *The Ruskins and the Grays*, 126–27.

17. Ibid., 232.
18. Ibid., 174n.
19. Ibid., 228.
20. Ibid., 180.
21. Ibid., 185.
22. "I have your precious letter here: with the account so long and kind—of all your trial at Blair Athol—indeed it must have been cruel my dearest: I think it will be much nicer next time, we shall neither of us be frightened." Lutyens, *The Ruskins and the Grays*, 185.
23. Ibid., 214.
24. Ibid., 218.
25. Quoted by J. A. and Olive Banks, *Feminism and Family Planning in Victorian England* (New York: Schocken Books, 1964), 22.
26. Lutyens, *The Ruskins and the Grays*, 229.
27. Ibid., 234.
28. Lutyens, *Young Mrs. Ruskin in Venice*, 28.
29. Ibid., 156.
30. One strange arrangement was that of Radetzky, the Austrian military hero who served as governor of the Lombardo-Veneto district when the Ruskins lived there. Radetzky and his wife had recently started living together again after a separation of thirty years. "They never quarrelled," Effie reported, "but wrote to each other always, and were very good friends. The other day Radetzky happened to pass through the town where she lived, called upon her and brought her here, and our friend thinks they will not separate again." Lutyens, *Young Mrs. Ruskin in Venice*, 61.
31. Ibid., 149.
32. Ibid., 175.
33. Lutyens, *Millais and the Ruskins*, 14–15.
34. R. H. Wilenski thinks that Ruskin's influence as an art critic in the 1850s has been greatly exaggerated. See R. H. Wilenski, *John Ruskin: An Introduction to Further Study of his Life and Work* (London: Faber and Faber, 1933).
35. Ruskin's *Modern Painters* was an important book for the PRB even though their way of achieving truth to nature, which was hard-edged, comparatively flat, and precise in style, differed so from Turner's fluid, impressionist fidelity, which Ruskin had particularly endorsed. These young artists admired the sincerity, piety, spirituality, and freshness of color characteristic of painters before the High Renaissance—hence the name Pre-Raphaelite. Instead of painting on dark grounds, in imitation of the antique, they painted on white grounds, as artists generally do now, producing (for the moment—they have not lasted well) brighter and clearer colors. One has to struggle to see what so shocked and irritated contemporary audiences about the work of the PRB. Much of it looks stagy and belabored, anything but "true to nature" as we now see nature. But in their opposition to idealiza-

tion and to prettifying, as well as in their technical innovations (bright color, hard outline), the Pre-Raphaelite painters in their time boldly challenged the hegemony of Academy painting. See Quentin Bell, *Victorian Artists* (Cambridge: Harvard University Press, 1972).

36. Lutyens, *Millais and the Ruskins*, 61.
37. Ibid., 60.
38. Ibid., 69.
39. Ibid., 97.
40. Ibid., 101.
41. Ibid., 108.
42. Ibid., 156. See also 186.
43. Ibid., 232-33.
44. Ibid., 185.
45. Ibid., 129.
46. Ibid., 150.
47. It was discovered by the widow of the successor of Rutter's successor. Its discovery precipitated a battle for ownership between Effie's descendants and Ruskin's literary executor. I can only guess how Ruskin would have proved his virility to the court. Although the law defined virility as the ability to perform the sex act with a woman, Ruskin probably thought it meant simply the ability to get an erection. Also, Rousseau had given a certain dignity to masturbation by mentioning it in his *Confessions*, and Ruskin was perhaps offering to show the court evidence of masturbation.
48. "Ruskin's Statement to His Proctor in the Nullity Suit" (April 27, 1854), in Whitehouse, *Vindication of Ruskin*, 16.
49. Lady Eastlake to Effie in Lutyens, *Millais and the Ruskins*, 196.
50. Lutyens, *Millais and the Ruskins*, 199.
51. Ibid., 197.
52. Ibid., 216.
53. "Decree of Nullity, Commissary Court of Surrey" (July 15, 1854), in Lutyens, *Millais and the Ruskins*, 230.
54. See "Ruskin on His Marriage: The Acland Letter," by Jeffrey L. Spear, *Times Literary Supplement* (February 10, 1978): 163, a report on a recently discovered letter. For other new Ruskin material, see Mary Lutyens, "From Ruskin to Effie Gray," *Times Literary Supplement* (March 3, 1978): 254.
55. Lutyens, *Millais and the Ruskins*, 248.

HARRIET TAYLOR AND JOHN STUART MILL

1. Ruth Borchard, *John Stuart Mill, the Man* (London: Watts, 1957), 41-43.
2. Mary S. Hartman, *Victorian Murderesses* (New York: Schocken Books, 1977). See particularly the case of Adelaide Bartlett, a victim of an arranged marriage, for some interesting ways to avoid having sex. Bartlett

consulted a woman named Mary Nichols who specialized in the problems
of unhappily married women and often advised platonic unions.

3. F. A. Hayek, *John Stuart Mill and Harriet Taylor: Their Correspondence
and Subsequent Marriage* (Chicago: University of Chicago Press, 1951), 77.
Henceforth referred to as Hayek.

4. Carlyle's account of how Mill met Mrs. Taylor, the source of all later versions, may be found in *The Letters of Charles Eliot Norton*, 2 vols. (Boston and New York: Houghton Mifflin, 1913), 1:496–97. Prof. Norton
moved through literary London between 1850 and 1880 keeping a running
account of his conversations with the great, particularly with Ruskin and
Carlyle, whom he most admired.

Fox's motives for introducing Mrs. Taylor to Mill are debatable. Michael
St. John Packe suggests that he wanted to get Mill to contribute to the
Monthly Repository and was using Mrs. Taylor as "a handsome sprat to
catch an exceptional mackerel" (Packe, *The Life of John Stuart Mill*
[New York: Macmillan, 1954], 128). And what did he imagine happening
after he introduced them? In what sense was Mill the cure for Harriet's
problem? Adelaide Bartlett's marital adviser, Mrs. Nichols, "for a time at
least . . . appears to have counselled that in some cases love unions which
the world labelled adulterous might be called for" as solutions to marital
unhappiness (Hartman, *Victorian Murderesses*, 200). Could the Unitarian
minister have been thinking along similar lines? His own domestic arrangement was unconventional, ultimately scandalous. He had taken into
his household two talented members of his congregation, Eliza and Sarah
Flower, upon the death of their father. Eliza Flower and Fox became
lovers. By 1835, Mrs. Fox brought a formal accusation against her husband
and forced him to defend himself in church. He was allowed to continue in
charge of the congregation and promptly left his wife, setting up a new
establishment with Eliza Flower. In later years, he disapproved of the con-
cessionary path that Mrs. Taylor and Mill chose to pursue in their conduct
towards Mr. Taylor.

Whatever Fox had in mind, it seems to have been a sincere interest in
women's rights that brought Mrs. Taylor and Mill together when they met.
Mrs. Taylor had probably been complaining to Fox that her husband was
insensitive in this area, and Fox thought of Mill as Taylor's opposite. This
would explain why Mill says in his *Autobiography* that his belief in the
equality of men and women pre-dated his acquaintance with Harriet and
was the reason she became interested in him (*The Autobiography of John
Stuart Mill* [New York: Columbia University Press, 1944], 173n.).

5. Mill, *Autobiography*, 94.

6. Ibid., 124.

7. Jack Stillinger, ed., *The Early Draft of John Stuart Mill's Autobiography*
(Urbana: University of Illinois Press, 1961), 199.

8. *Letters of Charles Eliot Norton*, 1:496.

9. Hayek, 58.
10. Ibid., 76.
11. Ibid., 73.
12. Ibid., 69.
13. Mill, *Autobiography*, 161.
14. Hayek, 49.
15. Ibid., 99–100.
16. Ibid., 46, 49, 50.
17. Ibid., 52.
18. Hayek, 80.
19. Ibid., 82.
20. Ibid., 85.
21. Ibid., 79–80.
22. Mill, *Autobiography*, 161.
23. Hayek, 122.
24. Ibid., 120–21.
25. Ibid., 130–31.
26. Ibid., 161.
27. Ibid., 162–63.
28. Ibid., 168.
29. Alexander Bain, *John Stuart Mill: A Criticism* (London: Longmans, Green and Co., 1882), 151.
30. Hayek, 177–78.
31. Ibid., 196.
32. Stillinger, *Early Draft*, 171. In the interest no doubt of tact, this passage did not survive the first draft. A milder version was substituted.
33. See, for example, on the non-consummation of the Mills' marriage, Ruth Borchard, 106, and Bruce Mazlish, *James and John Stuart Mill* (New York: Basic Books, 1973), 301–2. That the Mills' marriage should have been sexless fits all too neatly Mazlish's theory of infantile dependency in Mill. Borchard seems more disinterested, if less pretentious. For Bain's comments on Mill's sexuality, see Bain, *John Stuart Mill: A Criticism*, 149. For an interesting and amusing account of Mill's dream, see Hayek, 253–54.
34. See J. A. and Olive Banks, *Feminism and Family Planning in Victorian England* (New York: Schocken Books, 1964).
35. Alice Rossi, "Sentiment and Intellect," introduction to *Essays on Sex Equality by John Stuart Mill and Harriet Taylor* (Chicago and London: University of Chicago Press, 1970).
36. *The Letters of Sigmund Freud*, ed. Ernst Freud (New York: McGraw-Hill, 1964), 75–76.
37. Packe, *The Life of John Stuart Mill*, 318–19.
38. Mill, *Autobiography*, 171.
39. Rossi, "Sentiment and Intellect."
40. Packe, *The Life of John Stuart Mill*, 371. See also Hayek; Borchard, *John*

Stuart Mill, the Man; and Gertrude Himmelfarb, *On Liberty and Liberalism: The Case of John Stuart Mill* (New York: Alfred A. Knopf, 1974). An exception is H. O. Pappe, *John Stuart Mill and the Harriet Taylor Myth* (Melbourne: Melbourne University Press, 1960), which disputes Harriet Taylor's influence on Mill, but the work is short, silly, and dismissible.

41. Quoted in Hayek, 300. I am indebted to Packe for his treatment of this episode.
42. Hayek, 134–35.
43. Ibid., 300.
44. Ibid., 137.
45. *The Later Letters of John Stuart Mill, 1849–1873,* ed. Francis E. Minetka and Dwight N. Lindley, vol. 14 in *The Collected Works of John Stuart Mill* (Toronto: University of Toronto Press, 1972), 165.
46. Minetka and Lindley, *Letters,* 14:197.
47. Hayek, 192.
48. Minetka and Lindley, *Letters,* 14:197.
49. Bain, *John Stuart Mill,* 171.
50. Mill, *Autobiography,* 131.
51. Minetka and Lindley, *Letters,* 14:273.
52. "Mill's Intellectual Beacon," *Partisan Review* 19 (1952): 115–20. To Mrs. Trilling, the egregious New Year's greeting is a "transgression difficult to forgive even in the name of neurosis."
53. Mill, *Autobiography,* 131.
54. Mill was an inspired linguistic stickler in the service of feminism. Reviewing the first volume of Grote's history of Greece, he criticized his friend for using the words *masculine* and *feminine* to describe the scientific and artistic sides of the Greek mind. As Bain said, "Mill could never endure the differences of character between men and women to be treated as a matter of course." And later, as a member of Parliament, Mill initiated the first parliamentary debate on women's suffrage by proposing that the word *person* replace the word *man* throughout the Reform Bill of 1867, which extended the franchise.

On the issue of women's rights Mill stood firm and virtually alone among his male contemporaries. Even Auguste Comte, whose work Mill admired early for its progressive, scientific cast, differed from Mill on the position of women. Comte took the more usual determinist line. Character derived from physical properties of the brain (he was the originator of phrenology), and women were destined to inferiority because their brains were smaller than men's, although they compensated for their intellectual inferiority by moral and spiritual superiority. Mill was not surprised when Comte's later work became nightmarishly totalitarian, extolling a utopia in which no books would be allowed because none was necessary: truth would have been established. This view provoked Mill to write *On Liberty* (why did all systems of social reform seem to end in liberticide?) and he claimed it was predictable from Comte's belief in the inferiority of women. To believe that anything was innately true was, to Mill, a fatal flaw of thought on which no healthy structure could be built. If you got your epistemology right, the rest would follow.

55. Bain, *John Stuart Mill*, 171.
56. Hayek, 210.
57. Minetka and Lindley, *Letters*, 14:165.
58. Hayek, 195.
59. Ibid., 125.
60. *The George Eliot Letters*, ed. Gordon Haight, 9 vols. (New Haven: Yale University Press, 1954–78), 3:407n. They had previously stopped at Père Lachaise to see the tomb of Héloïse and Abelard, but it was being repaired.
61. Mill, *Autobiography*, 184–85.
62. See J. Hillis Miller, *The Disappearance of God: Five Nineteenth Century Writers* (Cambridge: Harvard University Press, 1963).
63. A friend has pointed out that we require an equivalent term for *henpecked*, referring to women. She suggests *peckerpecked*.

CATHERINE HOGARTH AND CHARLES DICKENS

1. See the engrossing *Dickens and Mesmerism* by Fred Kaplan (Princeton: Princeton University Press, 1975).
2. My account of this episode follows closely that of Jane Carlyle in a letter to her uncle of December 13, 1847. See *Letters and Memorials of Jane Welsh Carlyle*, ed. James Anthony Froude, 2 vols. (New York: Charles Scribner's Sons, 1883), 1:309–12.
3. Leslie Staples, "New Letters of Mary Hogarth and Her Sister Catherine," *The Dickensian* 63 (1967): 76.
4. *The Letters of Charles Dickens, Vol. I (1820–1839)*, ed. Madeline House and Graham Storey, The Pilgrim Edition (Oxford: The Clarendon Press, 1965), 689.
5. House and Storey, 1:630.
6. Staples, *Dickensian*, 77.
7. Charles Dickens, *Barnaby Rudge*, New Oxford Illustrated Dickens (London: Oxford University Press, 1948–58), 631–32.
8. Staples, *Dickensian*, 80.
9. *The Letters of Charles Dickens, Vol. II (1840–1841)*, ed. Madeline House and Graham Storey, The Pilgrim Edition (Oxford: The Clarendon Press, 1969), 310n.
10. House and Storey, 2:317.
11. Ibid., 322.
12. *The Letters of Charles Dickens, Vol. III (1842–1843)*, ed. Madeline House,

Graham Storey, and Kathleen Tillotson, The Pilgrim Edition (Oxford: The Clarendon Press, 1974), 9n.

13. House, Storey, and Tillotson, 3:629.

14. Ibid. I quote this letter because it is one of few written by Catherine Dickens that survives and because I like its unassuming sweetness of tone. In trying to reconstruct such a shadowy figure, one grasps at straws.

15. House, Storey, and Tillotson, 3:204–5.

16. Ibid, 206.

17. Ibid., 302, 302n.

18. Ibid., 613–14n. Jane noticed one of Dickens's small children gazing in awe at the plum pudding his father had just pulled out of the hat and saw him approached by Mrs. Reid, one of the "Friend-of-the-Species" people for whom the Carlyles had such scorn. Seeing the opportunity for a moral lesson, Mrs. Reid whispered loudly into young Master Dickens's ear, "Wouldn't you like there to be such a nice plum pudding as that in every house in London tonight? I am sure *I* would!" Jane was delighted by the uncomprehending look which the little boy cast up at his questioner, "a whole page of protest against *twaddle!*"

19. This terror of bankruptcy despite success was the reason he fought so hard for an international copyright law. He ended up making himself unpopular in America by taking this as the theme of many of his speeches there.

20. House, Storey, and Tillotson, 3:444.

21. Ibid., 575.

22. Ibid., 597. Birth rates were high at mid-century and came down towards the end of the century, probably in response to the inflation of the 1870s. Large families were simply no longer affordable, and people turned towards birth control, which had been resisted passionately for most of the century, although Francis Place began trying to spread information about it as early as the 1820s. The size of the Forsyte family, according to their historian, Mr. Galsworthy, varied with the interest rates, ten being the usual number of children when the interest rates were 10 percent and three being more usual later. The vulcanization of rubber in 1844 allowed the development of the diaphragm as a method of birth control, but the condom had existed much earlier, as well as the vaginal sponge, a device brought to England from France and the one which Francis Place was trying to popularize. But technology was not the crucial factor. (The most widely used methods of birth control in the nineteenth century—coitus interruptus and prolonged breastfeeding—depended on no technology at all.) Ideology kept middle-class people from using birth control until economic necessity forced them to it. On these matters, see J. A. and Olive Banks, *Feminism and Family Planning in Victorian England* (New York: Schocken Books, 1964) and Peter Fryer, *The Birth Controllers* (London: Secker and Warburg, 1965).

Even the use of chloroform to ease the pains of childbirth was resisted, as being contrary to the Biblical injunction that women must bring forth children in pain and suffering. But Queen Victoria, who detested childbirth, as she detested what she called the whole "shadow side of marriage" (anything having to do with sex), made chloroform respectable by using it for the birth of her eighth child, Prince Leopold, in 1853. Even before that, however, both Dickens and Charles Darwin had insisted that their wives be given chloroform for the birth of children, in 1850. Dickens insisted against doctors' advice, and Darwin administered the chloroform himself. This was only three years after James Simpson, the Edinburgh physician, had discovered and published the usefulness of chloroform as an anaesthetic.

23. *The Letters of Charles Dickens*, ed. Walter Dexter, 3 vols., The Nonesuch Edition (London: The Nonesuch Press, 1938), 2:625-26.

24. Ibid., 633.

25. Ibid., 649.

26. Charles Dickens, *Little Dorrit*, The Oxford Illustrated Dickens (London: Oxford University Press, 1967), 150.

27. Dickens, *Nonesuch Letters*, 2:785.

28. Daniel Levinson et al., *The Seasons of a Man's Life* (New York: Alfred A. Knopf, 1978), 199. See also Elliott Jaques, "Death and the Mid-Life Crisis," *International Journal of Psychoanalysis* 46 (1965): 502-14, reprinted in Elliott Jaques, *Work, Creativity, and Social Justice* (New York: International Universities Press, 1970).

29. "The Stages of Life," in *The Portable Jung*, ed. Joseph Campbell, trans. R. F. C. Hull (New York: Viking, 1971), 16-17.

30. Gladys Storey, *Dickens and Daughter* (New York: Haskell House, 1971; orig. publ. London, 1939). This book burst like a landmine into the placid fields of Dickensian biography, revealing for the first time details of Dickens's secret life, and particularly his affair with Ellen Ternan. Gladys Storey was a friend of Dickens's daughter Kate, and got her information directly from Kate, in conversations held in 1923. See also David Parker and Michael Slater, "The Gladys Storey Papers," *The Dickensian* 76 (Spring 1980): 3-16.

31. Storey, *Dickens and Daughter*, 219.

32. Dickens, *Nonesuch Letters*, 2:765.

33. See Stephen Greenblatt, "Ralegh and the Dramatic Sense of Life," in *Sir Walter Ralegh: The Renaissance Man and His Roles* (New Haven and London: Yale University Press, 1973), 22-56.

34. Dickens, *Nonesuch Letters*, 2:825; 859.

35. Ibid., 2:805.

36. See Ada Nisbet, *Dickens and Ellen Ternan* (Berkeley and Los Angeles: University of California Press, 1952), 11. Nisbet's book, through Edmund Wilson, who made use of the Ellen Ternan material in his essay "Dickens:

The Two Scrooges," in *The Wound and the Bow* (London: Methuen, n.d.), revolutionized contemporary attitudes towards Dickens.

37. Edgar Johnson, ed., *The Heart of Charles Dickens* (Boston: Little, Brown, 1952), 347–48.

38. Quoted by John Forster, *The Life of Charles Dickens*, 2 vols. (London: J. M. Dent, 1966; orig. publ. 1872–74), 2:198–99.

39. Forster, 2:199.

40. In the period 1876–80, there were about 460 petitions for divorce annually. See O. R. McGregor, *Divorce in England* (London: Heinemann, 1957), 36.

41. Edgar Johnson, *The Heart of Charles Dickens*, 349.

42. Quoted by Edgar Johnson, *Charles Dickens: His Triumph and Tragedy*, 2 vols. (New York: Simon & Schuster, 1952), 2:879.

43. Forster revealed the blacking factory episode in his biography of Dickens, quoting heavily from an autobiographical document Dickens had prepared for him. Dickens was so deeply ashamed of this episode that he had not told even his wife about it and the remembrance of it made him a child again in thought: "My whole nature was so penetrated with the grief and humiliation of such considerations, that even now, famous and caressed and happy, I often forget in my dreams that I have a dear wife and children; even that I am a man; and wander desolately back to that time of my life." Forster, *The Life of Charles Dickens*, 1:23. See 1:19–33 and Wilson's "Dickens: The Two Scrooges."

44. Quoted Nisbet, *Dickens and Ellen Ternan*, 46.

45. Dickens, *Nonesuch Letters*, 2:20.

46. Storey, *Dickens and Daughter*, 219.

47. See Nisbet, *Dickens and Ellen Ternan*, 64.

48. Dickens, *Nonesuch Letters*, 3:15.

49. He even broke with Bradbury and Evans, his publishers of many years, for not reprinting—although he had not requested them to do so—his *Household Words* statement in their magazine, *Punch*. They characterized this offense as the refusal to "take upon themselves, unsolicited, to satisfy an eccentric wish by a preposterous action" (Nisbet, *Dickens and Ellen Ternan*, 17).

50. Nisbet, *Dickens and Ellen Ternan*, 65–67.

51. See *New Letters and Memorials of Jane Welsh Carlyle*, ed. Alexander Carlyle, 2 vols. (London and New York: John Lane, 1903), 2:118. The various expressions in which *dickens* is used as a substitute for devil ("speaking of the dickens," "playing the dickens," etc.) are, however, very old. Some usages can be found in the sixteenth century.

52. *The Journal of Benjamin Moran, 1857–1865*, ed. Sarah Agnes Wallace and Frances Gillespie (Chicago: University of Chicago Press, 1948), 1:344, quoted Nisbet, *Dickens and Ellen Ternan*, 26.

53. Ada Nisbet did the extraordinary detective work needed to understand this

part of Dickens's private life. Dickens destroyed most of his diaries, but one, kept on his second American tour, slipped away from him and ended up in the Berg Collection of the New York Public Library, where Nisbet found in it Dickens's reminder to himself of his telegraphic code. See *Dickens and Ellen Ternan*, 54.

54. Aldo Carotenuto, *A Secret Symmetry: Sabina Spielrein Between Jung and Freud*, trans. John Shepley, Krishna Winston, and Arno Pomerans (New York: Pantheon, 1982), 177.

55. *The Letters of Charles Dickens, Vol. I (1820–1839)*, ed. Madeline House and Graham Storey (Oxford: The Clarendon Press, 1965), xxii.

GEORGE ELIOT AND GEORGE HENRY LEWES

1. Sir Charles Gavan Duffy, *Conversations with Carlyle* (New York: Charles Scribner's Sons, 1892), 222–23. See also Thomas Carlyle to John Carlyle, November 2, 1854.

2. The *Westminster Review* was founded in 1824 by James Mill with money supplied by Jeremy Bentham. It was to be the organ of philosophic radicalism. John Stuart Mill presided over it from 1838 to 1840, and, after various transfers of ownership, it passed to Chapman in 1850. He dreamed of providing a liberal review for readers on both sides of the Atlantic, but scarcely had the capital to support his ambitions and was always in financial trouble. See Gordon Haight, *George Eliot and John Chapman* (New Haven: Yale University Press, 1940), 28–30. Mill's connection with the *Westminster* explains why his biographer misunderstood Jane Carlyle's remark about the strong woman of the *Westminster Review*, assuming it referred to Harriet Taylor. See Michael St. John Packe, *The Life of John Stuart Mill* (New York: Macmillan, 1954), 325.

3. 142 Strand housed both Chapman's business and residential quarters. The house was so big that they often took in boarders, and the place was a favorite residence in London for visiting literary Americans, including Emerson, Greeley, and Bryant.

4. *George Eliot Letters*, 9 vols., ed. Gordon Haight (New Haven: Yale University Press, 1954–78), 7:42n. Both Marghanita Laski in *George Eliot and Her World* (London: Thames and Hudson, 1973) and Gordon Haight imply, quite unnecessarily, I think, that Herbert Spencer was homosexual because he was not attracted to Miss Evans.

5. *George Eliot Letters*, 8:42. The remarkable set of letters from George Eliot to Herbert Spencer has only recently been published. They were known to exist for many years but a librarian at the British Museum told Professor Haight they could not be seen until 1985, omitting the proviso, "without the permission of the trustees."

6. *George Eliot Letters*, 8:56–57.

7. Ibid., 2:22–23, 29.

8. Ibid., 2:14–15.

9. Ibid., 2:46.

10. Pronounced Lewis.

11. *George Eliot Letters*, 2:98.

12. The double standard was understood to have originated in order to protect the passing on of property from a man to his rightful children. A woman can always tell her own children, but a man has to invoke the power of law to make sure his children are his. Keith Thomas disputes this explanation in "The Double Standard," *Journal of the History of Ideas* 20 (1959): 195–216. He suggests that the true reason for the double standard is that the woman herself is property whose value is diminished when someone other than her husband shares in possession. It should be noted that even after the Matrimonial Causes Act, a woman couldn't divorce her husband simply for adultery. There had to be an additional cause, such as cruelty, desertion, or sodomy.

13. *George Eliot Letters*, 2:132, 151.

14. *George Eliot Letters*, 2:190.

15. "Linger! You are so lovely." (*Faust*, 1:1700). *George Eliot Letters*, 2:173.

16. Elizabeth Hardwick, "George Eliot's Husband," in *A View of My Own: Essays in Literature and Society* (New York: Farrar, Straus and Cudahy, 1962), 87–88.

17. A case in point is the story of how she came to publish an article on Weimar in *Fraser's Magazine*. She had written out in her journal some description of Weimar, and although she didn't think highly enough of it to send it out, she thought well enough of it to read it aloud to Lewes. He, liking it, urged her to try to sell it to *Fraser's*. "As this was a mode of turning it into guineas I could have no objection," she recalled. *George Eliot Letters*, 2:201.

18. *George Eliot Letters*, 2:206.

19. Ibid.

20. "How I Came to Write Fiction," reprinted from George Eliot's journal in *George Eliot Letters*, 2:406–10. When John Walter Cross edited George Eliot's papers for publication after her death, he removed the phrase "lying in bed" from her account of how she came to write fiction. Presumably he found the place and posture too private for the conception of George Eliot's career. I insist upon it for the same reason. The location of her epiphany about her own talents suggests to me that Lewes's connection with her creativity was more secret and intimate than is generally allowed.

21. *George Eliot Letters*, 2:408.

22. The "George" of her pen name was in honor of Lewes. "Eliot" was perhaps intended to echo her own name, Evans. That her pseudonym should be masculine was inevitable—the Brontë sisters had long since established

that books would be treated more seriously by reviewers if they were thought to be written by men.

23. Actual children would have been at the least awkward: illegitimate, potentially outcast. And Lewes already had more people to support than he could easily handle. He and Miss Evans resolved to practice some form of birth control. We know this because of an extraordinary confidence that Marian Evans made to Barbara Leigh Smith. See Gordon Haight, *George Eliot: A Biography* (New York and Oxford: Oxford University Press, 1968), 205.

24. Charles Bray, *Autobiography*, 74–75, quoted by Haight in *George Eliot: A Biography*, 51. See also *George Eliot Letters*, 1:265–66 and note.

25. *George Eliot Letters*, 1:284. For her fears about the unfortunate balance between her moral and animal regions, see 1:167.

26. Haight's nonetheless magnificent biography endorses this unsubtle view of George Eliot's character and relationship to men. One chapter is titled "Someone to Lean Upon," another, "The Need to be Loved," and the line "She was not fitted to stand alone" is repeated throughout the text.

27. *George Eliot Letters*, 3:186.

28. Ibid., 2:213.

29. Ibid., 2:182.

30. Ibid., 1:268.

31. See Haight, *George Eliot and John Chapman*, 87–92. Barbara Leigh Smith, who was to remain one of George Eliot's closest friends, was so far seduced by Chapman's arguments that she spoke to her father—in a general way—about her desire to practice free love. Her father said that would be fine, but she should go to America to do it. When she spoke more specifically about Chapman's proposal, he arranged to get her out of the country. In Algeria, she met Dr. Eugene Bodichon, whom she married. Her father, Benjamin Smith, had never married the mother of his five children, although he had no other ties and lived with his family, whom he loved very much. A wealthy man of advanced views, he endowed even his daughters with considerable fortunes, enabling Barbara eventually to be one of the principal backers of Girton College, the first women's college at Cambridge.

32. *George Eliot Letters*, 2:175–76.

33. *George Eliot Letters*, 8:130. The fascinating exchange of letters between Bray and Combe on the Lewes-Evans elopement has only recently been published in a supplementary volume of the *George Eliot Letters*.

34. Ibid., 2:214.

35. Ibid., 2:231. Mrs. Jameson was the author of many books, including *Loves of the Poets, Celebrated Female Sovereigns*, and her most highly esteemed work, *Sacred and Legendary Art*. Her first book was about her experiences as a governess, for she had spent many years working as one before she married Robert Jameson. The marriage seems to have gone badly from the start and Jameson went to America, first to Dominica and then to Canada.

At his insistence, she joined him in 1836 but returned to England in 1838, at which time their formal separation began.

36. *George Eliot Letters*, 8:124.
37. Quoted by Charles Bray in a letter to Combe. The letter from George Eliot has been lost. *George Eliot Letters*, 8:128.
38. Ibid., 2:214.
39. Ibid., 4:367.
40. Charles Dickens, *David Copperfield*, The Oxford Illustrated Dickens (London: Oxford University Press, 1960), 505.
41. Simone de Beauvoir, *The Prime of Life*, trans. Peter Green (Cleveland: World Publishing Co., 1962), 20, 89.
42. *George Eliot Letters*, 5:9.
43. Ibid., 322.
44. Ibid., 3:31.
45. Ibid., 208.
46. Ibid., 219.
47. Ibid., 363.
48. Ibid., 6:72.
49. Ibid., 5:357.
50. Ibid., 4:233, 235.
51. Ibid., 136.
52. Ibid., 5:450.
53. Ibid., 4:47. *Leaves from the Journal of Our Life in the Highlands* was published privately in 1867 and issued publicly the following year. George Eliot was sent a copy by Lewes's friend Arthur Helps, who edited it, and since she was reading it in January of 1868, it is likely she was sent a copy of the private edition. The queen was a great admirer of her work.
54. *George Eliot Letters*, 6:64, 5:110, 5:227.
55. Ibid., 7:121.
56. Herbert Lewes had died in Africa, leaving a widow and two children who insisted upon coming to England and lived at George Eliot's expense.
57. *George Eliot Letters*, 7:140, 141.
58. Ibid., 264n.
59. Her brother-in-law, Leslie Stephen, almost collapsed with the shock of seeing them kissing in his living room.
60. *George Eliot Letters*, 6:398.
61. Ibid., 7:284.
62. When Emily Tennyson, the poet's sister, who had been engaged to Arthur Hallam, decided eight years after Hallam's death to marry someone else, she was widely condemned as disloyal. Mrs. Brookfield said, "Only *conceive* Emily Tennyson (I really can hardly even now believe it) Emily Tennyson is actually going to be married—and to whom after such a man as Arthur Hallam. To a boy in the Navy, *supposed* to be a Midshipman. . . . Can you

conceive anyone who he had loved, putting up with another? I feel so distressed about this, really it quite *hurts* me, I had such a romantic admiration for her, looked at her with such pity, and now my feeling about her is bouleversé." See *Mrs. Brookfield and Her Circle*, ed. Charles and Frances Brookfield, 2 vols. (London: Pitman and Sons, 1906), 1:102–3; also Robert Bernard Martin, *Tennyson: The Unquiet Heart* (New York: Oxford University Press, 1980), 258. Opposition to re-marriage was an article of Positivist doctrine. Auguste Comte was chief among the Positivists who subscribed to the sentimental opposition to re-marriage. See W. M. Simon, *European Positivism in the Nineteenth Century* (Ithaca: Cornell University Press, 1963).

63. *George Eliot Letters*, 7:287.
64. Elizabeth Hardwick, "George Eliot's Husband," in *A View of My Own*, 87.
65. *George Eliot Letters*, 7:212.
66. Ibid., 211. (*Wenn du bist nicht da:* when you aren't there); 213.
67. Ibid., 283, 276, 273.
68. See Haight, *George Eliot: A Biography*, 544–45; and John Walter Cross, ed., *George Eliot's Life*, 3 vols. (New York: Harper and Bros., 1885), 3:293–94. Venetian fevers had likewise afflicted Alfred de Musset when he was on a romantic escape with George Sand, and before that, Lord Byron, who was nursed by pretty Marianna Segeti. See Curtis Cate, *George Sand* (Boston: Houghton Mifflin, 1975), 255ff.
69. *George Eliot Letters*, 7:302.
70. Quoted by Haight, *George Eliot: A Biography*, 545.
71. *George Eliot Letters*, 7:351. Around the corner, in Cheyne Row, Thomas Carlyle had been living without his wife for fourteen years. She too had died suddenly, not many months after Gavan Duffy came to call and they gossiped about George Eliot. Thomas Carlyle was now eighty-five and less than two months away from his own death.
72. Huxley to Spencer, *Life and Letters of Thomas Henry Huxley*, ed. Leonard Huxley, 2 vols. (London, 1900), 2:19.

JANE WELSH AND THOMAS CARLYLE
(THE MARRIAGE)

1. *Letters and Memorials of Jane Welsh Carlyle*, ed. James Anthony Froude, 2 vols. (New York: Charles Scribner's Sons, 1883), 2:41.
2. Quoted by James Anthony Froude, *Thomas Carlyle: A History of His Life in London*, 2 vols. (New York: Charles Scribner's Sons, 1892), 2:115; also Thomas Carlyle, *Reminiscences*, ed. James Anthony Froude (New York: Charles Scribner's Sons, 1881), 453.
3. Quoted Froude, *Carlyle's Life in London*, 2:116.
4. *Letters and Memorials of Jane Welsh Carlyle*, 2:27.

5. Ibid., 97.
6. Ibid., 357, 362–64.
7. Ibid., 51.
8. Ibid., 45.
9. Ibid., 37–38.
10. Ibid., 40.
11. Ibid., 47.
12. *New Letters and Memorials of Jane Welsh Carlyle*, ed. Alexander Carlyle, with an introduction by James Crichton-Browne, 2 vols. (New York and London: John Lane, 1903), 2:94.
13. Ibid., 97, 103.
14. Froude, *Letters and Memorials*, 2:47.
15. Carlyle, *New Letters and Memorials*, 2:103.
16. Froude, *Letters and Memorials*, 2:41.
17. Carlyle, *New Letters and Memorials*, 2:101. She also followed the trial of Madeleine Smith, accused of poisoning her lover. (See Mary S. Hartman, *Victorian Murderesses* [New York: Schocken Books, 1977] and entries for 1857 and 1861 in my chronology.) These murder trials, as Mary S. Hartman suggests, seem to have provoked public discussion about family life and its difficulties.
18. Froude, *Letters and Memorials*, 2:83.
19. Ibid., 88.
20. Quoted Froude, *Carlyle's Life in London*, 2:347.
21. Ibid., 349.
22. Thomas Carlyle, *Reminiscences*, 474–75, 504, 493–94.
23. Ibid., 509.
24. Ibid., 467.
25. Froude, *Letters and Memorials*, 2:388.
26. Quoted Froude, *Carlyle's Life in London*, 2:324.
27. Ibid., 349–50.
28. Carlyle, *New Letters and Memorials*, introduction by James Crichton-Browne, 1:lv.
29. Clifford Geertz, discussing the symbolic function of Balinese cockfights, says that spectators are aware that some fights are "deeper"—richer and more meaningful—than others. See "Deep Play: Notes on the Balinese Cockfight," in *Myth, Symbol, and Culture*, ed. Clifford Geertz (New York: W. W. Norton, 1974), 1–37.

POSTLUDES

1. Joseph Irving, *The Annals of Our Time: A Diurnal of Events . . . from 1837 to 1871* (London and New York: Macmillan and Co., 1890), 718; see also 717, 721–22. Based largely on newspaper accounts, but relying also on

memoirs, diaries, parliamentary debates, proceedings of learned societies, and so on, this volume is a fascinating and valuable daily record of Victorian history. On the Governor Eyre affair, see also James G. Paradis, *T. H. Huxley: Man's Place in Nature* (Lincoln and London: University of Nebraska Press, 1978).

2. Jane Welsh Carlyle, *Letters and Memorials*, 2:380–81.

3. Quoted Paradis, *T. H. Huxley*, 63–64.

4. See Helen Singer Kaplan, Clifford Sager et al., "The Marriage Contract," in *Progress in Group and Family Therapy* (New York and London: Brunner/Mazel, 1972), 483–97.

5. "The Golden Rule and the Cycle of Life," in *The Study of Lives*, ed. Robert White (New York: Atherton Press, 1963), 421–23.

6. See Stanley Cavell, *Pursuits of Happiness: The Hollywood Comedy of Remarriage* (Cambridge: Harvard University Press, 1981).

7. See Jessie Bernard's *The Future of Marriage*, rev. ed. (New Haven and London: Yale University Press, 1982), which points out how much better marriage works for men than for women. Bernard believes, however, that it is the role of housewife enjoined by traditional marriage rather than marriage *per se* which weakens women and helps men to thrive.

Selected Bibliography

ACKERLEY, J. R. *My Father and Myself*. New York: Coward-McCann, 1969.

ADRIAN, ARTHUR. *Georgina Hogarth and the Dickens Circle*. London: Oxford University Press, 1957.

BAIN, ALEXANDER. *John Stuart Mill: A Criticism*. London: Longmans, Green and Co., 1882.

BANKS, J. A. AND OLIVE. *Feminism and Family Planning in Victorian England*. New York: Schocken Books, 1964.

BARKER-BENFIELD, BEN. *The Horrors of the Half-Known Life: Male Attitudes Toward Women and Sexuality in Nineteenth-Century America*. New York: Harper & Row, 1976.

BASCH, FRANÇOISE. *Relative Creatures: Victorian Women in Society and the Novel*. Trans. Anthony Rudolf. New York: Schocken Books, 1974.

DE BEAUVOIR, SIMONE. *The Prime of Life*. Trans. Peter Green. Cleveland: World Publishing Co., 1962.

———. *The Second Sex*. Ed. and Trans. H. M. Parshley. New York: Alfred A. Knopf, 1953.

BERNARD, JESSIE. *The Future of Marriage*. Rev. ed. New Haven: Yale University Press, 1982.

BLISS, TRUDY, ed. *Jane Welsh Carlyle: A New Selection of Her Letters*. New York: Macmillan, 1950.

BLUM, LÉON. *Marriage*. Trans. Warre Bradley Wells. London and Philadelphia: Lippincott, 1937.

BODICHON, BARBARA LEIGH SMITH. *An American Diary, 1857-8*. Ed. and with an introduction by Joseph W. Reed, Jr. London: Routledge & Kegan Paul, 1972.

BORCHARD, RUTH. *John Stuart Mill, the Man*. London: Watts, 1957.

BRANCA, PATRICIA. *Silent Sisterhood: Middle-Class Women in Victorian Homes*. Pittsburgh: Carnegie-Mellon University Press, 1975.

BROOKFIELD, CHARLES AND FRANCES, eds. *Mrs. Brookfield and Her Circle.* 2 vols. London: Pitman and Sons, 1906.

CALDER, JENNI. *Women and Marriage in Victorian Fiction.* New York: Oxford University Press, 1976.

CARLYLE, JANE WELSH. *The Collected Letters of Thomas and Jane Welsh Carlyle.* Ed. Charles Richard Sanders, Kenneth J. Fielding et al., Duke-Edinburgh Edition. 9 vols. to date. Durham, N.C.: Duke University Press, 1970–.

————. *Letters and Memorials of Jane Welsh Carlyle.* Ed. James Anthony Froude. 2 vols. New York: Charles Scribner's Sons, 1883.

————. *The Love Letters of Thomas Carlyle and Jane Welsh.* Ed. Alexander Carlyle. 2 vols. London: John Lane, 1909.

————. *New Letters and Memorials of Jane Welsh Carlyle.* Ed. Alexander Carlyle. 2 vols. London and New York: John Lane, 1903.

CARLYLE, THOMAS. *Reminiscences.* Ed. James Anthony Froude. 2 vols. New York: Charles Scribner's Sons, 1881.

CATE, CURTIS. *George Sand.* Boston: Houghton Mifflin, 1975.

CAVELL, STANLEY. *Pursuits of Happiness: The Hollywood Comedy of Remarriage.* Cambridge: Harvard University Press, 1981.

CHITTY, SUSAN. *The Beast and the Monk: A Life of Charles Kingsley.* New York: Mason/Charter, 1975.

COCKSHUT, A. O. J. *Truth to Life: The Art of Biography in the Nineteenth Century.* New York and London: Harcourt Brace Jovanovich, 1974.

COLLIS, JOHN STEWART. *The Carlyles: A Biography of Thomas and Jane Carlyle.* New York: Dodd, Mead and Co., 1973.

COLP, RALPH, JR. *To Be an Invalid: The Illness of Charles Darwin.* Chicago and London: University of Chicago Press, 1977.

CRAIG, DAVID. *Scottish Literature and the Scottish People.* London: Chatto and Windus, 1961.

CROSS, JOHN WALTER, ed. *George Eliot's Life.* 3 vols. New York: Harper and Bros., 1885.

DAWSON, CARL. *Victorian Noon: English Literature in 1850.* Baltimore and London: The Johns Hopkins University Press, 1979.

DEGLER, CARL. "What Ought to Be and What Was: Women's Sexuality in the Nineteenth Century." *American Historical Review* 79, no. 5 (December 1974): 1467–90.

DELAMONT, SARA, AND LORNA DUFFIN, eds. *The Nineteenth-Century Woman: Her Cultural and Physical World.* London: Croom Helm; New York: Barnes & Noble, 1978.

DICKENS, CHARLES. *The Letters of Charles Dickens.* Ed. Walter Dexter. 3 vols. The Nonesuch Edition. London: The Nonesuch Press, 1938.

————. *The Letters of Charles Dickens.* Ed. Madeline House, Graham Storey, Kathleen Tillotson, K. J. Fielding. 5 vols. to date. The Pilgrim Edition. Oxford: The Clarendon Press: 1965–.

DICKENS, SIR HENRY FIELDING. *Memories of My Father*. New York: Duffield and Co., 1929.

DICKENS, MAMIE. *My Father As I Recall Him*. New York: Dutton, n.d.

DOUGLAS, MARY. *Purity and Danger: An Analysis of the Concepts of Pollution and Taboo*. New York and Washington, D.C.: Praeger Publishers, 1966.

DREW, ELIZABETH. *Jane Welsh and Jane Carlyle*. New York: Charles Scribner's Sons, 1928.

DUFFY, SIR CHARLES GAVAN. *Conversations with Carlyle*. New York: Charles Scribner's Sons, 1892.

DUNN, WALDO HILARY. *James Anthony Froude: A Biography*. 2 vols. Oxford: The Clarendon Press, 1961.

ELIOT, GEORGE. *The George Eliot Letters*. Ed. Gordon Haight. 9 vols. New Haven: Yale University Press, 1954–78.

ELLMANN, RICHARD. *Golden Codgers: Biographical Speculations*. New York and London: Oxford University Press, 1973.

ERIKSON, ERIK. "The Golden Rule and The Cycle of Life." In *The Study of Lives*, ed. Robert W. White. New York: Atherton Press, 1963.

FADERMAN, LILLIAN. *Surpassing the Love of Men: Romantic Friendship and Love Between Women from the Renaissance to the Present*. New York: William Morrow, 1981.

FLEISHMAN, AVROM. "Personal Myth: Three Victorian Autobiographers." In *Approaches to Victorian Autobiography*, ed. George P. Landow, 215–34. Athens: Ohio University Press, 1979.

FORSTER, JOHN. *The Life of Charles Dickens*. 2 vols. London: J. M. Dent, 1966.

FOUCAULT, MICHEL. *The History of Sexuality; Volume One: An Introduction*. Trans. Robert Hurley. New York: Pantheon Books, 1978.

FOX, CAROLINE. *Memories of Old Friends: Extracts from the Journals and Letters of Caroline Fox, 1835–1871*. Ed. Horace Plym. London: Smith, Elder, and Co., 1882.

FROUDE, JAMES ANTHONY. *Thomas Carlyle: A History of the First Forty Years of His Life*. 2 vols. New York: Charles Scribner's Sons, 1882.

———. *Thomas Carlyle: A History of His Life in London*. 2 vols. New York: Charles Scribner's Sons, 1892.

———. *My Relations with Carlyle*. New York: Charles Scribner's Sons, 1903.

FRYER, PETER. *The Birth Controllers*. London: Secker and Warburg, 1965.

GEERTZ, CLIFFORD. "Deep Play: Notes on the Balinese Cockfight." In *Myth, Symbol, and Culture*, ed. Clifford Geertz. New York: W. W. Norton, 1974.

GILBERT, SANDRA M., AND SUSAN GUBAR. *The Madwoman in the Attic: A Study of Women and the Literary Imagination in the Nineteenth-Century*. New Haven and London: Yale University Press, 1979.

GOFFMAN, ERVIN. *The Presentation of Self in Everyday Life*. Garden City, N.Y.: Doubleday, 1959.

HAIGHT, GORDON. *George Eliot: A Biography*. New York and Oxford: Oxford University Press, 1968.

————. *George Eliot and John Chapman.* New Haven: Yale University Press, 1940.

HALEY, BRUCE. *The Healthy Body and Victorian Culture.* Cambridge and London: Harvard University Press, 1978.

HARDWICK, ELIZABETH. *Seduction and Betrayal: Women and Literature.* New York: Random House, 1973.

————. *A View of My Own: Essays in Literature and Society.* New York: Farrar, Straus and Cudahy, 1962.

HARRISON, BRIAN. "Underneath the Victorians." *Victorian Studies* 10 (1976): 239–62.

HARRISON, FRASER. *The Dark Angel: Aspects of Victorian Sexuality.* New York: Universe Books, 1977.

HARTMAN, MARY S. *Victorian Murderesses.* New York: Schocken Books, 1977.

HAYEK, F. A. *John Stuart Mill and Harriet Taylor: Their Correspondence and Subsequent Marriage.* Chicago: University of Chicago Press, 1951.

HAYTER, ALATHEA. *A Sultry Month: Scenes of London Literary Life in 1846.* London: Faber and Faber, 1965.

HIMMELFARB, GERTRUDE. *On Liberty and Liberalism: The Case of John Stuart Mill.* New York: Alfred A. Knopf, 1974.

HIMES, NORMAN. *Medical History of Contraception.* Baltimore: The Williams and Wilkins Co., 1936.

HOLME, THEA. *The Carlyles at Home.* London and New York: Oxford University Press, 1965.

HUDSON, DEREK. *Munby, Man of Two Worlds: The Life and Diaries of Arthur J. Munby, 1828–1910.* London: John Murray; Boston: Gambit, 1972.

IRVINE, WILLIAM. *Apes, Angels, and Victorians: Darwin, Huxley, and Evolution.* New York: McGraw-Hill, 1955.

IRVING, JOSEPH. *The Annals of Our Times: A Diurnal of Events, Social and Political, Home and Foreign, from the Accession of Queen Victoria, June 20, 1837, to the Peace of Versailles, February 28, 1871.* London and New York: Macmillan and Co., 1890.

JAMES, ADMIRAL SIR WILLIAM, ed. *John Ruskin and Effie Gray.* (In England, *The Order of Release.*) New York: Scribner's, 1947.

JAQUES, ELLIOTT. "Death and the Mid-Life Crisis." *International Journal of Psychoanalysis* 46 (1965): 502–14. Reprinted in Elliott Jaques, *Work, Creativity and Social Justice.* New York: International Universities Press, 1970.

JEWSBURY, GERALDINE. *Selections from the Letters of Geraldine E. Jewsbury to Jane Welsh Carlyle.* London, 1892.

JOHNSON, DIANE. *The True History of the First Mrs. Meredith and Other Lesser Lives.* New York: Alfred A. Knopf, 1972.

JOHNSON, EDGAR. *Charles Dickens: His Triumph and Tragedy.* 2 vols. New York: Simon & Schuster, 1952.

————, ed. *The Heart of Charles Dickens, as Revealed in His Letters to Angela Burdett-Coutts.* Boston: Little, Brown, 1952.

JUNG, C. G. "Marriage as a Psychological Relationship." In *The Portable Jung*, ed. Joseph Campbell, trans. R. F. C. Hull, 163–77. New York: Viking, 1971.

KAMM, JOSEPHINE. *John Stuart Mill in Love.* London: Gordon and Cremonesi, 1977.

KANTOR, DAVID, AND WILLIAM LEHR. *Inside the Family: Toward a Theory of Family Process.* San Francisco: Jossey-Bass, 1976.

KAPLAN, FRED. *Dickens and Mesmerism.* Princeton: Princeton University Press, 1975.

KAPLAN, HELEN SINGER, AND CLIFFORD SAGER, eds. *Progress in Group and Family Therapy.* New York: Brunner/Mazel, 1972.

LASCH, CHRISTOPHER. *The Culture of Narcissism: American Life in an Age of Diminishing Expectations.* New York: W. W. Norton, 1979.

————. *Haven in a Heartless World: The Family Besieged.* New York: Basic Books, 1977.

LEDERER, WILLIAM J., AND DON JACKSON. *The Mirages of Marriage.* New York: W. W. Norton, 1968.

LEVINSON, DANIEL et al. *The Seasons of a Man's Life.* New York: Alfred A. Knopf, 1978.

LEWIS, R. W. B. *Edith Wharton: A Biography.* New York: Harper & Row, 1975.

LUTYENS, MARY. *Millais and the Ruskins.* London: John Murray, 1967.

————. *The Ruskins and the Grays.* London: John Murray, 1972.

————. *Young Mrs. Ruskin in Venice: Unpublished Letters of Mrs. John Ruskin written from Venice between 1849–1852.* (In England, *Effie in Venice.*) New York: The Vanguard Press, 1966.

MACKENZIE, NORMAN AND JEANNE. *Dickens: A Life.* New York and Oxford: Oxford University Press, 1979.

MARCUS, STEVEN. *The Other Victorians: A Study of Sexuality and Pornography in Mid-Nineteenth Century England.* New York: Basic Books, 1966.

MARLOW, JOYCE. *The Oak and the Ivy: An Intimate Biography of William and Catherine Gladstone.* New York: Doubleday, 1977.

MARTIN, ROBERT BERNARD. *Tennyson: The Unquiet Heart.* New York: Oxford University Press, 1980.

MAYHEW, HENRY. *London Labour and the London Poor.* 4 vols. London: Griffin, Bohn, and Co., 1861. Reprint ed. New York: Dover Publications, 1968.

MAZLISH, BRUCE. *James and John Stuart Mill: Father and Son in the Nineteenth Century.* New York: Basic Books, 1973.

MCGREGOR, O. R. *Divorce in England: A Centenary Study.* London: Heinemann, 1957.

MILL, JOHN STUART. *The Autobiography of John Stuart Mill.* New York: Columbia University Press, 1974.

Selected Bibliography

————. *Earlier Letters of John Stuart Mill, 1812–1848.* Ed. Francis E. Minetka. Vols. 12 and 13, *The Collected Works of John Stuart Mill.* Toronto: University of Toronto Press, 1963.

————. *The Later Letters of John Stuart Mill, 1849–1873.* Ed. Francis E. Minetka and Dwight N. Lindley. Vols. 14–17, *The Collected Works of John Stuart Mill.* Toronto: University of Toronto Press, 1972.

MINUCHIN, SALVADOR. *Families and Family Therapy.* Cambridge: Harvard University Press, 1974.

MITCHELL, JULIET. *Woman's Estate.* New York: Pantheon, 1971.

MORLEY, JOHN. *Nineteenth Century Essays.* Ed. Peter Stansky. Classics of British Historical Literature Series. Chicago and London: University of Chicago Press, 1970.

NISBET, ADA. *Dickens and Ellen Ternan.* Berkeley and Los Angeles: University of California Press, 1952.

NORTON, CHARLES ELIOT. *The Letters of Charles Eliot Norton.* 2 vols. Boston and New York: Houghton Mifflin, 1913.

ORIGO, IRIS. "The Carlyles and the Ashburtons." In *A Measure of Love*, 117–85. New York: Pantheon, n.d.

PACKE, MICHAEL ST. JOHN. *The Life of John Stuart Mill.* New York: Macmillan, 1954.

PAPPE, H. O. *John Stuart Mill and the Harriet Taylor Myth.* Melbourne: Melbourne University Press, 1960.

PARADIS, JAMES G. *T. H. Huxley: Man's Place in Nature.* Lincoln and London: University of Nebraska Press, 1978.

QUENNELL, PETER. *John Ruskin: The Portrait of a Prophet.* London: Collins, 1949.

RAY, GORDON N. *H. G. Wells and Rebecca West.* New Haven: Yale University Press, 1974.

————. *Thackeray: The Uses of Adversity, 1811–1846.* New York: McGraw-Hill, 1955.

————. *Thackeray: The Age of Wisdom, 1847–1863.* New York: McGraw-Hill, 1958.

REDINGER, RUBY. *George Eliot: The Emergent Self.* New York: Alfred A. Knopf, 1975.

RITCHIE, ANNE THACKERAY. *Chapters from Some Unwritten Memoirs.* New York: Harper and Bros., 1895.

ROSENBERG, JOHN D. *The Darkening Glass: A Portrait of Ruskin's Genius.* New York: Columbia University Press, 1961.

ROSSI, ALICE, ed. *Essays on Sex Equality by John Stuart Mill and Harriet Taylor.* With an introduction by Alice Rossi. Chicago and London: University of Chicago Press, 1970.

ROWBOTHAM, SHELIA. *Hidden from History: Rediscovering Women in History from the Seventeenth Century to the Present.* New York: Pantheon Books, 1974.

RUSKIN, JOHN. *Letters from Venice, 1851–1852*. Ed. John Lewis Bradley. New Haven: Yale University Press, 1955.

———. *Ruskin in Italy: Letters to His Parents, 1845*. Ed. Harold Shapiro. Oxford: The Clarendon Press, 1972.

RUSSELL, BERTRAND AND PATRICIA, eds. *The Amberley Papers*. 2 vols. London: George Allen and Unwin; New York: Simon & Schuster, 1966.

SCANZONI, JOHN. *Sexual Bargaining: Power Politics in the American Marriage*. 2d ed. Chicago and London: University of Chicago Press, 1982.

SCARF, MAGGIE. *Unfinished Business: Pressure Points in the Lives of Women*. New York: Doubleday, 1980.

SCHEIBE, KARL. "In Defense of Lying: On the Moral Neutrality of Misrepresentation." *Berkshire Review* 15 (1980): 15–24.

———. *Mirrors, Masks, Lies, and Secrets: The Limits of Human Predictability*. New York and London: Praeger, 1979.

SEIDENBERG, ROBERT. *Marriage Between Equals*. Garden City, New York: Doubleday, Anchor Press, 1973. Orig. publ. as *Marriage in Life and Literature*. New York: Philosophical Library, 1970.

SHORTER, EDWARD. *The Making of the Modern Family*. New York: Basic Books, 1975.

SHOWALTER, ELAINE. *A Literature of Their Own: British Women Novelists from Brontë to Lessing*. Princeton: Princeton University Press, 1977.

SIMON, W. M. *European Positivism in the Nineteenth Century*. Ithaca: Cornell University Press, 1963.

SIMPSON, ALAN AND MARY, eds. *I Too Am Here: Selections from the Letters of Jane Welsh Carlyle*. London, New York, and Melbourne: Cambridge University Press, 1977.

SPEAIGHT, GEORGE. *Punch and Judy: A History*. Boston: Publishers Plays, 1970.

SPEAR, JEFFREY. "Ruskin on His Marriage: The Acland Letter." *Times Literary Supplement* (February 10, 1978): 163.

STANG, RICHARD. *The Theory of the Novel in England: 1850–1870*. London: Routledge & Kegan Paul; New York: Columbia University Press, 1959.

STAPLES, LESLIE. "News Letters of Mary Hogarth and Her Sister Catherine." *The Dickensian* 63 (1967): 75–80.

STEPHEN, LESLIE. *George Eliot*. The English Men of Letters Series. London: Macmillan and Co., 1902.

———. *The Mausoleum Book*. Oxford: The Clarendon Press, 1977.

STILLINGER, JACK, ed. *The Early Draft of John Stuart Mill's Autobiography*. Urbana: University of Illinois Press, 1961.

STONE, LAWRENCE. *The Family, Sex, and Marriage in England 1500–1800*. New York: Harper & Row, 1977.

STOREY, GLADYS. *Dickens and Daughter*. New York: Haskell House, 1971. Orig. publ. London, 1939.

SYMONS, JULIAN. *Thomas Carlyle: The Life and Ideas of a Prophet*. New York: Oxford University Press, 1952.

THACKERAY, WILLIAM MAKEPEACE. *The Letters and Private Papers of W. M. Thackeray.* Ed. Gordon N. Ray. 4 vols. Cambridge: Harvard University Press, 1945–46.

THOMAS, KEITH. "The Double Standard." *Journal of the History of Ideas* 20 (1959): 195–216.

TRILLING, DIANA. "Mill's Intellectual Beacon." *Partisan Review* 19 (1952): 115–20.

VICINUS, MARTHA, ed. *Suffer and Be Still: Women in the Victorian Age.* London and Bloomington: Indiana University Press, 1972.

———, ed. *A Widening Sphere: Changing Roles of Victorian Women.* London and Bloomington: Indiana University Press, 1977.

WALLER, WILLARD. *The Family: A Dynamic Interpretation.* New York: The Dryden Press, 1938.

WEEKS, JEFFREY. *Sex, Politics, and Society: The Regulation of Sexuality Since 1800.* London and New York: Longman, 1981.

WHITEHOUSE, J. HOWARD. *Vindication of Ruskin.* London: George Allen and Unwin, 1950.

WILENSKI, R. H. *John Ruskin: An Introduction to Further Study of His Life and Work.* London: Faber and Faber, 1933.

WILLEY, BASIL. *Nineteenth Century Studies.* London: Chatto and Windus, 1964.

WILLIAMS, RAYMOND. *Keywords: A Vocabulary of Culture and Society.* New York: Oxford University Press, 1976.

WILSON, EDMUND. "Dickens: The Two Scrooges." In *The Wound and the Bow,* 1–93. London: Methuen, University Paperbacks, n.d. Orig. publ. 1941. Rev. ed. 1952.

WOHL, ANTHONY S., ed. *The Victorian Family: Structure and Stresses.* New York: St. Martin's Press, 1978.

WOODHAM-SMITH, CECIL. *Queen Victoria: From Her Birth to the Death of the Prince Consort.* New York: Alfred A. Knopf, 1972.

WOOLF, VIRGINIA. "Geraldine and Jane." In *Collected Essays,* 4:27–39. 4 vols. New York: Harcourt, Brace and World, 1967.

ZARETSKY, ELI. *Capitalism, the Family, and Personal Life.* New York: Harper & Row, Colophon Books, 1976.

Index

Index

Index